# Math
# Panic

DISCARDED
JENKS LRC
GORDON COLLEGE

# Math
# Panic

## Laurie Buxton

### With a Foreword by Lynn Arthur Steen

JENKS L.R.C.
GORDON COLLEGE
255 GRAPEVINE RD.
WENHAM, MA 01984-1895

**Heinemann**
**Portsmouth, New Hampshire**

**Heinemann Educational Books, Inc.**
361 Hanover Street, Portsmouth, NH 03801–3959
Offices and agents throughout the world

© 1991 by Laurie Buxton. Portions previously © 1981 by L. G. Buxton under the title *Do You Panic About Maths?* All rights reserved. No part of this book may be reproduced in any form or by electronic or mechanical means, including information storage and retrieval systems, without permission in writing from the publisher, except by a reviewer, who may quote brief passages in a review.

Chapter 12 was previously published in *Visible Language*, Vol. XVI, no. 3 (Summer 1982), and is reprinted with permission.

Every effort has been made to contact the copyright holders for permission to reprint borrowed material where necessary. We regret any oversights that may have occurred and would be happy to rectify them in future printings of this work.

**Library of Congress Cataloging-in-Publication Data**
Buxton, Laurie.
    Math panic/Laurie Buxton.
        p.    cm.
    Rev. ed. of: Do you panic about maths? 1981.
    Includes bibliographical references and index.
    ISBN 0-435-08313-9
    1. Math anxiety.    I. Buxton, Laurie. Do you panic about maths?
II. Title.
QA11.B89 1991                                                                    90-28874
510′.7—dc20                                                                          CIP

Designed by Maria Szmauz
Printed in the United States of America
91  92  93  94  95  6  5  4  3  2  1

To Pam, Carole, Claire,
Joanne, and Jackie

# Contents

# Section Four

## Additional Group Sessions

# Foreword

Terror, frustration, despair, anxiety, anguish...words of panic, rarely used by competent adults in ordinary life, stream forth when people are asked to describe feelings evoked by mathematics. Strange it is that mathematics, the epitome of objective rationality, should elicit such emotion-laden language.

Yet however strange it may seem, it is actually quite common for mathematics to carry with it intense emotional baggage. For some, the emotive impact is primarily positive — a "pleasurable obsession" that provides what Bertrand Russell called an "intense delight" in the beauty of reason. But for most adults the emotional baggage of mathematics is an overwhelming burden without apparent redeeming value — a ladder to the past filled with remembrances of mind-numbing boredom and embarrassing frustration.

The subjects in this book are successful adults of varied backgrounds who share a profound anxiety about mathematics. Although these particular individuals are all British, they could as easily be American or French — or Russian or Japanese. Their reactions to mathematics — whether remembering their previous educational experiences or working on problems as adults — are authentic reflections of human experience. Listen to their voices, and you hear the genuine emotions of mathematics:

> The thing I remember about math, of course, is a *fantastic* lack of comprehension.

> Cachunk, down comes the blanket like a green baize cover over a parrot's cage.

> If you are really sure that you cannot do math, there are many ways of refusing to admit that you might.

The theses of this pioneering study is that emotion often blocks the faculty of reason to prevent otherwise capable adults from coping with mathematics. By probing the psychological roots of panic—a sudden mental discontinuity that disables rational thought—Laurie Buxton establishes a credible case that mathematics education must take as much account of emotion as it does of cognition.

Pressure of timed tests and risk of public embarrassment have long been recognized as sources of unproductive tension among many school students. Buxton adds to this a thorough analysis of the special role that authority plays in children's learning of mathematics. These three ingredients—imposed authority, public exposure, time deadlines—combine to create true panic in many adults when they face even very simple mathematical problems. Yet these same ingredients feature prominently in most traditional mathematics classes—which, of course, is precisely why there is so much panic about math in our society.

Even simple strategies that teachers take for granted can contribute in unintended ways to emotions that block rational thought. Asking questions, offering praise, enlisting parents—all generally accepted as good teaching practices—can in some cases provoke an emotional revolt against authority that erases any hope that the mathematics that follows will be engaged or understood.

Alone among subjects children study in school, mathematics is its own ultimate authority. Neither teachers nor answer books are needed to confirm the correctness of a typical school mathematics problem. Yet common teaching strategies too often enhance rather than emancipate pupils' emotional dependence on teachers for approval. Such practices may, according to one of Laurie Buxton's more tantalizing suggestions, account in part for the observed differences between men and women in mathematical achievement—since it is well known that boys and girls are socialized to respond differently to imposed authority.

Although the investigations on which this book is based were conducted in England, they speak directly to the present crises in U.S. mathematics education. The roots of adult panic are planted by American schools just as they are in England. Schooling in both countries leaves many lacking confidence that their efforts at mathematics could ever produce correct results. Many emerge personally diminished from their encounter with school math, as if one of their faculties had been excised.

Educators have always known that effective teaching must educate the whole child, not just the child's mind. Being of a pragmatic bent, Americans recognize the importance of motivation to success in school, whence so much emphasis on preparation for jobs and future careers.

Laurie Buxton adds to this an insight well worth studying—that the response of pupils to mathematics teaching is as much emotional as cognitive. Failure to learn may as easily result from emotional blocks created by school practice itself as from any of the other sources (for example, curriculum, motivation, pedagogy, textbooks, or tests) more commonly found on the agenda of the school reform movement.

This volume's focus on emotions associated with the study of mathematics provides a valuable complement to the current reform agenda in mathematics education. Indeed, the interviews and ideas in this volume open an important new frontier for research in mathematics learning. Laurie Buxton's analysis adds a challenging new voice to the American dialogue about mathematics education — the voice of emotion.

Lynn Arthur Steen<br>Professor of Mathematics

St. Olaf College
Northfield, Minnesota

# Preface

If your math lessons at school were generally fruitful, rewarding, and full of interest, then some of the views expressed by the people in this book may seem surprising. If, on the other hand, you sat out these lessons in a mixture of fog, fear, bewilderment, and occasional panic, then you will learn that there are many like you.

From this book you will learn a little math and a great deal about why you feel so uncomfortable about it. If you have the nerve to explore within yourself why you should have fears quite out of proportion to the significance of the subject, you will be well on the way to removing them. You should finish the book knowing more about yourself, more about what math is really about, and ready, if you want to, to approach the learning of it in a completely fresh state of mind.

Different readers will respond best to different parts of this book. For the general reader who has great anxiety about math, the first section (chapters 1 through 6) and the third section (chapters 11 through 13) are the most relevant.

Teachers generally will benefit in addition from chapter 10 and the final section (chapters 14 and 15). Those with a research bent will find the theoretical background to the single issue of panic in chapters 7 through 10, and possible starting places for further research in the second half of the book, which begins with section 3.

In plan, therefore, the first section of the book has much anecdotal information, of interest to all; the second section proposes the theory of panic. A surprising consequence of the attitude taken to authority is developed in chapter 10. From there the discussion is widened to the general area of emotional responses, and to some new approaches to the teaching of mathematics that embrace the emotional element.

A few words on the English educational system are also in order here. By law children enter school at the age of five, although some receive monitored nursery education before this. In most parts of the country — and in the references in this book — the schools for children between the ages of five and eleven either are integrated primary schools or are subdivided between infants and juniors, with the transfer occurring at age seven. In any year the children are normally taught the full curriculum by one teacher, although there may be some special arrangements for music or physical education.

At eleven, students transfer to secondary schools, which normally enroll those of all ability levels. Here they are taught most subjects by specialists, so the pattern of the day they meet is very different from that in primary school. At sixteen, students had traditionally been offered comprehensive (but not compulsory) examinations, which were given different names at different times. In this book there are references to the *O-level* (or ordinary) examination, which was aimed at students in the top twenty-five percent in terms of natural ability. This was supplemented by a (sometimes limited) Certificate of Secondary Education (CSE), awarded to those with lower levels of ability. Results provided information to prospective employers and served as a basis for selecting students to receive further education. The most able proceeded to an *A-level* (advanced) examination at eighteen. The system is more flexible now, catering to all abilities, but the people in this book passed through this earlier system.

Since the majority of the population leaves school at sixteen (in the past, often without taking an examination), there is in England nothing comparable to the American high school, nor to graduation from high school. In England, and in this book, any reference to a graduate means someone with a college degree.

Two further notes: The terms *English* and *England* (rather than *Great Britain* and *British*) are used throughout, since the Scottish system is different. All those mentioned in the book (unless it is clearly stated otherwise) have gone through the English system. Also, the above description applies only to the state system. The arrangements for private education are different and need not concern us.

# Acknowledgments

My thanks to the Inner London Education Authority (now alas destroyed by a malevolent government), for allowing me a sabbatical to start the task of which this book is a beginning—in particular to Peter Newsam and Michael Birchenough, but most particularly to the memory of Ina Chaplin. Thanks also to the Leverhulme Foundation for a postdoctoral research grant to continue this work.

Those who provided me with material appear throughout the book, some by name (for example, Mike Brearley, Edward de Bono, and Warwick Sawyer) and some anonymously. It is evident that I owe them much and my thanks are recorded in the text; they know how I valued what they told me. My thanks also for the typing and deciphering skills of Rosita and Barbara.

Finally, it has been a pleasure and a privilege to work so closely with my friend, Richard Skemp, professor of educational theory at Warwick University, and to help develop his model of learning into this area.

# Math
# Panic

# Section One

## The Experiment

# Chapter One
## Panic in the Mind

It may seem somewhat overdramatic to talk about "panic." Certainly I would have thought so before I began research in this area; I did not lightly accept that many people feel panic when faced with a mathematical problem. Only after a number of those whom I interviewed *volunteered* that word did I begin to take it seriously, and even then I did not realize that it might lead to a central issue. The clue to its importance lay in just how specific the word "panic" is. It would not be surprising if people said that they were worried, anxious, or perhaps bored with math, but the word "panic," apart from its dramatic force, is narrower, more precise in meaning than these more general terms — and this suggests purpose and intent in its use.

As far as possible in my early interviewing, questions were open-ended. I had decided against a very set structure of questions since I wanted to be able to follow answers wherever they led, but I did explain that I was concerned with feelings about the subject rather than with what people actually knew. A typical response was: "Whenever I think back to it, it's always that dreadful numbing panic." Where feelings were less readily recalled, they quite rapidly surfaced when I actually gave the person some mathematics to do: "Now, yes...good God...straight away I'm panicking...not straightforward ...that makes me panic." The manner and intonation were quite as important as the actual words spoken, and generally confirmed that the word was appropriate and chosen with deliberation.

After a while I became interested in whether people who did not volunteer the word would do so with some little pressure. There was an evident danger in feeding in answers that I sought; once people have agreed to cooperate in being interviewed they tend to become cooperative in giving the answers they think you want. Nonetheless, a little probing seemed legitimate, and the following anecdotes illustrate this.

One Sunday, after we had been canvasing for the local elections, I sat in the local pub having a drink with some of the party faithful. Interest was shown in my study and I was soon launched upon a description of my work. One of those present, an Oxford history graduate now studying for a Ph.D., acknowledged (as about half the people I meet seem to do) that he had considerable concern about math.

"How does it make you feel?" I asked.

"Worried," said he.

I wanted to go beyond this stage, and I felt confident that he would not offer any description that he did not mean.

"Suppose I were to sit you down to do a math problem, what would be your state of mind. Is there something specific you would feel?"

"Panic!" (with a slightly nervous laugh).

I had directed him in two ways—one in insisting that he be specific and the other in bringing back the image of a classroom situation. Both I felt to be fair, and the word "panic" was his own.

In a larger group one can practically guarantee that panic is mentioned. When I was first becoming particularly interested in this reaction I spoke at a parents' meeting at a primary school, on the general topic of mathematics. I asked them how they felt about math, and how they would react if I made them do a test. There was general slightly nervous laughter, and the word "panic" was offered from several quarters and agreed to by others. On occasions like this people often come up to me afterward to pursue the point about their terror of the subject.

It was still possible that people were exaggerating and that my sensing that people genuinely meant "panic" was not to be trusted. The next step was to discuss it in greater depth and with some objectivity. So I posed the question, "Is it really panic?" both to those individuals whom I met regularly, and also to an early session of the group I recruited as part of my research project. You will meet these people often in the book; at this stage let us simply pick up some of the points they made about panic, both in its mathematical and in its more general context.

Peter was most solidly against the idea that he could panic about a school subject. His feelings, he said, were of irritation and at times a deep frustration expressed forcibly as "Why can't *I* do it?" But he claimed they did not approach the level that a word like "panic" implied. He felt this was much better reserved for life-and-death situations, and was clearly slightly embarrassed at the use of such a term unless the situation was genuinely desperate. He described such an occasion when on a climbing expedition he found himself losing his grip on a sheer cliff face. This, he said, certainly involved panic; fortunately he escaped by a sudden convulsive movement to a safe hold.

Roger once had actually fallen fifty-five feet on a mountain climb. During the fall he had not panicked but had thought calmly and clearly. At the bottom was a dog on which he was in danger of falling and, conscious of this, he had placed his feet apart to avoid the animal! Fortunately he escaped with remarkably little damage and went back on the cliff face the next day. Again he found himself coming off, and this time he did panic, freezing into total immobility; he was aware that his fingers were slipping but was unable to take any action. This time he was roped to others and rescued by them, but was totally unable to help himself.

At first sight, it seemed that we were making an extravagant leap from the classroom experiences we wished to study to such extreme dangers. I felt rather uncomfortable till several of the group assured me that the *feelings* were similar and the discussion therefore was probably relevant. So we explored more anecdotal material to do with panic, in an attempt to pin it down a little. It became apparent that panic as a *type* of feeling may relate to a variety of situations, both desperate crises of survival, and less serious ones — all evoke similar reactions.

Perhaps we should look more closely at the question of "survival." Falling off a cliff is clearly a survival issue, but are there smaller "deaths" one can die? Certainly the comic who is not found funny by his audience "dies a death," and it may well be that some classroom experiences strike so directly at us as to involve survival of a part of ourselves. In response to Peter's restriction of the use of the word "panic" to physically perilous situations, Barbara said that if she was "up against closed doors" it *was* a matter of protecting her safety: "Oh my God, I'm going to make a fool of myself — or be found out!" This is a very pertinent point. Dangers are by no means always physical.

On reflection it was felt that the more dramatic situations did not always result in panic. Peter would not in fact have escaped from the peril on the cliff face if he *had* panicked. No doubt there was at one stage intense fear, but when it came to the point a solution was found relatively calmly. This state of calmness, the antithesis of panic, was something that several of us recalled in various automobile crises. No less than three of us could remember going downhill without brakes (which does not say very much for our cars), but in every case the imminence of a serious crash did not produce panic. It *was* genuinely present, however, in the reaction described by Roger when he froze on the cliff. It had seemed natural to search for what was really meant by panic in these episodes, and this relates to the somewhat dramatic nature of the word. Now let's see how this fits in with people's feelings about math.

Certainly Peter's frustration was shared by other people, but generally it was not considered adequate to describe what was felt. Sue said that she quite commonly felt frustrated in art classes when she could not get something right, but that panic was quite different, and it was something she did experience with math. Rosita agreed, saying that frustration does at least mean that you are having a go, whereas when she felt panic she could not even get started. She also wondered if women expressed this feeling more than men, but this is the sort of question that the present study is not suited to answering; it is statistical and we do not have statistics. There is also the belief, darkly mentioned by various of the women subjects, that men would be less willing to acknowledge panic—and this I believe! Barbara felt that the word "panic" *might* be too strong, though it would be appropriate for her if she were asked to *teach* math. She went on to say that she and Susan ran their school on the basis of "We never panic," yet here we all were "using it so solemnly about math."

What did the other men in the group feel? Roger was positive that "frustration" and "irritation" were not strong enough, and he was clear that "panic" was appropriate for him. Richard said that he did experience a gradually increasing frustration and irritation and that then something cut out, though he was hesitant to acknowledge panic. When pressed further by Roger he described a statistics examination in graphic terms. The subject for him had involved learning a series of procedures, with no knowledge of why he was doing them. Came the examination and he completely dried up and could not go on. He was in panic.

At the end of this session with the group I did feel that there was a clearly recognizable (if not easily definable) state of mind called panic, and that for all of them except Peter math could bring it about. It may seem a long road to travel merely to accept the word, but for me this point needed establishing before we sought to analyze further.

But there was a final "clincher" for me, which came with Elaine. This at last made me understand the extremity of feeling that math could occasion. She identified the feeling in math with that occurring in a situation clearly far more desperate and threatening. Earlier she had spoken to me of her terror in an exam when she did not know seven times seven. She resorted to adding up seven lots of seven and then got stuck in the middle of the column in total panic. This memory and the feeling attached to it have remained etched in her mind since childhood. Quite recently her husband had been on a business trip to Israel and was much delayed in returning. He was unable to warn her and her fear gradually mounted to panic as she became convinced that he had been killed: "And I had exactly the same symptoms, now I look back on it, as I had in that exam when I was trying to add those seven sevens."

The association of matters so different in importance by this common response of panic has, in cold print, a touch of the ludicrous about it—but it rings true. After all, the strength of our emotional responses does not in fact always match the significance of the event. Minor annoyances can sometimes result in explosions of anger more dramatic than reactions to matters far more serious.

Later, in chapter 8, I will attempt to develop a model of the mind that suggests how we can interpret panic, but for now let us stick to a descriptive approach and pick out some mental and physical symptoms, some related emotions, and some of the causes, again largely in the words of my subjects rather than myself.

The buildup to a state of panic may be long or short and seems to involve a mounting tension until a critical point is reached at which things may go either of two ways. There is a sudden discontinuity in behavior, not unlike that seen in the studies of aggression in dogs by Lorenz and described in catastrophe-theory terms by Zeeman. Within the mind, something happens with almost a click of a switch. The best way to describe it may lie in the various images that have been offered.

**Sue:** You get so far and then the wall comes up.

**Richard:** It brings the shutters up.

**Martin:** But nevertheless, cachunk, down comes the blanket like a green baize cover over a parrot's cage.

**Roger:** Pushing the button that cuts out logic.

Perhaps the imagery is superfluous in the sense that if you have experienced it, you know how it is for you.

Before this point there may be tension in varying degrees; this may mean irritation, frustration, or anxiety—but beyond it lies panic. There seem to be two different states that one might properly call panic, yet they are *very* different. One is a sort of turbulence in the mind, a type of frenzy (though this is not a word anyone in the group used), of which the best image is Martin's "mind in chaos." Within, nothing is stable, information "topples out of the mind," to use Sarah's phrase. The state of mind may be accompanied by violent physical activity, such as flailing about when drowning. More common in the math classroom is a sense of paralysis, a freezing of the mind, linked often with physical tension and rigidity. It really does seem as if something locks together in the mind, rather as a car engine without oil may seize up; and this is the image we shall later follow in our analysis.

People may pass through the chaotic to the frozen stage or may simply enter paralysis directly. Rosita expresses it succinctly as "Panic means you can't start," and Sue puts it: "Panic is when you dry up before you start. Finished — done! I've never really tackled anything in math." This idea of "drying" occurs again when Roger describes two different ways of learning a play. These two ways provide a valuable metaphor for the more general processes of learning. In one, the play is learned by rote so that lines are triggered as they are cued. In the other, the general theme of the play is learned in gradually increasing detail until finally the words are filled in and committed to memory. In the first method, if one "dries" on stage it is not easy to escape and panic may rapidly ensue. The more general approach allows one to say something appropriate, to *ad lib* until one is back on track and to avoid the panic situation.

Under certain pressures therefore we arrive at a critical point where a sudden change occurs, and beyond this point our performance as an organism changes abruptly. As Roger put it: "Panic is the point where your normal logical responses cut out. Therefore you perform significantly less well than you are capable of because you can't bring all your experience to bear on the problem." This is extremely relevant in mathematics, in which students are constantly asked to demonstrate their performance in solving problems.

Interestingly, beyond the critical point may lie not panic (either of the chaotic or of the frozen kind), but a sudden enhancement of awareness, a slowing down of the world and the solution of problems normally *beyond* one's capacity, all accompanied by an unusual *calm*. This was the case in Roger's descent from the cliff and the experiences in runaway cars. Any theorizing we may do later must seek to explain both these phenomena.

Many emotional states have related physical ones, as in the connection between "mind in chaos" and physically thrashing about. Physical responses to anxiety are the basis of such things as lie detectors, though there is a long path to travel before we can assess with any real accuracy what a person is thinking from physical symptoms. This is not a line we shall pursue far, but it is worth recording the reactions of two people as they approach panic. First:

**Susan:** I feel cold and sweaty. My hands get clammy. Brain freezes and I would like to go and sit in a corner.

**Roger:** What about your guts?

**Susan:** They turn over.

Second, Elaine, who was recreating the physical symptoms as she spoke:

> Physiologically it's a tightening of the throat, with feeling a lump in the throat, feeling that you would get some release if you could cry, but "What's the use of crying? That's not going to add seven sevens or get Steven back," so you don't cry and...tension all through your limbs and a light sweat—so that's anxiety, isn't it?

Probably it is; but it is well on the road to panic.

There is an important issue here for the teacher. If a student does feel panic approaching when confronted with a piece of math there should be recognizable signs. When a person's eyes go slightly glazed and a certain rigidity enters his or her posture, here are clear warning signs. An awareness of such changes in manner can, interpreted sensitively, help us to avoid creating uncomfortable situations. We can never be sure of what is going on in the mind of another and we must rely on these outward physical signs. (See chapter 11.)

Elaine's statement leads us to ask how we may disentangle panic from other emotions, and in particular from strong anxiety. Without attempting an extended analysis of emotion we must try to characterize panic. A range of other feelings, including embarrassment, irritation, frustration, anxiety, and fear had all been mentioned in connection with math, and any or all of them might be either elements of, or precursors to, panic. Peter described how it might be possible to run the gamut of them before arriving at panic; in so doing he seemed more accepting of the word than before. Susan stated succinctly that "panic implies fear." It certainly does seem that this is true, but it may arise only from the very general nature of the emotion of fear, which may be connected with most negative and unpleasurable experiences. Acute embarrassment might lead to disordered flight, one form of behavior associated with panic, but it is certainly not an *essential* element of it. In short, to discover the elements of panic we would need a theory, rather like a chemical one, defining certain basic emotions and describing how others are compounded of them (see chapter 11). At this stage the best we might say is that it is a highly specific feeling and, most important, that it lies beyond a certain critical point. The rapidity with which a person reaches this point will depend upon how strongly the preliminary negative feelings have been reinforced in the past.

# Elements of Panic

The next major issue is to describe some of the circumstances that may bring it about. We all differ in the pressures that we can resist and in those that make us fray at the edges. It is easy to think of circumstances that cause us anxiety; the stronger pressures may lead to panic and among the range of them three seem to carry great weight.

The first is the presence of someone seen as an *authority figure*. It does not matter that this figure is not seen by him- or herself in this light; even the mildest of teachers may represent authority to some. The essence is that the figure will make *judgments* about right and wrong. The pressure that this can create, and the state of confusion and actual panic that ensue, are not easy to credit.

My friends in this work have contributed a number of telling phrases showing their awareness of authority and the pressure it puts on them. The group's evening work sessions were accompanied by drinks, and during one break Rosita was trying to work out the unit costs of sherry. She commented how much harder it would have been had I been there "looking over my shoulder." She then generalized this to the telling phrase, "The figure that knows better than you." Barbara also felt strongly about this and spoke of math as being right or wrong, with the very strong *moral* implications these words carry; she remarked that "you can be found out." Susan too said that it is all right if no one is looking on and "judging." She went on to say: "Before you get far into it someone says, 'That's wrong,' and so you don't start it after that." With Sarah I found that pressure of demands made — even if not associated with time — break up her thought patterns completely. Both Lynn and Elaine found it difficult to deal with even a suggestion of authoritarian harshness.

The second circumstance arousing panic is the emphasis which many math teachers place on *speed* as well as perception. I remember that in "training" A-level candidates I too emphasized speed, with the slightly paradoxical wish to make the time given in the examination seem ample. I would test the very able at much higher speeds than would be required in the exam, but on one occasion I reduced a boy (now an original researcher in mathematics) to a state of disintegration by this process. At the time this greatly surprised me; it does no longer, but I am pleased that I managed to repair the damage. It is a common misapprehension to believe that mathematics should be done in a hurry. Much of it requires concentrated and uninterrupted attention, but it does not generally need speed. It may well come as a surprise to those who were constantly urged to hurry at school to learn that that particular pressure is highly counterproductive.

One of my subjects had as a child been regularly tested on the tables by her father, who demanded instant response. She had the highest level of anxiety and the most rapid entry into panic that I have met. When I got her to do genuine mental arithmetic she believed that she had to answer quickly; she was very soon saying, "I can't, I can't," and clearly beginning to disintegrate. By luck I struck upon the calm phrase "No hurry" and she managed to complete 15 × 12 in her head, no mean task. (See chapter 6.) Richard's main recollection of panic was in a statistics exam, and an essential element, though not the only one, was his consciousness of the time ticking away.

Tests of mental recall of facts (often wrongly referred to as mental arithmetic) have much to answer for. In an interesting experiment done by Richard Skemp some twenty years ago, students were faced with sorting tasks in which the method of sorting had constantly to be changed. Not surprisingly this created confusion and tension, but one student reported "waves of panic." We shall later see this as a breakdown in a planning process and interpret it in terms of a model of our minds. (See chapter 9.)

In all these cases the pressure of time is enhanced by the presence of an authority figure, for even in the exam, where such a person is not actually present, someone will indeed mark and judge the work. It is not easy to remove this element, though there is evidence that some people may get very upset when they are stuck, even if they are alone and have unlimited time. They have come to believe their math will be judged and also that they must demonstrate speed in solving the problems, so that even when these conditions are absent they still believe them to hold.

Time also enters into the question of panic in a rather different way, one that at first almost seems to contradict what we have just said. Richard comments, "To panic you have to have time to panic." In this statement he is describing the gradual approach of an undesirable eventuality which you know you cannot avoid; the delay increases the fear and increases the chance of panic. More than one of the group described having to speak at some future meeting at which there was bound to be conflict or possibly exposure of one's inadequacy. Perhaps the most powerful example, however, was given by Susan. Some years ago, on a school journey, she had a fall from a loaded tractor and crushed one hand. The events of this time seemed to occur in slow motion and are deeply etched in her mind, but with no sense at any time of panic. After surgery, however, while waiting to see the eventual result, she remembers a growing tension with bouts of panic as the moment of truth approached.

These examples are more dramatic than those that the classroom might normally offer, but the panic induced by a gradually approaching threat can certainly occur there. I still remember the feeling almost of suffocation when as first-year pupils at grammar school some forty years ago we were tested on our singing and had to stand up one at a time and perform to get our exam mark. I am in fact noted for my singing, but not in the sense that would get me high marks in an exam! It was inexorable in its approach and I too felt "waves of panic." This was echoed for me just recently when I was presiding in court. In this case it was a boy in the juvenile court who had committed some offense when skipping school. He had not played hooky in the sense of taking the day off, but had missed a certain lesson. Not really expecting an answer I asked why. He explained that in English they had to stand and read in turn in front of the class and that this frightened him. This in no way mitigated his villainy once out of school, but it was wholly convincing (to me at least) as a reason for being out of school.

Sue recalled a very similar experience in gym class. The teacher insisted that they do cartwheels and she could manage only a bunny jump. She was told to do it "and they would all watch her." Sue's reaction to this was to stick her fingers down her throat to induce physical sickness before the next gym class. Her parents and teachers were all unable to understand why she was sick at ten o'clock every Thursday morning!

These examples illustrate the fact that it is not only math that causes pain, but the elements of time pressure and of judgment do seem to be more regularly present there. There are other pressures that matter, and Sue's experience in gym class did involve being watched.

This leads on to the third circumstance that can arouse panic. Susan said that an essential feature of panic is the *public situation*. She could admit failure to herself, and would be prepared to come and talk privately about it to me, but there was agreement that the public nature of an occasion could be one of the strongest pressures leading to panic; Peter said he was relatively at ease when prepared with all his material but would hate to face such a situation unprepared. The classroom *is* a public place. The child is surrounded by peers, and a question asked in front of them can be totally exposing. This applies in all class-teaching situations in all subjects, but questions tend to come thicker and faster in math than elsewhere. (See chapter 11.) I cannot go along with Susan's statement that publicity is an *essential* feature, however, for there is evidence that people do panic privately. Roger certainly says he can panic in a problem without public pressure, and this is confirmed by Richard's example of the statistics exam and by Elaine's seven sevens. Nonetheless, exposure *is* daunting, and one of the surest ways of causing panic.

A smaller point but perhaps one with some significance is how people feel if asked to teach rather than to learn math. This certainly shifts the balance of authority but is not very helpful if you feel you don't have authority! Both Susan and Sue regularly teach math to primary school children and find this reversal of roles positively helpful. Susan's trenchant attitude on starting her job was "I can teach *this* little lot," and the confidence of her professionalism even encompassed the fact that she had to teach them mathematics. Barbara, on the other hand, who has been a headmistress for some time, teaches regularly but does not teach math and would feel panicky if required to do so. Roger "could not conceive of teaching it."

A lost child, particularly in an unknown and mysterious place, rapidly panics. This may (though it is only speculative) be at the root of some of the adverse response to mathematics. Certainly some attitudes to math convey this sort of image. It is seen as a vast mountain of unknown material that has to be remembered. The material is somehow mysterious, cannot be coped with, and there is no way through it. From the time of Pythagoras, there has been a certain mystique about the subject, and this is reflected in Barbara's view that this mountain is peopled by those who *do* know about it and claim what fun it all is. A couple of remarks from Roger indicate the feeling: "Out in realms you know you are not familiar with," and "The pressure is provided by the things that I don't know."

There may be a chance here to distinguish some elements of fear and panic. Fear can derive from perfectly clearly understood situations; panic-producing situations may more often have in them the element of the unknown or the incomprehensible, so that one cannot possibly behave appropriately. It is difficult to capture the range of feelings in this area and clearly it would help to get many more people to express themselves about it; of course this book in itself is part of the exercise.

We have got ahead of ourselves in this first chapter. It was necessary to make a point, but now let us get back to how it all began.

# Chapter Two
## An Idea for an Experiment

There is disquiet at the moment about mathematics teaching. This is not new; it arises with distressing regularity. Nonetheless, there is good reason for undertaking a study of certain ill effects that our math teaching has had and is perhaps still having. The ultimate aim must be to improve what goes on in the classroom, though if others also benefit, that is a most desirable bonus.

Three different strands led to the beginning of this study. Those people working in math rapidly become aware not only that few share their interest, but also that the subject is regarded with some distaste. This consciousness, accepted but largely unexamined, was the first strand. The second was a constant desire to know more about what teaching and learning mean. Through my own professional development, and then through the opportunity to observe a vast range of teaching styles and techniques, I became aware that there was little organized thought about how people *felt* about learning, and the emotional responses that math might generate in the classroom. The third strand lies in my involvement over many years with the ideas of my friend Richard Skemp and in particular with his new model of intelligence (Skemp 1979). More needs to be said about each of these strands.

## Feelings of Distaste

There is much evidence that many adults greatly dislike math. The feelings of uncertainty and anxiety are constantly expressed to me at parents' meetings at schools, and also in many casual conversations. Bad experiences at school are well remembered and the statements made about them are very explicit. Some of these expressions come unbidden, but the flow is greatly increased when people realize how genuinely interested I am in the way they feel. It is this change in my attitude from a mere awareness of the negative feelings to a positive desire to know about them that releases the floodgates of information from others. The things that are said may not individually seem remarkable, but few of those who told me how they felt had been able to express those feelings at the time they were undergoing them. Their teachers may have been kindly, but the discussion of emotional response was not seen as part of the teaching process. This was most unfortunate.

The evidence goes beyond the direct and explicit. Feelings are not strongly expressed in most social situations, but that does not mean they are not strongly felt. Experience in behavioral studies, particularly in leaderless groups, shows how powerful feelings may be when not covered by social convention or by the demands of an explicit task. In more usual circumstances one must look for hints about how people feel. The information is there but it is necessary to look positively for it. The pretense of a shudder that people give when they hear you are a mathematician, accompanied by a laugh meant to indicate the reaction is only in fun, is then seen to have a clear meaning — expressed by the shudder, not the laugh. Similarly the reaction of backing away, with hands raised as if to ward you off, may not exactly mean that the person regards ability in math in the same light as a social disease, but it does imply that you should not parade it if you wish to win friends and influence people. The fear and anxiety expressed in these semi-humorous ways are in fact present. We should not exaggerate their extent, but, like "panic" in our introduction, they are perfectly proper words to use. The spoken response seldom varies. When you state an interest in math it is rarely met with the invitation, "Oh, how interesting; do tell me more." Rather there is the fairly obvious "let's talk about something else" ploy expressed in one of two ways. There may be the defensive "Oh, I was never any good at mathematics," or alternatively, we have the surface compliment "You must be very clever," said with the evident accompanying meaning that you may also be a threat and a bore.

# Developments in Math

There have been many changes in teaching in the last forty years (though some teachers have not changed). To understand how these, too, lead up to this study we need to know something of them, and this will involve a slight digression. Most people know that "school" math in particular has changed. These changes encompass the *content* of what is taught, the *method* of teaching it, and the *relationships* between teacher and taught and the degree of control asserted in the classroom.

**Changes in content.**   Mathematics is a constantly developing subject, and at the time of the great period of Greek civilization it was regarded differently from the way in which we see it now. Yet much of what was taught in classrooms until the 1960s would have been clearly recognizable to the classical Greeks. Then began the move toward new material, and topics such as sets, transformation geometry, and topology began to appear on syllabuses, causing great disturbance to those teachers who did not understand them, and the usual reactions from all those who do not wish to see any change at all. It was not necessary that the methods used in teaching them should be different, though the material often demanded more conceptual understanding with less emphasis on manipulative techniques.

**Changes in method.**   Yet new thinking did then lead to changes in method. We saw the growth of activity methods, in which children actually did things with concrete materials; discovery methods, in which they were expected to find things out for themselves; and the breaking down of the idea that a class must be taught as a whole. We saw the development of group work and individualized learning. I myself remember starting as a teacher more than thirty years ago, seeing the task as one of clear exposition to a class which sat attentively (I hoped) receiving my words. There is still room for good expositors; a lecture given to a large audience by someone who really knows the subject has clear value and can give great pleasure. It is not the only way; a person who can do this but cannot cope with other forms of organization is obviously limited as a teacher. New and diverse skills are now needed.

**Changes in relationships.**   When we come to the matter of authority and control the changes are more complex. Relationships between teacher and taught have become less formal. This is evidenced by less show of deference on the part of the pupils. It neither needs nor should involve any decrease in courtesy. The freedom of movement that certain methods imply is sometimes interpreted as lack of control by those who prefer their charges to remain seated in formal lines. Control may indeed be more difficult in active classrooms but it is no less necessary. For me, control is measured purely and simply by the proportion of purposive work that is achieved. In these terms a class that is bored but motionless, with shutters down behind apparently open eyes, is not in control, in that it is not doing what it is supposed to do. It can be as unfruitful as the other extreme, that of a room in chaos with the pupils doing what they choose, which will by no means always be valuable to them.

Classes, then, can vary in all these parameters: in type of material, from the highly traditional to the way-out modern; in method, from the rigidly uniform (be it new or old) to the interestingly varied; and in style and weight of control. The three are to some considerable extent independent. It is possible, for instance, to teach traditional material in varied ways and with informal relationships. Equally, new material can be presented solely through the medium of class teaching and with the rigid "control," which may be the antithesis of control in the terms I have defined it.

All changes along these three lines are presumably intended by the teacher to achieve greater learning by the pupils, and each teacher has his or her own idea as to which is the best way to do it. Some teachers will make explicit the criterion that their students should *like* what they are doing, and that their choice of approach has that in mind. It is claimed by proponents of one or another style that behavior is better with a certain mode, and that this indicates that it is better liked. But the views of liking or not are general, not specific. There has been no detailed consideration of what is enjoyed and what is not, nor of the very specific emotional response that content, method, or relationships may induce. There are many and varied ways of testing what has been *learned* but not what has been *liked*. There may well be a high correlation between the two, but we can only speculate; we do not know.

This consideration has brought us to the point of departure. It is necessary to know not only what our pupils learn through our various methods of approach, but what their emotional reactions to it are.

# Math and Emotion

Mathematics is commonly seen as a study based on reason, with the emotions rarely engaged. There is a belief in its firmness, precision, and fixity; this is associated with a feeling in some that it is not created, is certainly not man-made, but is external and intractable. This was confirmed by someone who learned early on that he could not manipulate it as he could people — and felt aggrieved. He now works as an educational psychologist.

A mathematician would not accept these views, but that such beliefs are widely held is a fact. They lead to an odd antithesis — that math is not connected with emotion and that in many people it demonstrably evokes decidedly strong emotional responses of a very negative sort. It raises in a pointed fashion the question, old but largely unresolved, of the relationship between reason and emotion. The aim now is to suggest an initial model that will represent the ways in which they interact, and eventually to extend it as the result of our study, in order to offer explanations of some of the causes of success and failure in math. Mathematics is an appropriate field for such a study because of the clear demands it makes on the cognitive processes, but some of the following observations may also prove relevant to the study of other subjects.

**Reason and emotion.** It would be sensible to ask whether we can treat reason and emotion in any sense separately. Certainly the fact that language, which develops to match concept formation, distinguishes between reason and emotion, between thinking and feeling, and classifies separately the cognitive and the affective, permits us to speak of them as distinct. In this area language is a most important guide.

Both character and behavior are often expressed in terms with emotional bases; in the mediaeval view, Man was compounded of "humors," such as the choleric or the melancholic. We may speak of someone as being a "frustrated" or "angry" person, and beside these is sometimes placed the image of a "rational" person as if this were one of a range of humors; but there is, in fact, a fundamental distinction between reason and the other characteristics. Alternatively, human behavior is sometimes seen as ranging in a spectrum between the highly rational and the deeply emotional (and the adverbs used may be significant). This can lead to a position at which reason and emotion are regarded as so integrated that they cannot usefully be distinguished.

The view taken here is that although reason and emotion cannot exist independently, it may be helpful to treat them as conceptually distinct (even to the extent of representing them in different boxes in diagrams). This does not mean that they should be theorized about separately, and indeed the whole purpose of this study is to consider their interaction. A change in one induces change in the other. This implies that behavior cannot be considered as resulting from one or the other, but that both must be taken into account. It is essential in all learning situations that what the students are feeling should be regarded as being as important as what they are "thinking," even in subject areas such as math that are believed to be largely concerned with the cognitive. People can remember their feelings about math at school with some intensity, but can recall almost none of the content of the subject. The message is clear.

Our model will therefore treat reason and emotion as distinct but once they are operating as being strongly interactive. The study will be directed mainly at this interaction and less at the nature of reason and emotion.

**The nature of a model.**   Before setting up a model it is worth making some observations about the purpose of model making. It is certainly a very important human activity, and may in fact be the single mental attribute that gives us our present dominance over other species. No model can properly represent actuality, but nonetheless, we do seem to improve our understanding by constructing speculative models, even when they attempt the difficult task of modeling our own understanding.

Models of the solar system, such as those of Ptolemy and Copernicus, sought to explain the motion of the heavenly bodies and to *predict* where they would be. However many accurate predictions are made, the truth of a model cannot thereby be established. If sufficient complications are introduced into the Ptolemaic system it may predict the position of the planets reasonably well; but there are good reasons for our abandonment of it. It is curious that the fact that we now regard it as conceptually wrong to place the Earth at the center of the planetary system does not alter the fact that the geocentric system was useful in predicting the position of planets—and could still be used to do so within certain limits. Succeeding models do this better and are applicable to a wider range of situations.

Theories about human behavior are likely at this stage to have a different status from those relating to the physical world. There may be narrow areas where the stimulus-response theories of the behaviorists seem to afford some explanations and prediction, but the position taken in this book is different. Such theories as we construct will not be *scientific* in the sense in which Karl Popper defines the word (see Magee 1973). A scientific theory seeks to make exact predictions, albeit sometimes over a limited range. It can be tested by its predictive capacity, but the important criterion is that it makes forecasts that may be proved false in the event. If they are, then the theory has to be modified. Einstein's model of the universe offered predictions that could be tested. Had they failed, the superiority of the model over Newton's would not have been established.

In dealing with human behavior the situation is somewhat different. A psychotherapist may, as a result of background theory, help someone in emotional difficulty. The information the therapist receives from a patient may suggest a theoretical explanation and also a response that, the therapist predicts, will be helpful. The matter is far less cut and dried than is the position of a planet at a particular time. Justification may lie merely in its helping more people than it harms! We may be at a pre-Ptolemaic stage in this particular field. Our models will not offer clear predictions, the failure of any one of which would lead to a modification of the model.

In constructing a model of the interaction between reason and emotion we are tackling a very difficult problem. At best, it can offer us some insights, explain and predict some forms of behavior, and suggest that some modes of behavior are unprofitable. We must speculate from what we see of others and from what they tell us. We have the very valuable experience of our own inner workings, though both in this and in working with others, the process of observation affects behavior. This is of course true in the physical sciences, where the instruments we choose and the way in which we use them can affect our observations, but the difficulty is likely to be much greater in interpersonal reactions. If, however, some people eventually say, "Yes, that is how it seems to be to me; it explains something of myself," an end has been achieved, for that is the basis on which people can move forward and make changes in the way they learn and understand.

Finally it should be said that Popper does not use "unscientific" as a pejorative term in describing a theory, but rather uses the word of theories that do not conform to certain criteria. Freudian theory is unscientific in Popper's sense, but its value is not in doubt.

**Skemp's theory.**    Some theorizing by Skemp (Skemp 1979) will be the basis for our examination of the relationship between mathematics and emotion.

In seeing much of our activity as goal directed and to some marked degree under our control, Skemp adopts a stance very distinct from that of the behaviorists. The extent to which our lives are goal directed is a legitimate area for argument and may depend on exactly how we are to define a "goal." But in the study of attitudes toward math it does seem clear that goals, defined either by ourselves, or more often by others, are regularly present, and this line of approach is therefore highly appropriate. The central activity of intelligence Skemp sees as model building, and it is the quality of these models and of the plans we make in using them to achieve goals that distinguishes us from the other living species. He further sees the activities of model building and goal seeking as strongly linked to survival, and indeed these abilities allow us to plan ahead and to avoid dangers to a marked degree. It would be possible to argue that they are as much concerned with dominance as with survival. They certainly are the basis for our present dominance in this world, although it may well be that some of the consequences of our model building could just as well lead to our own destruction as to our survival! But we will concentrate on the simple starting point that we do in fact make models in our minds and use them to achieve certain goals.

An added characteristic we have is the ability to reflect upon what we are doing, and in particular to monitor our progress toward some goal we have set ourselves or have been set. This feedback information then generates *emotion*, and this makes the first important step to a link between cognitive activity and emotional response. Difficulty in reaching a goal may generate feelings of frustration or perhaps disappointment, while approaching it may afford feelings of confidence and elation. We are not yet at a stage where we can ascribe very specific feelings to particular goal-directed situations, and we should perhaps offer only the two broad responses of pleasure or unpleasure (sometimes called "hedonic tone") at approaching or receding from a goal. This in simplistic terms directly relates goal achieving to pleasure, and the spectrum of pleasure/unpleasure to the assessment of how near our present position is to a desired goal. This response is somewhat more intellectual than the feelings of pleasure and unpleasure resulting from the satisfaction or otherwise of basic instinctual drives such as hunger and sex. Koestler comments, in *The Ghost in the Machine* (1967): "The hedonic tone depends on several factors and could be described as the feedback report on the progress or otherwise of the drive towards its real, anticipated or imaginary target." This general position we can accept, but will extend in a more analytic form.

**Motivation.**   The feedback process, being a continual one, has further consequences. It is no new thought that success in reaching goals breeds confidence, but, before we have reached a goal, a feedback report that we are approaching it appears to lend weight to our reasoning powers and enables us to drive through difficulties we might not otherwise overcome. This "weight" appears to be lent by the emotions. We feel ourselves to be strongly *motivated*. Motivation then becomes internal and related to continued success or the expectation of it, rather than an inducement offered by someone else. The teacher must provide opportunities for success that encourage this internal experience and do not rely on external rewards.

Activity that is apparently purely cognitive can certainly result in strong emotions, as evidenced by some comments made by Bertrand Russell, the first of which many people may find almost unbelievable: "At the age of 11 I began Euclid...this was one of the great events of my life, as dazzling as first love. I had not imagined there was anything so delicious in the world" (1967, 36). Elsewhere he says, "My work goes ahead at a tremendous pace and I get intense delight from it."

(Characteristically, he adds in a footnote that this piece of work turned out to be all nonsense!)

The contrast with the experience of math that most people have had is somewhat marked. If success in reasoning gives such emotional pleasure, it is not surprising that it is then pursued with more energy and with the weight of the emotions behind it. The relation of the emotions to cognitive processes is expressed slightly differently by Einstein, who at the same time emphasizes the model-building activity.

> Man tries to make for himself in the fashion that suits him best a simplified and intelligible picture of the world; he then tries to some extent to substitute this cosmos of his for the world of experience. This is what the painter, the poet, the speculative philosopher and the natural scientist do, each in his own fashion. Each makes this cosmos and its construction *the pivot of his emotional life*, in order to find in this way the peace and security that he cannot find within the all-too-narrow realm of swirling personal experiences. (Italics mine)

Certainly this suggests that the cognitive drive derives from an emotional need, and transcends the notion that this drive is supported simply by the pleasure engendered by its own success. Such evidence from very profound thinkers makes it clear that their emotions are strongly locked into their reasoning activities in a positive manner. A number of creative mathematicians experience such obsessive pleasure in "thinking" that they will ignore the ordinary creature comforts for long periods at a time while absorbed in their passion.

To most of my subjects pleasurable obsession with anything remotely connected with mathematics would be quite foreign, but it was achieved with Elaine on one occasion, and the problem is worth recounting. I had asked her to visualize a cube and she had answered a string of questions about the number of faces and edges. (See appendix A.) I asked her to see it as three inches each way and that it had to be cut into one-inch cubes. How many saw cuts would this take? She worked very contentedly with this problem; the cube kept returning to her mind and she felt real pleasure that it should do so. Though she did not in fact solve this problem, she was successful with several other spatial problems, content that she had explored this particular one, and felt happy to have it explained to her. She later reported: "The next day, on the way to County Hall for an interview that I thought was absorbing my thoughts, an image of the cube correctly cut appeared suddenly and with apparent irrelevance in my mind."

The experience of pleasurable absorption in a problem is so satisfying that were we able to achieve it with any regularity in our students they could face the many inevitable failures they will experience without emotional revulsion from the subject.

┌─────────────────────────────────────────────────────────────┐
│                                                             │
└─────────────────────────────────────────────────────────────┘

**Figure 2-1**   The relationship between mathematics and emotion

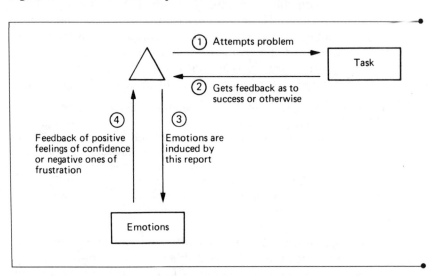

**A first model.** At this stage then let us merely make the cautious assumption that, whatever one's reasoning capacity, its effectiveness is strongly dependent on the degree to which the emotions aid or impede it in the particular task upon which it is engaged. The emotions provide an important survival function. They ring danger bells when some undesired end (antigoal) approaches. So not only do emotions influence the performance of our reason in tackling a task, but they also tell us which tasks should be tackled and which not. Some people will find that setting this out in diagrammatic form will help, although our study has shown that this may certainly not always be so. One subject, on seeing an article of mine illustrated with diagrams, remarked with some distaste, "It made it seem like a textbook." Let the words speak if the diagram shown in figure 2-1 does not. In the diagram reason is denoted by a Greek letter delta ($\Delta$).

At this point then, an area of study based on experimental work became delineated. There were three strands to the study. The first strand at this time was largely one of casual observation, yet it was from this that the "subjects" for my study would emerge. The second strand was experiential, a considerable backlog of accumulated knowledge that needed sorting and making explicit. The third strand was the beginnings of some theory that needed to be modified and extended as I reflected on what people told me. This led on to the experiment described in the following chapters.

# Chapter Three
## The Experiment Begins

## Design and Rationale

The natural approach might have been to discover how a large number of children think—so perhaps we need to justify a study of how *a few adults feel*. The former approach is widespread in mathematical education. We shall examine one by one the features of the present approach: why "few," why "adults," and why particularly, "how they feel" rather than how they think.

**Why "few"?** The number of people studied is clearly important. To make comments with genuine statistical validity implies the mounting of a fairly large-scale operation, and if this is not done one cannot even support terms such as "most" or "many," though presumably "some" is acceptable! Broad attitudes may in fact be the conclusion of many years of listening to many people, but certainly not in a respectably organized fashion. In statistical approaches, however open-ended the initial exploratory work, it is necessary at the end to produce some standardized tests or questionnaires to distribute to a substantial number of people and on which the statistical results would be based. Such information is almost always interesting and useful, but it is not the only way of finding out. Most questions depend considerably on what has already been said, and they form sequential chains different for every interview. Naturally a questionnaire will often be designed to take into account likely sequences, but it does ultimately constrain. It may be that returning to the same few people, with more and more questions based on what has gone before, elicits different information, and that it is neither a more nor a less valid approach, but simply a different one. There is in the long run a test involving large numbers—and that is if many people read this book and then find it relevant or otherwise.

There is another problem involved in close work with few people, and that is that one is bound to affect the situation far more than a detached observer. Affecting an experiment by observing it is a standard difficulty in the natural sciences. In psychological work the difficulty is even more evident; this is accepted rather than avoided. What people say about what they feel is affected by the fact that they are speaking to a particular person. Again the appeal must be simply to a larger audience, with the question, "Is this how you feel?"

It is interesting that the statistical approach has been particularly evident in the United States, where it is difficult to appear academically respectable without a great number of figures and cross-referencing to other authorities. On the other hand, the important work of Krutetskii in the Soviet Union has a much more "individual" approach, in which the work of various children is followed (Krutetskii 1971). This approach has influenced what I have done, and there is much one can learn from it. It is amusing that a society that claims to emphasize the individual should resort to heavy statistical work while one that extols the collective examines individuals.

**Why "adults"?**   For this experiment I worked with intelligent, articulate adults, most of them involved with the education world. It is not easy to define what is meant by either intelligent or articulate, and we should accept these words in their ordinary everyday sense, with the implied vagueness entailed. These adults had mostly failed O-level math (an examination taken at age sixteen in England; slightly below high school graduation in the United States) or its equivalent at school. In some sense, that might suggest a relatively high level of performance in math, since if one is even allowed to enter for an exam designed for the top 25 percent of the population one is likely to be above average for that population! There were some who were not allowed to take the exam, others who refused to do so, and some who succeeded after three or four attempts. The failure in math was specific; they had strings of other O-levels and many much higher qualifications. They also claimed to be apprehensive in varying degrees about working at math, but all would have liked to be able to do it.

There were therefore various criteria for their selection, but the main one was whether they were willing to help. Great kindness was shown by everyone in their willingness to give the time involved in the initial survey. The commitment of time and energy of the ten who eventually worked throughout the year was enormous. They hoped to learn, and I believe did so, but there was nothing else I could offer these very busy people, except my thanks.

Why then, these particular adults? The brief was to find out why people were frightened of math, or, in rather more academic terms, to study the cognitive-affective interaction. It was necessary therefore to have people who could describe their emotional reactions in a rational manner, who could remember, or even directly experience at that moment, anxiety about math—and then speak about it. The ability to discuss emotion in this way is present in some mature adults but in few children.

There was another most important ethical consideration. Since we were looking at the problem of stress in doing math it was clear that such stress was going to be created at times. In fact it was only occasionally in the group, and more frequently with the individuals, that stressful situations occurred. It would have been unacceptable to do this with children deliberately, though it must be said that they encounter plenty of stress already.

**Why "how they feel"?**   The adults who worked with me had left their school days well behind, and their feelings of those times were overlaid with many subsequent experiences. These feelings were also seen through adult minds, themselves skilled in teaching, and reinterpreted in the light of this. The distancing involved had some advantage in that the experiences could be seen with more objectivity, but of course the view may have been distorted for the reasons suggested. There were several counters to this. First, it does seem (though this will need more substantiation) that memories of feelings are less likely to be distorted than those of actual events. Secondly, the points remembered from school have been subjected to the selectivity of the memory process, and those recalled may be the more significant ones. Thirdly, the actual mathematical material helped us into the past. One of the group felt at one time that I was pressing on some point that caused pain in adolescence because the material used was that learned at that time. This idea was an important one, and the notion of math offering a ladder back into the past is developed further in chapter 7. However, the most important reason for not being overconcerned with the distance from the original learning (or nonlearning) situation was that we were in fact mostly studying feelings experienced in the here and now. If someone recoiled from tackling a piece of math, their feelings *at that moment* were the object of study. It may be that as adults these reactions were different from those that children experience in the classroom, but it seems unlikely. Certainly as adults they not only had the power to articulate their feelings, but were also in a situation where they were expected to do so.

The quality of the findings depended heavily on the quality of those who helped. I myself have not generally had negative feelings about mathematics, so I simply did not know, and still do not know in the genuine experiential sense, what it is like for them. It was necessary that they should tell me, and that I should try to make sense of what I

was told. I am confident that a great deal that is important has been
told to me, whatever I have made of it.

In all, there were three modes of inquiry. In the first, which was
mainly preparatory, various people talked for an hour at a time,
somewhat discursively, offering hints and suggestions to explore in
greater depth. The next mode was the group work, which we shall
shortly discuss in more detail. This involved finding seven or eight
people who had not participated in the earlier introductory conversations. This optimal group size was determined in the light of general
observations on groups, which indicate that difficulty in communication is experienced by some people once this number is exceeded.
The final group of seven — eight if I include myself — was balanced as
far as the sexes were concerned, although in the study of math there
is, for whatever reason, quite a sharp sex differentiation. Finally, it
was decided to have weekly two-hour sessions to maintain the
momentum. We met thirty-six times.

The third mode of inquiry was the individual "in-depth" series of
interviews. So interesting were some of the initial individual conversations that this method seemed sensible; it was found to be extremely
fruitful. Ideally it would have been good to work with two men and
two women. In the event it turned out to be three women, but they all
had much to tell. The intention was to have interviews at intervals of
not less than a week; they were obviously more flexible in arrangement
than those of the group, and if one session needed to be cancelled
because of illness or for any other reason, that did not create a problem.
Two of the subjects were interviewed roughly two dozen times each
during the academic year; the third, whose extended case study appears
as chapter 6, only a dozen times.

All individual sessions were taped, as were most of the group
ones. Some were transcribed in full, but from most extended notes
were made. These were then available for examination. As the year
progressed, ideas that had been discussed were written up in the form
of a series of reports, eventually numbering twenty, ranging from two
to twenty-four typewritten sides. These too were distributed for
comment to all ten of the subjects. They form the basis for
many sections of this book. The total volume of work was therefore
considerable, but the pace and concentration were enjoyable.

## The Initial One-on-One Interviews

The first step was to find out what needed to be investigated in depth.
Among the two dozen people who were willing to give up an hour or

more of their time to discuss the matter (a stressful exercise for one or two of them) were heads of three major London secondary schools; several other heads; a range of people in advisory work, including two of my colleagues in the London Inspectorate; two well-known educational journalists; a number of teachers; and several others not connected at all with the educational world. They were all willing to do so first because they hoped it might help others to understand how bad an experience attempting to learn math can be and also to help perhaps improve it for our present young generation. What they told me I found immensely relevant; it is to be hoped that others will too. Every person was successful in what he or she was doing, and it may be a surprise to some that failure to understand math need not inhibit a career in education!

Hints and suggestions for ideas that needed to be looked at more closely constantly arose from their comments. They are discussed here under four broad headings, but many contain points that were later categorized in different ways.

**School life.** Attitudes toward their schooling varied from affection to horror. For some their relative failure in math was a matter of puzzlement in an otherwise enjoyable school life, for others the lowest spot in a generally disastrous experience. Some liked their teachers; others did not. Reflections of mature adult minds on those teachers are very telling: "All assumed that what they were saying was comprehensible. The math teacher only explained anything once and then it was very difficult for anyone to ask questions, because she always gave the impression that anyone who didn't understand the thing the first time was quite stupid." And from someone else: "If you responded correctly to the marks he made on the blackboard you evidenced understanding; if you responded incorrectly you were somehow breaking a code that he had established which you were supposed to conform to."

When we reach chapter 4 we shall see such remarks fitting naturally into categories. They are sophisticated observations, made in retrospect. As children, the speakers could not have expressed them in these terms, but they remain valid. Perhaps there are fewer teachers now like those characterized — but there are *some*. Another remark, related perhaps more to algebra than to the teacher's attitude, exemplifies a sense of bewilderment that characterized many people's attitudes: "Seeing a math teacher writing letters on a board seemed to be a very odd thing to have him doing at all."

Sanctions were usually directed at lack of understanding (and not, as might have seemed more fair, at laziness or some other fault that could possibly be corrected by sanction). Parents sometimes reinforced these sanctions at home, and a number of people had felt in consequence that there was no escape. Punishment varied from mild and oblique expressions of dismay or disappointment (sometimes carrying great weight in the child's mind) through blatant derision ("I was being singled out as a ludicrous object") to savage beatings. The apparent strength of the sanction did not always match the strength of the effect on the child. Expressed disappointment could have a much greater effect on a sensitive child than could a beating on a child inured to that treatment.

Two people, whose early experiences were not in fact in English schools, make comment. The first says, "The teachers believed in caning in primary school and that put the fear of God in me and I was never at school." He notes about his father: "When I was between seven and ten he must have realized my arithmetic was very bad and he set me long division while my friends were playing outside. I was crying my eyes out. He locked me up for two to three hours, but I just couldn't do them." The other revealed: "I've always associated math with fear and trembling. I managed to escape with a beating once a term." He later went on to say: "It was the whole school ethos. You got your figures in nice lines and you had vertical lines in the math books (which my handwriting didn't 'fit' into anyway), and if you didn't do it, it was a mark of insolence and deviation and all sorts of things."

Many people had very clear memories of their performance at school; some could remember grades in particular examinations, others exactly where they gave up in the subject. I asked one person at what point he first felt uncertain and unhappy about it. His reply: "When I was asked to do the two times tables." An early starter! Another lasted longer: "Well, I know the point where understanding switched off. It was somewhere just beyond quadratic equations and I learned the formula." For another it was when $\theta$ first appeared. He asked the teacher what it was and was told it was a circle with a line across! He felt that it must be something rather grand, but gave up trying to understand.

One person, remarkably unsuccessful at math, but with a good degree and a senior post in the educational world, had very detailed recall of his performance. His father was a carpenter and believed that math was the only school subject that mattered. He accepted his father's view and worked very hard at the subject, with no success, but, he claims, with no distaste whatsoever. The whole experience of math has been one of a sense of frustration and yet not upsetting. He wanted to do math, he still wants to do math and he does not know why he cannot do it. At primary school he had no difficulty with addition, subtraction, multiplication, and division but "problems" were another matter. In his homework he used to get three out of five right and make stupid mistakes in the other two. In the "scholarship" exam, the 11 + — formerly taken to determine whether one went at the age of eleven to a grammar school (having passed) or to a secondary modern school (having failed) — he got three completely right and he remembers to this day the stupid mistake he made in another. His father was very cross and he himself was very upset. At his grammar school there were four math sets and he was shocked at being in the fourth. He had to conceal it from his father, regarding it as shameful. He was determined to work to get out of it. The following year there were five math sets. He was in the fifth! At General Schools (the forerunner of O-level) he could not get a pass, let alone the credit necessary for matriculation. In the sixth form he took math as an elective, slaved at it, spending more time on it than anything else, and again met with dismal failure.

His determination, and his deeply etched memories, are quite remarkable. I have a great desire to teach him some math!

**Personal reactions.**   Later it was possible to be more detailed and specific about feelings generated. Oddly enough, to understand emotion, we need to have it expressed in as articulate a manner as possible in *cognitive* terms. At this stage many remarks had emotional content, and a few may show their variety. One very curious ambivalence was expressed in remarks widely separated in one interview: "A string of figures and my brain seizes up," and then later: "I don't really know whether I do in fact like numbers or not. When I see numbers on doors I add or multiply them. An obsession with me. For a person who doesn't like math why should I do that?"

A feeling of frustration is widespread: "My frustration at not being able to do math then led to a frustration at being obliged to spend time on it which might be used better elsewhere." This feeling is often allied with bewilderment: "And the thing I remember about math of course is *fantastic* lack of comprehension." When pressed further for his reaction to a particular problem he explained: "Well, it's a bugger's muddle is what goes on in my head when I'm faced with that." And one last reaction, from another person: "Early on I was given the clear indication that I was a mathematical buffoon and I acted on that principle and I quite consciously gave up."

There was generally some disquiet about early authority relationships, both with teachers and with parents. Some of this was not easy to follow up because of its personal nature. The importance of math had often been emphasized, and this added the weight of the teacher's authority to that of the subject, so that some reactions to math were therefore standard reactions towards authority. Some people had been submissive and when not able to do things had sought to cover it up. They experienced shame. Others, more rebellious, sought to deny the importance of the subject and paraded the fact that "I can't do math." These modes were not sharply defined and an individual might move back and forth between them. The lack of balance that can be produced by an authoritarian approach was expressed by the remark, "Authority figures often ask about unimportant matters and thereby give them a cachet they do not deserve." This has certainly affected the view of many people about what is and is not important, and is shown in the earlier quotation about keeping figures in neat horizontal and vertical columns.

At this stage the question of reaction to time pressure did not come through as strongly as later, but in retrospect, people did feel they were supposed to answer quickly when I asked them a mathematical problem. One, when taxed about this, said he did think it had to be done quickly. Another person, a woman, was more explicit and said that, when rushed, "I just *blank off.*" The various pressures were clearly intertwined and it was only later that the significance of authority and time pressures emerged more strongly.

**The nature of mathematics.** Mathematics was spoken of as cold, precise, formal, and abstract. One person said of a problem, "I can't think abstractly enough for this sort of thing," though he later claimed to get pleasure from formal algebraic procedures. There was a general belief in its firmness, precision, and fixity. In one case the latter two notions were regarded as identical and this meant that the idea of variation, an important one in math, could not be accepted. These feelings were associated with the belief that math is not created, is certainly not manmade, but is external and intractable. This term was introduced by someone who stated, "I felt I could not actively impose my own personality on the material which was being presented," though later he said, "I realize now that it has got some importance in terms of what it is to be a human being."

There was an acceptance that there were "rules of the game" in math, but it was not understood how many of these were dictated by our own choice and what a high degree of tractability in fact exists in the subject. Perhaps the general feeling was summed up in the comment: "Mathematics has been presented to me as a fixed body of knowledge, which has been handed down, which embodies certain abstract truths, and which one has been expected to imbibe of and reproduce." One comment that proved particularly helpful in later work contains an important truth: "It seems to me to be a very private occupation whereas writing, speaking, drawing, are partly communicative."

Some saw math as having a sort of mystique, and this was strongly put: "I dislike doctors because they seem to have wrapped themselves round in magic — mystique — and I feel mathematicians have the same quality." Pursuing this, I asked him if he saw mathematicians as priests and he replied "Yes" very firmly. To my question, "And do they have power?" he replied, "Priests always have power, don't they?" This view was supported, quite independently, by someone who saw mathematics as a sort of esoteric religion, with its gurus and their enthusiastic disciples. Some were envious of the power that mathematicians (supposedly) had, and two saw math as a secret garden denied to them.

It was not easy for people to reconcile these ideas of mathematics as an ivory tower with the evident usefulness of some aspects of it. A number of discussions centered on its "relevance" and whether this determined if it was interesting or not. One person remarked that she had failed math at O-level but got the higest mark the school had had in "Physics with Chemistry" — a combined O-level exam available at that time. This was most unusual, and she explained:

> The important distinction here is that in the classroom, math was a matter of juggling around with symbols and numbers, where it had no meaning at all in my mind. In physics your $u$'s and $v$'s represented certain quantities, and you had a purpose in working out a formula to find a focal length. In a sense because the symbol wasn't abstract, because it represented focal length or whatever, it had a reality it lacked in math lessons.

A geographer took a similar view. He had been involved in a study of a projected new line on the London Underground and its likely effects. He found this study strongly motivating, despite its mathematical content. Indeed, he even enjoyed the math involved.

At a more basic everyday level there were a number of comments like this one: "I'm the accountant at home. I do the accounts perfectly, of course!" Matters such as decorating, arranging a kitchen, and the demands of a job selling calculators ("Once I realized I had to earn a living by it, I really got my nose down and learned") were all coped with and even enjoyed. Two people felt that the outcome had to be more than practical, it had to be *concrete*, something had to be made as a result of using some math. Yet I believe that these people were capable of abstract and formal thinking in other areas.

All this would seem to argue for the importance of "relevance" in the subject in order to interest, yet there were counterindications. I offered people a number of mathematical problems of doubtful practical relevance and asked them not to do them, but to say if they were intrinsically interesting. Generally they were found to be so. A typical question was, "Do the prime numbers go on forever?" I am unaware of any practical use of knowing the answer, but most found it an interesting question. (See chapter 14.)

There was a sharp distinction between my interviewees and those who like math, with regard to remembering. For those who take readily to math it is a lazy person's subject, with not much remembering and with little revision before exams. It was not seen like that by the people who spoke to me. The main bugbear was geometry:

> We had to learn the theorems by heart (fifty or so) and then regurgitate them. In no way was I going to pass the geometry exam.
>
> You just had to remember them...lots of them.
>
> By learning the rules I got by in arithmetic and it didn't work there.

It was not only in geometry, however. The subject as a whole was seen as a mountain of material, formulas, routines, and facts: "I think of math as an attempt at remembering routines, and I gained no cohesive view of the subject. However, I now get an impish pleasure in asking questions about numerical information presented to me."

There was another issue, never properly explained, and directly in contrast to the intractability discussed earlier. It was a feeling of "control." This cropped up later in other contexts and was not clarified: "That is why I have an allotment. It is the one place where I am absolute boss and absolutely independent and I can order things exactly as I want. In a tiny way I get that pleasure in adding a column of figures or in working out exactly how much income tax I should pay in the year. I get a real pleasure out of doing simple calculations." It does sound comfortable!

In talking with all the people I saw I felt that somehow they *ought* to be able to do math. There is a serious practical danger in confusing *ought* and *is*, let alone the philosophical pitfalls one may encounter. But I felt it worthwhile to explain some logical processes I thought of as mathematical activities. Perhaps the most interesting was creating schedules. Three "nonmathematical" heads of large secondary schools expressed a very positive pleasure at making a schedule. It was something they could have delegated, but they *enjoyed* it.

One other area produced very positive feelings. Several of those interviewed expressed strong interest in astronomy and in particular the questions of infinity in space and time. These seemed to fire the imagination—but they were not seen as connected with math. The stimulation of the imagination certainly leads to the belief (right or wrong) that important ideas, often with a strong mathematical content, can be understood.

**Mathematical points.**   Though the emphasis in the study lies in how people *feel* about what they are doing in math, a few significant points of practical mathematics came up, which were developed later in the group meetings.

Some experienced difficulty early on. The first big hurdle for most (except the character who did not like the two times table) was long division. It was remembered as a complicated routine, the underlying principle of which was not understood. There is a serious danger in rote-learning methods of this sort. Even telling people something about these routines, such as that division is repeated subtraction, can make them far more acceptable.

Place value, which is a central issue, was another problem: "I missed out on hundreds, tens, and units and never understood it, and it had to be the vertical columns which I couldn't manage anyway." We later spent an interesting session on it in the group. Most people, if pressed, feel less than certain about all the underlying concepts of place value.

The most serious stumbling block for most came with the introduction of $x$, called the "unknown" and therefore invested with mystery! As an initially unknown but fixed and findable number, it has few terrors. For instance, given that $x + 2 = 5$, most people can see that $x = 3$. This does not conflict with the idea of fixity of number. Using letters to express general results, however, seems much less acceptable. To contain all arithmetic results such as $9 + 4 = 4 + 9$ and $25 + 11 = 11 + 25$ in a single algebraic statement $x + y = y + x$ is not an easy step. This seems to be because the letters no longer represent fixed numbers but *any* numbers.

It is a further step to regard $x$ as a variable, taking all values. Even the idea that a quantity may vary with time seemed to offend ideas of fixity and precision.

Is it just possible that the development of a variable is seen as conflicting with an early and perhaps hard-won Piagetian concept of the conservation of number? It does seem that it is a step that few had made and this failure may extend far beyond the group of avowedly nonmathematical people seen.

There is a wider issue than $x$. The symbols and notations of mathematics may be strong inhibitions to learning for many people. Even the phraseology may have a strong effect. One person to whom I offered the phrase "Let $n$ be the number such that..."interrupted: "The shutters come down." This is a very large topic, on which work is in progress, but there is too much for us to handle here. (See chapter 12.)

One person mentioned that compound interest was something he could not cope with. When I asked him what the idea was about, he knew perfectly well and explained it clearly. He simply could not get the right answers. This was in sharp contrast to most mathematical issues, where it was the *idea* that people did not grasp.

If I had to select the two most difficult issues from what people told me I would say "place value" and "variable." That is no surprise.

There is an important issue, not exactly a piece of mathematics but a necessary ability in some areas of it: an individual's power of spatial perception. Some of the problems used were directed at this (see appendix A), partly out of general interest and partly because a number of people were interested in art and I thought that an approach through space and shape might help. In an area where they may have had little specific teaching, abilities were very varied. In the problem about building a three-by-three-by-three cube out of unit cubes, some answered immediately that twenty-seven were needed, whereas one person had no idea and when asked how many were needed for the "floor" said, presumably at random, "Thirty-six." Asked to work at it she said: "There are four on each side — that's twelve round the perimeter — and then some in the middle."

When I arranged square ashtrays on the table to show the bottom layer she was surprised — but not surprised that she had been wrong. If an intelligent person has such poor basic visual perception (for whatever reason) how can she hope to tackle certain aspects of mathematics?

For many people, diagrams can greatly simplify the presentation of certain ideas, and while many concepts may be readily expressed in words, some can not. For those who have facility both in words and in spatial perception most presentations are improved by using both, yet a significant proportion of people do not easily interpret a diagram. The effect of this is that even if one uses both, the mere existence of diagrams through the text can put some people off.

Krutetskii (1971) has shown that there can be a marked imbalance between people's skills in the numerical, analytic area and their understanding of geometric and diagrammatic forms. How much lies in teaching, how much in early experience in play, and how much in innate ability (or innate "inclination" as Krutetskii insists) is an open question.

It would be impossible for me to organize everything I was told by the two dozen people interviewed, but what they said gave me the seeds of many ideas to follow. I was in a position to investigate in greater depth and find out how we should change our classroom practice. It may be that it is destined to be fruitless, for we shall end this chapter on the one and only quote from a school child: "I *think* in the playground, when I go out to play."

# Chapter Four
## The Group

The group consisted of Barbara, Peter, Richard, Roger, Rosita, Sue, and Susan—and myself. Two had in fact passed O-level (see the Preface if you need to refresh your understanding of the English school system) but it was felt their credentials were established by the fact that they had chalked up five previous failures between them and had eventually struggled through only when they were eighteen and taking A-levels in other subjects. We met in a mathematics center, in a rather plain discussion room, seated on comfortable chairs in a circle, with a roller blackboard and chalk available. When we needed other material, such as paper or scissors or electronic calculators, they were at hand somewhere in the center. The occasions were sociable. We had a short break and a drink halfway through each session. At Christmas, Easter, and at the summer halfterm we went on to a meal in a local restaurant where we were sometimes joined by one or more of the other three individual subjects.

Before the sessions began I knew three of the people well and two slightly. By the end of the year we all felt we knew each other rather closely. During that time we became aware of various changes in personal situations. People changed houses or jobs, had children, and got married. These events are not relevant to this study but were part of the general existence of the group, for they were talked about, both outside and inside the two hours we set aside every week. When someone arrives breathless and late to the group, hot from the purchase of a new house, it is not sensible to expect them to remain silent about it. A good teacher absorbs many such extraneous concerns of pupils in much larger classes than this; it is time consuming but necessary.

The attendance rate, considering the extensive commitments of these very busy people, was extraordinarily high, though there were occasions when people had to arrive late or leave early. During the first two terms there were twenty-three sessions with a possible at-

tendance of eight people on each occasion. Of the 184 possible attendances that this gave, there were only eight absences. At Easter the
demands of a new job forced Peter to leave the group. This was quite
unavoidable, but a considerable loss. During the fragmented summer
term we still had thirteen sessions, with a maximum possible weekly
attendance of seven. Of these ninety-one possible attendances there
were only ten absences. In view of the fact that Barbara and Susan
both went on school journeys during the year and that Peter and
Richard had jobs in which evening demands could be made on them,
the total number of absences was very small. I was ill on two occasions
and on both the group carried on without me, and I listened with great
enjoyment to the tape of the sessions. Everyone had been told that
joining the group was meant to involve a very high commitment. But
it says a great deal for the group members, none of whom enjoyed
math initially (and not all by the end!) that they should manage to
restrict absence to a level not much higher than might be expected
from the casual incidence of illness.

Although in one sense the group might have been expected to be a
rather poor teaching prospect, because of their attitude to the subject,
there were many advantages. The fact that they had joined in volun-
tarily is an important feature, though initial willingness is not always
easy to sustain over a whole year. Their power to communicate was
enormously important. All were articulate and there were a number of
vivid turns of phrase. They also brought some important skills in
teaching. It is of very great benefit in a learning situation if teaching
problems are understood. There was a high degree of cooperation
between those who had grasped something and thus moved into a
teaching role, and those who had not. All members of the group were
able to examine and discuss their own feelings with a very welcome
openness. All in all it was a very "enhanced" teaching situation, and
one in which some things could be done that could not be done in an
ordinary class. The description of how we operated it is not therefore
intended as a model of how teaching should be done, not only because
the situation was an unusually favourable one, but also because the
purposes were different from those of a normal teaching group.

## Aims and Purposes

The aim in the group, as in other aspects of the study both practical
and theoretical, was to explore the negative feelings people had about
math and the reasons they had arisen. In doing so, it was evident that
we should also seek to remedy these feelings. Back in the classroom
our solutions must be both preventive and remediative, since however

much we have modified our own teaching to avoid unnecessary fears developing, we shall always be faced with students who have had them created by others. Perhaps the emphasis on discovering reasons was partly because that is the obvious first step, and also because prevention is in the long run more important than cure.

We could not explore the feelings without actually doing some mathematics, and this was another important aim. I had hoped to teach for understanding and to get people to a stage when they might feel they could tackle O-level. This was not achieved, though some did advance substantially. In part it was too ambitious, and in part it was precluded by the proportion of the time we spent (profitably in the event) discussing matters other than math but related to our first aim. In addition, what we learned about time pressure suggested we could not afford the demands that would have been imposed by a goal such as O-level at the end of a year. We did do some math however; what we actually did is indicated later.

The group acted as a sounding board for developing ideas — ideas arising from the practical work, written up in the reports and notes, and finally discussed in the group and with individuals. In describing feelings and attitudes to math which I did not share it was necessary to check constantly with everyone, and also to see if my speculative theories were regarded as relevant. All the work which appears in chapters 7, 8, and 9 was tested in this way, and modified in the face of clear disagreement.

The tasks of the group were therefore varied, and the total time they used rather less than seventy-two hours. In that time they did a great deal.

## Style, Ethos, and Activity

A group much above this size, if it is to work cohesively rather than individually, would need a controller (presumably the teacher) who determines who speaks when, and controls the rate of input of contributions and also possibly their nature. Most school classes that work as a class, rather than in groups or individually, cannot manage collective exploration, and neither can the teacher adopt a passive role. With the group, its maximum size being eight, it was possible to allow extended periods without intervention. These periods were among the most satisfactory, particularly when the group was exploring ideas rather than solving routine problems. The temptation to intervene is very strong. In my own classroom experience, at this time fifteen years out of date, I had been accustomed to directing. To hold back when a point was missed or, worse, when something wrong was accepted, was a sore trial. In fact I think I intervened too much. But input was necessary from time to time; math cannot be explored without a guide. The intent was to pose questions for consideration, rather than to explain ideas. At times their exploration seemed excruciatingly slow — to them as well as to me. Yet the value of thinking things through was manifest both in doing the math and in shifting attitudes. After one successful episode, when I had been able to leave the circle and sit back listening, I was moved to say, "You're the best group I've ever had." "And the slowest," replied one of them.

Both were true. At times they were prepared to shut me up, particularly if one person in the group wanted to explain a point rather than me. They would also take initiatives in what they wanted to do. On one occasion, when they had dealt with a problem, I wanted to move on. "No — I want to do another one." "All right — make one up for yourselves and then do it."

The deliberate lack of formal control (not completely achieved) occasionally meant that more than one person was speaking at a time. The men were noisier than the women and tended sometimes to talk through them, but the group gradually achieved its own courtesies, and the enthusiastic and forceful contributions of some were treated indulgently by others. Tensions and aggressions can easily manifest themselves in these circumstances, but despite all the rough speaking and occasional forceful contradictions, the underlying tone was remarkably harmonious; nothing worse than irritation was present, and that seldom.

The principle that I should be a provider rather than a director worked well initially. Later I began to operate more didactically, perhaps because of a shift of emphasis from exploring attitudes to finding out whether they could learn some math. Even so, it was necessary to stand aside when the internal mechanisms of the group, or sometimes of one member, seemed ready to take over. Throughout, however, we tried not to move on till something had been understood by everyone. This was the most important policy in the way of working and is not easy to establish.

Every individual is concerned with his or her own speed of comprehension and finds it difficult to admit failure to understand. This is evidenced at a simple level when we are faced with someone speaking in a strong dialect. The pressure is a social one and relates to a fear of seeming stupid in front of others. In a group the pressures are stronger and it is also easier for one's lack of comprehension to go unnoticed. Many of us must at times have sat through lectures and understood very little. This was probably something most of the rest of the audience was also experiencing, yet most people diminish themselves by believing that they are the only one, or perhaps one of a few who do not

understand. Within the group three people at different times characterized themselves as being the "dummy" of the group. If one believes
that everyone else has understood, it takes a great deal of nerve to stop
the proceedings and ask for further explanation. It is perfectly possible to
have a situation where no one in fact understood, but each believed
her- or himself to be the only person in that state. The difficulty is
enhanced when one believes that the issue is a very simple one —
although it has not been grasped. Certainly many teaching situations
create a belief that one's foolishness will be demonstrated if any
question is asked. It was important that this should not be the situation
in the group.

Stating it as a policy and getting agreement was a help, as was the
fact that it seemed likely at the beginning we would not have any
"know-it-alls" before whom it would be difficult to parade ignorance.
As we progressed it became clear that when they were interested and
involved, people were prepared to hold things up to work at understanding. The real danger was when someone was bored or distracted.
Then to demand explanation meant admitting that one had not been
listening, and also the effort of getting back into something in which
one had lost interest. Generally the dual role of student and teacher
was accepted. Once a person had understood, he or she sought to help
others to do so. This was very supportive, but did mean that people
were not always afforded the peace and quiet in which they might
have thought it through themselves. Mostly the group worked as one
group, and this was the general intention, but sometimes individuals
helped one other person, or three people tried to argue through a
point together.

Of the three activities — talking about feelings, discussing a developing theory, and doing math — there was a shift through the year, but
it would not be possible to quantify this. Toward the end we did seem
to spend more time on math, but we regularly discussed all three
issues. Sometimes and for some people it was a relief to move from
mathematics to more general matters. At other times there was genuine
enthusiam for pressing on with the math.

# The Mathematics

None of the group had been brought up on modern math, and the
wrangle over whether traditional or modern content was "better"
seemed to have little relevance to this study. It seemed sensible to
look back at the sort of material on which they had failed. This would
often trigger memories about how they felt, and if some degree of
remediation were possible, it could be done on that work. So our

**Figure 4-1** The focus-directrix property relative to a parabola

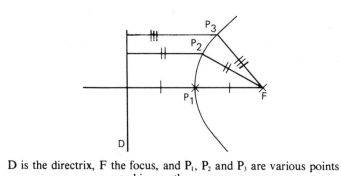

D is the directrix, F the focus, and $P_1$, $P_2$ and $P_3$ are various points making up the curve.

content was largely traditional, including the Euclid proof of Pythagoras and square roots done by the long method (an amusing episode). After many meanderings we ended up doing selected examples from recent O-level examinations, but we were not confined in what we tackled, nor did I seek control over what we did.

We made a curious start by plunging into the conic sections. This arose because Roger was designing helmets for a film and the designer wanted them (for some unknown reason) to be elliptical. After we had discussed the conics for some time as sections of a cone, I introduced the focus-directrix property in the simplest case, that of the parabola (see figure 4-1).

Briefly, if you take a fixed line (directrix) and a fixed point (focus), and find all positions the same distance from each, you get a shape called a parabola. This work of course is well beyond O-level, and seems an odd thing to do with a group who claimed not to understand any math. There were two reasons for doing it. First and most important, it had come from one of them. Second, it allowed us to pursue what seemed from the initial survey to be a significant issue—that of variation. Most people think that points, like numbers, should stay fixed. It is necessary to grasp that they may vary if progress is to be made. During the successive sessions we plugged the theme of "variation under constraint." We drew all the conics, using different proportions for the distances from focus and directrix. The work was practical and generally very satisfying.

Pushing the idea still further we sought to find out the path traced

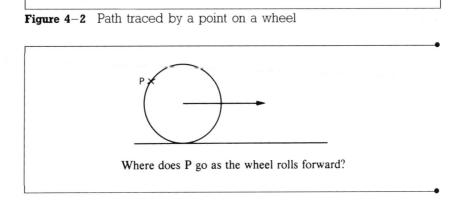

**Figure 4-2** Path traced by a point on a wheel

Where does P go as the wheel rolls forward?

by a point on a wheel as it rolled along a flat road (see figure 4-2). They worked with great interest at this and eventually arrived at the general shape of the cycloid, getting at the width and height of the arch and the angle it made with the road when it touched it. Peter is an enthusiast for railway engines and we became entangled with questions of the shape traced out if the wheel slipped. We could hardly handle this with full analytic rigor but the level of understanding was high. The following remark suggests considerable sophistication of perception: "If it came in at more than a right angle it would have to loop to get on to the next revolution."

From here I wanted to move, retaining the idea of a moveable point under constraint, to the notion that the constraint could be in the form of an algebraic equation. Eventually we did so, but only after an excursion occasioned by Peter's birthday. He arrived at the session asking to put a problem to the group. It turned out to involve a series, the connection being that a fixed number was expressed in successive number bases. We all failed to do the problem and Peter then explained it with great delight. Though we were slightly disappointed not to do it, we enjoyed the session and his explanation. From here we did persevere into the idea of a base and really sorted out what place value was about. A second major conceptual step had been made, yet by now we were at the seventh session and had done no work on O-level!

We gradually moved in on graphs and by about session twelve could draw and interpret straight-line graphs. The slow pace enabled us to examine not only feelings and attitudes, but also some unusual points about the math. One is described in chapter 8 where Rosita has a most curious way of reaching the right answer. Another was the failure to understand the symbol $2x$. Most did not distinguish between it and the statement $x = 2$. Two of the group were geographers and for

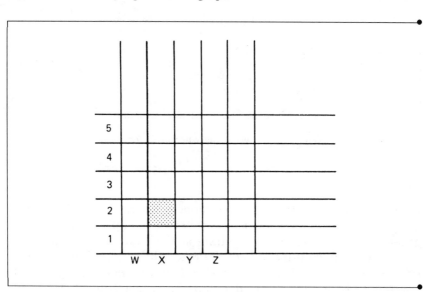

**Figure 4–3**   Plotted square on a graph

them 2x meant plotting a point, or finding a square on a map with one
axis marked in numbers and the other in letters (see figure 4–3). For
them the shaded square was 2x, and the idea of plotting a line $y = 2x$
proved difficult! We all made it eventually. By session seventeen we
had managed to tackle several "B" section questions (difficult O-level
problems, each worth 17 percent of the total grade) on graphs, with
occasional mistakes but, for most of the group, with fair understanding.
It seemed important for them to realize that a single question at that
level was accessible. If they could tackle that, it implied that they had
the cognitive power to do others—even if it took time.

Directed numbers are not easy. There is no problem in getting
people to agree that in some real situations it is appropriate to attach a
sign to a number. All are aware that their bank managers know about
negative amounts of money. The geographers are happy with negative
temperatures and measurements below sea level, but the difficulties
we encountered in dealing with operations between negative numbers
were legion. They are not the main theme of this study, but some are
worth mentioning. We tried to relate these devilish numbers to reality,
to the number line, to their internal consistency, to language, and to
graphs. Never get involved with "taking away a debt"—it doesn't pay!
To most of them, the idea of bigger or smaller related to the number
line was not accepted. They would accept that I believed + 2 to be

larger than $-8$, and that I might be right, but it did not mean it fitted their way of thinking. Going up or down the number line seemed to some to depend on which side of zero you were. In language terms there was agreement that a rise in employment and a fall in unemployment might be equated; the terms "no rise" and "negative rise" (why I introduced that I shall never know) were not distinguishable. Internal consistency was compelling but in some way a "con." The totally mystical saying, "A minus times a minus gives a plus," was remembered and not remotely understood. Eventually through graphs of house and car appreciation and depreciation, taking time hence and time ago, we got some measure of acceptance and agreement. We were at session twenty-two.

Undeterred, we went for indices, intending to show how a conventional agreement to write, for instance, $5 \times 5 \times 5$ as $5^3$ could lead to curious results in fractional and negative indices and to the idea of logarithms. We got sidetracked twice. One led (from this idea in fact) to factorizing whole numbers and to the previously unrealized idea that there was only one way in which a number reduced to its prime factors. This surprised and pleased some. We found some square roots in this way and then, almost predictably, had to show how to find square roots of numbers not themselves perfect squares. I have on occasion derided the teaching of square roots by the "long method." I taught them—they enjoyed it—and they learned why it worked.

We got back to indices and made great progress, ending on a graph of $2^x$. At one stage I commented that if $10^1$ was 10 and $10^2$ was 100, all the numbers between 10 and 100 were powers of 10 that were "one point something or other." Richard awoke from a snooze (he claimed he worked harder than any of us) and said: "Bloody hell! It is never taught in that way. That actually makes it simple. Ludicrous!" Between sessions of sleep he gained through the year various deep insights such as this.

In session twenty-seven we started geometry. I have long felt that the Euclidean geometry many of us sweated over at school could all be grasped in visually compelling ways if the verbiage were discarded. This has been shown to some extent through transformation geometry, and during the next sessions up to the thirty-fifth, we showed that this could be so. A number of problems at O-level standard were understood if not all solved in these sessions, remembering that by no means all the time was spent on math. We had dealt with the angle sum of a triangle (on which Rosita commented: "That's the nicest thing we've had in the whole year—I love that"), and the angle sum of a polygon, and successfully solved some examples on them. Then they read the original formal statements of these theorems. Even after the meaning had been grasped in conceptual terms, their response was: "Even now

I can hardly understand the theorem on the polygon. In one sense it has a lilt—on the other hand it is gobbledegook." It was perhaps too much to tackle Pythagoras in the "old" way: "It puts me off, still, to look at it—the number of lines. Just looking at it I think I can't do it." But we struggled through, and certainly managed a number of problems using it. An interesting point arose in that some people were unable to accept areas that crossed lines. Once a line was there it cut the area and that was that. In the proof about parallelograms on the same base and between the same parallels, one area was used in each dissection. It was not felt that it *should* be used twice.

We finished with a session on series, generally quite successful but involving a long and amusing episode about "gaps." In an arithmetic progression in which the terms go up in equal steps and in which the gaps are all 4 (such as 3, 7, 11, 15...), it is possible to find, say, the 100th term by adding 99 steps of 4 on to the first term, 3. So we get $3 + (4 \times 99)$ or 399. There were two ideas that prevented us from reaching correct answers. Some people were unwilling to count the first term as 3 and started counting only when we got to the dots. We overcame that. But Richard simply could not see that the number of gaps was one less than the number of terms. Though this resulted in a fair amount of frivolity, he had a genuine difficulty, that was somehow involved with the Roman way of counting, the Chinese habit of counting ages from "one" at birth and the different ways in which the British and the Americans number the floors in a building. It was not always easy to follow, and we did not eventually get through, despite spirited attempts. One good result, however, was gained from an explanation based on the fact that in traveling six stops on the Underground you saw seven stations. Sue saw that the result could be directly perceived. Until then she had invented a rule (a favorite game) that said, "You take one off from the number of terms." This was a rule that had to be remembered. It was a good level on which to end.

As far as the mathematics went, then, we reached a level where several of the harder questions on an O-level paper were within grasp. Certain central conceptual issues had been hammered hard, on the grounds that the detail would then more easily become accessible. In fact the amounts of math we covered in thirty-odd hours was quite surprising. It was not easy for them to assess, but given another dozen sessions the math would have advanced very well.

# Teaching Issues

Throughout the sessions we nagged away at various educational points, returning to them again and again as they were brought up by different mathematical material, and as they were developed in the reports I was writing. We probably spent more time on nonmathematical issues than on learning math. As we moved on, ideas shifted or developed, and strands of thinking began to emerge. It was possible to connect many, if not all, of these ideas with a growing theory, or with well-developed ideas of schematic learning and relational and instrumental understanding.

There was a related cluster of ideas, not easy to disentangle, on interest, relevance, understanding, and remembering. Early on we discussed whether or not performance was determined largely by interest. As to where this interest arose we had little to say, though a good deal about how it could be killed off. Krutetskii claims that innate inclination can exist; from there we could assume that much of the interest arises from success in reaching goals. Certainly spatial ability varied greatly; this may have been innate but is more likely related to early play experience. The only point constantly put by several of the group was the need for relevance. Slightly uncertain attitudes about this had been revealed in the initial survey but there are at least five instances where the issue of relevance was pursued and seems to have been an important feature either in getting started on a topic or in making some results within it acceptable. They are worth mentioning.

The first example is the discussion on the conics, which started from Roger's need to make a certain hat. This need was not shared by others, but got us under way. Though the Greeks had largely studied the conics simply because they wanted to, their later use in planetary motion made them practical, at least for some. At one stage we discussed the difficulty we would have with focusing a beam of light or of dropping missiles accurately upon each other without a knowledge of the parabola. Stirred by this, they were able to construct parabolas. Once done however, Susan's payoff and enjoyment with what she had done arose from explaining about the focus-directrix property to a mathematician friend. The "relevance" was forgotten.

The eventual breakthrough in directed numbers came from variation in house and car prices and was happily linked to Susan's arrival fresh from the purchase of a house. Several people had also been planning to change their cars, and with a little artificiality directed numbers were linked to these and at last made acceptable.

The Pythagorean theorem, tackled head-on, did not seem very relevant, despite the fundamental statement it makes about the space we live in. Some down-to-earth practical situations were adduced but not with great success. Here Sue said she was only really satisfied when you *made* something at the end of it all, yet earlier she was satisfied to make drawings of shapes which they did not then use.

The other two examples yielded a different sort of relevance, in some way secondhand but at the same time more useful through generality. When we started indices, in part leading on from the consistency proofs in directed numbers, we saw that what arose was the result of our agreement to represent something $(5 \times 5 \times 5)$ in a certain way $(5^3)$. This took the "rules of the game" approach to math and it was clear that there was no direct external relevance in being able to say that $(9/16)^{3/2}$ was equal to $27/64$. Nonetheless, when faced with the question "What use are logs, anyway?" it was easy to discuss how greatly they had simplified computation at a time when it threatened in science to become overwhelming. This was a second-order usefulness, but crucial at the time.

Another form of relevance came in a discussion of graphs. Again the question was asked, "What use are they?" and Peter and Richard launched into a discussion of their value in sociopolitical terms. This was convincing, but in fact the importance of graphs is more generally related to our thinking processes. To see things in graphical rather than numerical or verbal terms simply adds to one's powers of perception. I asked if they could all draw pupil performance against class size, making what assumptions they chose. This led to a lively discussion, with Barbara eventually drawing the most acceptable general shape of curve (see figure 4–4), with little improvement in the case of very high numbers, marked improvement when numbers were below forty or so, and a decline again when the class was too small (perhaps below ten). To see such a change as a picture can be an asset in holding information and is of general relevance in thinking—but it is not specific as were the first three.

**Figure 4–4**   Simple graphical curve

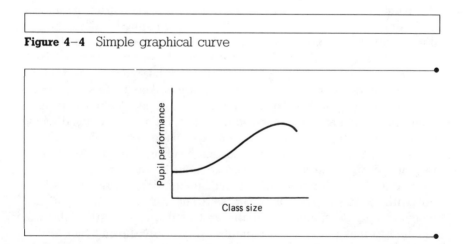

Relevance had thus to be asserted at times, but was not always an essential element. Some work simply seemed intrinsically interesting, and other work not so — and we could not say why. The shift indicated in the five examples as to what is meant by relevance led through to the general acceptability of information and what is meant by understanding. It was agreed that material that "made sense" internally did not need a justification in purely practical matters. If it somehow fitted established patterns, and possibly made them clearer, then that was interesting, as with thinking in graphs.

The need for understanding varied. For some initially it was enough that a method worked, though we all gradually shifted from that position. Even later on there was great pleasure at being taught, with no understanding, to find square roots by the long method. Yet the question arose: "Why do you double that last figure?" There was generally a wish to know why as well as how something worked. "I don't like applying something when I don't know why it does what it does."

We became increasingly aware of how long it could take for understanding to come, and to be sure that we had in fact understood. This slow pace, so difficult to establish, paid off in the classroom for some. Sue was pleased to report that subtraction had gone better with her class by waiting for understanding. Occasional quite false perceptions led to correct answers to problems, and this is very difficult to detect. At other times people were faced with contradictory ways of looking at things, both of which seemed right. Peter had on one occasion drawn a graph that everyone explained to him was incorrect. Roger explained clearly and with conviction how it should be done. Peter then explained he understood what the correct answer should be, saw that Roger's method was correct and understood it, but still did not know where his own view of the way to do it was wrong. Discovering such errors, rather than seeing how a thing should be done, is essential to learning.

At one stage a distinction had to be made between pattern spotting and understanding. In the group the realization that all the multiples of 9 up to 90 had digits that added up to 9 was greeted with surprise, and was felt to give new understanding to the 9 times table. In fact, this pattern then itself needs an explanation. When I somewhat inadequately gave one and asked, "Do you think that is a deeper level of understanding?" there was a chorus of rather derisory "No"s.

"That *what* was a deeper level?"

"The number line on the board rather than the pattern."

"The pattern is much neater."

One measure of thorough understanding is whether you can defend the point against someone who knows more (and perhaps argues better) than you. This did not turn out to be a very valuable criterion since it depended more heavily on the person than on actual understanding. Nonetheless, members of the group did during the year engage other people outside in discussions on math, and this in itself generally aided confidence and improved understanding.

In the geometry sessions we concentrated upon the notion of a thing being "visually apparent." In most of the theorems commonly taught at this level it is possible to work at the diagram until the reasons for the fact that is to be proved flit through our minds as our eyes travel round the diagram. This was strongly illustrated in the proof of the angle sum of a triangle. It was agreed that, taking a triangle by itself (see figure 4−5a), there was no apparent reason why the three angles should have a fixed sum. Extending one side to provide a straight line (see figure 4−5b) still did not make it at all clear. When, however, the left-hand side was moved along parallel to itself (see figure 4−5c), it *was* clear that it made the same angle with the base (because that was the way we moved it) and that the two angles marked with a cross were equal, because of the Z shape they made. The three angles of the triangle were then seen as clustering together at a point to make a straight line.

This proof is well known of course by all teachers — but it was not known by our group, and they were suitably pleased at gaining an understanding that they could hold within themselves, not simply

**Figure 4−5**   Proof of the angle sum of a triangle

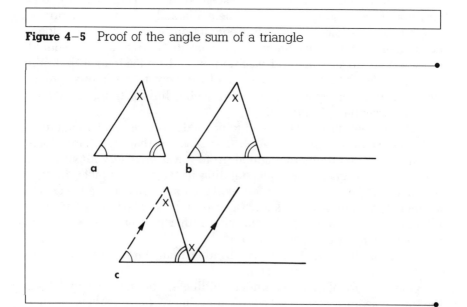

remember as a page of writing. It *is* satisfying to grasp something in this way. As Richard said: "I see that now — what fun!"

The view of math as a subject to be presented only in formalistic style and in stilted language is in fact strongly inhibiting to the understanding that is possible. In relation to a problem about a swimming pool, discussed later, Richard commented: "They would in fact knock out your common sense way of doing it. I don't think I'm particularly stupid about mathematical concepts, but you looked at that and it was ABCD and there was a formula somewhere and you applied it — and yet it was very obvious in doing it in practical terms." And Rosita followed up with, "The formula cuts out your own thinking process."

We felt then that we had made advances in understanding math, and knowing something of what understanding meant, but Sue put clearly and positively her difficulty: "Understanding it is not the same thing as doing it." This again makes the distinction between "reception learning" and problem solving. A knowledge of principles is essential to problem solving but it is by no means enough. To start out on a journey from given information through a hazy area to some goal requires both confidence and tools different from those necessary "just" to understand. On several occasions members felt let down when an explanation was given: "It was obvious, and I couldn't see it."

Skemp, in 1971, described an experiment in which children learned either by rote or schematically; and their powers of recall, when tested, showing markedly better performances in those who had organized the information with understanding. The question of remembering is a very important one in our educational system. Passing examinations puts a premium on remembering, perhaps too large a premium, though clearly there is much material that should be ready for recall. Certainly, organized knowledge will be more easily available, as a library will be more useful than random piles of books. In one session Peter described how modern theories in geography used a basic hexagonal pattern to explain the growth of major towns and their subsidiaries. An underlying theory of this sort will be of great value in storing information even at the level of locating the towns. It became apparent in the group that math had never been presented as if it had any structure above the very detailed level. The rigid form in which a single geometric theorem was to be presented may have been heavily emphasized, but not the structure of groups of theorems and certainly not what geometry was about. This observation of structure at various levels is essential to a proper understanding and provides the shelves on which the library books can be placed.

The relation between understanding and remembering was discussed regularly. Early on I had taken the view that once something was fully understood it would not be forgotten. I was soon disabused of this notion by several people, but came gradually to more diverse conclusions. Before we started, the idea of a variable point was foreign to them. After a long time on the conics, and then a gap of two or three weeks, one member said she could remember nothing at all about the conics, though she mentioned the idea of a "floating point." This very general notion had been grasped. So too, later, was the fact that certain types of equations produced certain types of graphs. The detail was lost, at least temporarily. Though some of these general ideas were both grasped and remembered, there was no general structure in their minds to which to attach new information. Building this would take time. Tests might reveal that little was remembered, unless the subject did some revision and reinforcement.

Two clear advantages did emerge, however, which suggest that experiments different from Skemp's might be performed. Though work was forgotten, the *speed of retrieval* seemed much higher than might have been expected. This was a purely subjective impression but the reaction of group members when prompted seemed very much more positive than in many classes where work, recently taught, is revised. The other advantage related to attitude, of which we need to say more. For the moment we may pick up an important point from a paper on self-appraisal by Ruth Eagle (1978). She comments on the ability to recall and deal with matters in which people once had mastery. The memory is not of the material, but that it had been mastered. This lends the confidence that allows them to thrust through again. Memories of feelings are often stronger than those of events or learned material. This is an important issue. Most of my colleagues in this work experienced sinking feelings about pieces of math, reflecting those felt at the time. Failing to remember something actually mastered is disappointing, but the revision of it becomes assured of success.

Other matters concerning teaching cropped up, though the intertwined ideas of interest, relevance, understanding, and remembering were the main theme. The most substantial was on the use of symbols, which is discussed in chapter 12. They can be powerful inhibitors to understanding.

Another issue concerned the environment. Roger, an art lecturer, wondered if the more cheerful surroundings in other subjects helped to create a positive attitude. This received little support; despite our general belief in display work, it was not felt to be a serious matter in putting people off math.

Lastly we discussed the transmission and reception of information. It was often clear that what was said was distorted when received — or else simply not received. It would be interesting to make a few remarks and then collect from a group what they thought had been said.

Perhaps it was best summed up by Rosita: "You know what we do — we don't listen."

## Attitudes and Reactions

Most of our second session was spent on a conversation about "panic," and many of the comments appear in chapter 1.

Two of the group explained how at school they took the role of clowns, as did one other person in the initial survey. This is a fairly common escape mechanism for someone who has been made to feel foolish and who therefore emphasizes that view of themselves. It is surprising how often this is not understood in the classroom, and the teachers treats the behavior as deliberately mischievous, not induced.

Individuals were not always explicit when upset, as people certainly were at times. Two members experienced intense disappointment on occasion, which was explored with them individually outside the group. This is one of the most damaging of emotions, the reaction to which can be complete withdrawal. A theoretical consideration of this is begun in chapter 11, under "Goals and Feelings." Another felt at one stage that a sore point in her teens was coming to light, presumably because of the math we were involved in at the time. Yet another had strong feelings of inertia at several stages during the year and the reaction "Why should I do this?" It did not prevent her continuing, and it would have provided a most valuable contribution if between us we had been able to break through it. We attempted this outside the group, in the hope that full understanding in one area would release the inertia, but we were unsuccessful. It is so prevalent a feeling in the classroom and so negative and difficult that a closer understanding of it would have been most helpful. (An attempt is made in chapter 11, under "Analyzing Emotion.") A rather similar attitude with another individual was overcome, as we shall see, but again without any understanding of how. The development in confidence of some people was quite remarkable. It tended to wax and wane with the material under consideration, but the attitudes clearly showed themselves. Anxiety in one that this might be her final chance to understand math hindered advances at times, though on the whole considerable gains in confidence were made.

It remained fairly easy to create overt anxiety even in so relatively easy a setting. I did not set out to do this but I occasioned it at times, as did others. Three occasions come to mind. On one, pursuing the idea that explaining an idea to others in the group would demonstrate that one member understood it, I started to ask someone to do this and became aware that all were in a panic. On another I came in with pencil and paper, and on another with a test! They became anxious. The word most commonly used was that they found it too "demanding." This theme was pursued to some extent and discussed particularly in relation to questions posed in chapter 13 under "Sex Differentiation in Mathematical Ability."

Once when Susan arrived late she was persuaded to go to the board and work things out that had been done just before she came. She was laughingly hurried by everyone and retorted: "You're trying to make me go faster than I can." She forced the pace to slow and coped with the work.

There was a last point. At times the presentation of problems was seen as an attempt to trick or embarrass, and this was a great deterrent to working at them. It is an awkward situation always when one person understands and another does not. Peter was in this position in his "birthday" problem, and I was considered to have been "smirking" in giving another problem. (See chapter 11 under "Goals and Feelings.") Perhaps there is something in this. Certainly there is at times a distrust of "teacher"; and a comment on an explanation was, "It's clever, but it is still a con." This may well be a general feeling about authority figures.

# Chapter Five
## Lynn and Sarah

Three people—Elaine, Lynn, and Sarah—worked with me on an individual basis. Elaine, who was at that time a headmistress of a secondary school, I generally visited at work; this investigation is given in detail in chapter 6. Lynn was working as an advisory teacher and it was therefore convenient for us both to meet in my office. Sarah, a primary teacher, came to the office after school roughly once a week. The work, particularly with Lynn and Sarah, was interwoven with that of the group. In most weeks, there were three sessions—one each with Lynn and Sarah, and one with the group—during which the same ideas and mathematical material might be involved. This focused thinking to some extent and allowed each to serve as sounding boards for the others. The in-depth sessions, as we began to call them, yielded rather deeper personal insights into these three people than were obtained in the group. These may at times have been idiosyncratic, whereas personal attitudes generally prevalent in the group have more likelihood of being widespread in the population at large. Views expressed in one type of session could, however, always be tested in another.

With all three in-depth subjects it became apparent that areas in their personal background, which one might not expect to enter through a study of anxiety in mathematics, did in fact surface. In retrospect it may not seem surprising, since many people clearly remember parental attitudes to math, because of feelings about authority connected with it. Yet I had not expected to embark on psychotherapy, which some sessions verged upon from time to time. All three, however, seemed perfectly capable of preventing discussions from entering areas into which they did not wish to go.

Many of the matters that we shall describe now in the sessions with Lynn and Sarah have been categorized to some extent already, but the views expressed always have an individuality and sharpness that adds to the perception of the problems. In these descriptions, as in the more sharply specific study of Elaine (chapter 6), the sessions are followed *seriatim*, with important issues therefore returned to several times.

# Lynn

At O-level Lynn gained seven passes and failed only in math. She remembers this "failure" beginning in the final year of junior school, though there was no suggestion that she would fail the 11 +. Her junior school was a large one, grouped by ability into three classes of the same age. Within classes they were also grouped by ability, again into three. Effectively then they were tightly streamed into nine sets. Lynn was in the top class, and within that class was in the top group for everything until she was "put down" into the second one for math. This in fact was the second of nine bands, yet it took her away from friends who were in the top group and she regarded it as failure and felt diminished. It would seem that by drawing barriers in appropriate places, almost anyone can be made to feel stupid.

She did pass the 11 + and went on to a rather high-powered and pressured grammar school. She went into lower sets and completely lost interest as she began to fail. If she did not understand she did not bother to ask. She corrected herself: "Well, not bother, a certain embarrassment." In the history of math teaching the number of questions that *should* have been asked by so many people defies calculation. When she reached mock O-level she was on the borderline of a pass. Her reaction was *not* to work.

Quite often during these sessions Lynn would say, "Can't remember," and we both came to accept that, true though it was, the memory was in fact inhibited by some internal unwillingness to bring unpleasant memories to the surface.

Early in our interviews I asked about whether certain mathematical ideas or facts seemed interesting. These ideas were both numerical and geometrical and there was no suggestion at first that she would have to do any serious work on them. Lynn seemed more responsive to geometry and later in the sessions very competent at traditional geometry problems. Tangency and also the golden rectangle were topics that appealed. When asked whether it seemed surprising that angles in the same segment were equal (presented of course in a diagram and without that terminology) she said she thought it obvious, and when shown an ellipse with similar angles drawn she did not expect them to be equal: "No, because it narrows down there." On the numerical side, she knew her tables, but when asked about primes generally thought numbers such as 91 or 93 to be prime because they were not in the tables. When asked if she thought the question about whether primes went on for ever interesting (as most people did), she said: "No—I don't care. It doesn't matter to me or my life."

Throughout the one-to one encounters with all three people, reactions of this sort, honestly given, were perhaps less related to the actual question than to the state of mind the person was in as a result of earlier questions. Here, for instance, Lynn had wrongly answered about primes just before and was ready to express boredom. It might be that if it had been asked more directly after her successful and accurate geometrical comments, her reaction might have been different. A feature not commented upon later and perhaps worth exploring further is the fluidity of emotional response that most people exhibited.

Early on Lynn commented that there was a mathematical principle in Greek statues and that this was "magical." This, almost an aside at this stage, was returned to later on.

At the end of the second session Lynn was asked how many little cubes there were in a big one three by three by three. She very rapidly responded fifty-four. This was arrived at by seeing that nine were visible on each of six faces and that $9 \times 6 = 54$. Two recurrent themes developed from this, and were reflected in others. The first was her belief that things must always be done quickly; the second, the idea that there must always be a formula for any calculation involving numbers, which can be expected to give a correct answer. In defence to this "formula" approach she said: "But I see the whole of mathematics as remembering."

The hope with everyone was to get them to experience the pleasure of working at a problem, preferably with success. So at the end of this session I explained what a "perfect" number was, giving 6 as an example, and asked that Lynn find the next one up, given that it was below 30. In fact she did this right after she left, as a chore to be gotten rid of: "I was beginning to get curious. I was tempted to ask somebody— lack of confidence. Then...might as well do it. I didn't get much enjoyment out of doing it, because I thought I'd get it wrong... wouldn't be able to find it." Her reaction when she did it was that it must be wrong, and to check and recheck. I said that we had to get to a stage where a problem was pleasurable to play with. She replied: "I can't possibly imagine it."

The real glimmer was the curiosity expressed at the beginning, but the route from burdensome chore to pleasurable play is a very long one. This relates to the overall view that the person has of what math is about. In particular for Lynn there was the difficulty about creativity, and this led us all at times into discussions about whether math was created or objective knowledge that was somehow always there. It is a philosophical problem and cannot be discussed at that level here, but what the person believes it to be, rightly or wrongly, matters considerably. Lynn's view on objectivity was: "We recognized 'five'—but it was always there." Math was also always rushed for Lynn. When I suggested it could be calm and contemplative, she said: "I've never been able to see it in that way."

Lynn began to talk about math to her friends (probably to their amazement), and gained great support from one who is a mathematician. She set them some of the problems she had been given, which, "gleefully, when they don't get it," she was able to explain. One particular problem on which she was successful was painting the outside of a three-by-three-by-three cube black, and visualizing how many of the twenty-seven small cubes had no paint on them. She spoke of constant failure, and when it was pointed out that she had demonstrably succeeded in a number of questions, she said, "Yes, but that is just a relief." The view that failure was to be expected implied that the most favorable reaction would be relief; this point is developed in chapter 11 under "Goals and Feelings." Nor could even success be fully admitted: "[It's] taken a long time to get me to understand."

We returned again to how different math was from other subjects. In writing an essay, a teacher suggests: "You have a certain freedom in that. If you get a low mark you can think they don't understand. You can question their judgment because it is so uniquely their judgment." I asked whether one could question the judgment of a math teacher. "No, he is totally right and you are totally wrong." One of the most difficult tasks was to persuade Lynn that some solutions in math could be seen as correct and not dependent on the agreement of another person. I introduced the phrase "the authority of the subject."

Lynn is a very organized person, who likes things to be under control. It reflected the view of the headmaster who liked his allotment, and columns of well-balanced numbers, but for Lynn math was certainly not in control: "Everything has its place and it's put back in it, and math is the one area where things don't have their place. That's obviously why I blocked it out for so long."

At about the fifth session we ran into difficulties. We had touched upon relationships with her mother (which we did in fact manage to discuss later in so far as it was relevant to the math), and later in the interview she said she found the situation demanding. It also happened in the group at times. She didn't mind demands that she could meet, but, as she put it, I was probing where she did not wish to be probed. It was a few weeks before we resumed.

She still found problems daunting but gradually there were new perceptions. We tried some de Bono problems on shapes, in which irregular shapes had to be cut into two that matched each other (see appendix A). They were not easy. They involved speculation rather than a routine approach—but they required no mathematical knowledge, which was why they were used. When I showed her the solution of one of them she said, "What proof have you that you are right? Oh...you have your own proof," showing that she had fairly grasped the point about internal checking.

It was during the eighth session that some important shifts began. We discussed drawing graphs and successfully plotted $y = x + 3$. Lynn asked, "Why is the three so important? Couldn't it be anything?" and she drew graphs with various constants giving a series of parallel lines. It was the first exploratory question—and she was able to answer it herself. I pursued it:

"Can you alter any other number?"

"It just puts me off even thinking about it."

"Your first question just arose."

"Because I wasn't asked about it. A moment of pure curiosity. I wanted to know. As soon as you said that, I didn't want to look at it any more."

Throughout, Lynn put on the brakes when fearful that she might have made a step forward. This time I did in fact persuade her to draw $y = 2x + 3$, but there she stopped. The twin problems of inertia and boredom are central to the classroom situation and I had hoped we might find mechanisms for getting through them. I was unsuccessful with one of the group, though quite successful with Lynn, but even then I was unable to speculate as to the means. Lynn found sustaining a flicker of interest exhausting: "I've been useful, it's benefited me a little—oh God, I don't want to do any more now." She further commented that other tensions were creative and involved response. That indeed specified the problem of boredom. Nonetheless, the growing ability to state her discontentments was in fact removing them: "For the first time I'm being honest about math. It won't be an issue any more—it's clear now."

The question of the use of symbols constantly recurred. It became possible to clear some thinking about them, but there are issues that remain unresolved. The work on directed numbers and then on indices provided a range of symbols to be coped with. Lynn in fact found them less confusing than some people did. One of the more difficult points about negative numbers is that the minus sign can be an instruction or an integral part of the number. Lynn was swift to see this and when I said of one sign. "It is not an instruction to do something *with* a number," she immediately responded, "It *is* the number." Very accurate. Even later when faced with $\pm 8 * \pm 2$ as a condensation of sixteen instructions she was not put out. At first she said, "I know it, to a degree I understand it, but I don't feel it," and later admired the brevity of the notation.

With indices the problem can be acute. Most people are rather unhappy when confronted with $(9/16)^{-3/2}$! Susan had commented, "There's so much going on there." Lynn found them acceptable at first but later, with $8^{2/3}$, she said, "Oh God, I can't think, can't think." Part of this arose from a self-imposed time pressure, but the use of symbols was an important element. It led us into an odd discussion.

Symbols may be familiar or unfamiliar, which will certainly affect the learning process, but some symbols, even if they are familiar, have a "strangeness" about them. Lynn (and others) disliked the square root $(\sqrt{\ })$ sign because "it conveys a confusion." She was in no difficulty about the concept of a square root, certainly at the level of knowing the square roots of 64 and 81 for instance, and she was able to recognize the sign and relate it to the instruction. I explored the notion of "strangeness" with various people. The Greek letter $\rho$ is unfamiliar to most people — but not strange. Another Greek letter, $\Sigma$, is seen as both unfamiliar and strange. Of a group of student teachers, asked which letter of our ordinary alphabet was most strange, seven out of fifteen plumped for $q$.

The work related to symbols provided a branch-point in my study, and some further experiments are discussed in chapter 12.

Between the fourteenth and fifteenth sessions we took another step. At the end of one session I gave Lynn a number of problems on indices. A variety of different issues arose from this:

**Laurie:** Do them if it is fun to do them.

**Lynn:** It *won't* be fun but I will do them. Maybe if I get a few out I'll be pleased. I'll be pleased at the end but not in the process. It'll be a relief if I get it out and if it is right.

**Laurie:** If you do, you'll feel delighted with yourself.

**Lynn:** Yes, but I won't want to do them again.

When she returned for the next session she described how the math had fallen out of her bag when she was with a friend, Georgina.

**Lynn:** I've been doing that with Laurie Buxton and you'll never believe it, I'm quite enjoying it.

**Georgina:** Oh I can't believe it. Even looking at those fractions my stomach turns.

Almost a script for a TV commercial!

Lynn then went on to say to me that she had found the work satisfying: "You were correct and I was wrong — though it was honest when I said it." But there were further defenses Lynn had against revising her view of her own incompetence at math. When I had set the index problems I had said that she would probably not be able to do them all. This was partly a direct assessment of their difficulty, but partly to guard against her being disappointed if she failed. When she had done the problems she immediately assumed that they must in fact have been easy: "It took the pleasure away the moment I had it." She also felt that I had been dishonest and manipulative, that I must have known they were easy and told her she wouldn't do them only to make them a challenge. This distrust of the teacher was apparent in several people and led to an interesting point about the degree to which a teacher does manipulate, or indeed should. My remark had been intended to guard against disappointment and to that extent, even though differently interpreted by Lynn, could be said to be manipulative. But was it wrong?

From here on we began to tackle questions from CSE and O-level papers, selected for topic but not all from the lowest level of difficulty. Lynn was generally successful, though needing to be supported. The work on geometry went particularly well, for although her initial description of the subject was "lines on a page that had rules to go with them," she was quick on visual understanding, which was emphasized heavily. We moved through the theorems quickly. One week, after she had done the angle sum of a triangle, I asked her to show it to me the next time. She started, made a mistake, but stayed cool and got it right. That was a real triumph. She promptly "put down" what she had done: "It's only because I remember the diagram easily." One of her most interesting observations came when we worked on Pythagoras' theorem. I told her of the Egyptian rope-stretchers who took a rope with knots along it making twelve equal gaps which they then pulled into the shape of a 3, 4, 5 triangle.

Laurie: They knew they would have a right angle there.

Lynn: But they didn't know why? I wonder why they didn't think. Perhaps they just had all they needed.

It is a remarkable change of attitude from the start.

During the last session we worked on problems involving circles, and we closed on her summing up, "That's nice — when you have a little bit of knowledge and it works out. Like the work on the circle."

# Sarah

Originally Sarah had been particularly keen to join the group, and only the considerable difficulty of finding a day of the week when everyone could come led to her exclusion. She remained interested in what they were doing, but accepted the alternative one-on-one interviews, which provided an opportunity to follow up certain interesting observations she had made.

When we began, Sarah was thirty-two and at the beginning of her third year of teaching. She had taken three O-levels at school, and then spent two years in France becoming fluent in the language. She had worked for some while for a photographer and then, deciding to go to college to train as a teacher, she had taken two further O-levels. She said she did not take math at all at O-level. In fact she could remember very little about school, though she recalled getting a lower grade than she ought in English because "spelling has always been my greatest bugbear." A number of the people interviewed had been able to establish where their math "failure" had started. Sarah could not do so. From her primary school days all that came back was: "One teacher I liked very much — very kind to me. The other teacher used to send us out to get peppermints in the lunch hour, and one teacher hit me around the ear for nothing at all — and that is all I remember." The only other general point was that she had been good at games but early on disliked competition and almost deliberately avoided winning: "I was always second." This attitude proved a significant one.

Two quite different experiences in math seemed to have interested her more recently. She had read C. P. Snow's *Variety of Men*, in which he relates the story, well known to mathematicians, of G. H. Hardy arriving to see Ramanujan, his collaborator, who was ill in bed. They shared a keen interest in relationships between numbers. Hardy remarked that the number of the taxi bringing him there (1729) was a particularly boring one with no special feature of interest.

"Not at all," said Ramanujan. "It is the smallest number that can be expressed as the sum of two cubes in more than one way."

$$1729 = 9^3 + 10^3 = 1^3 + 12^3$$

The somewhat esoteric nature of this piece of information is rather amusing and had caught Sarah's interest — less perhaps the fact itself, than that someone could think like that.

Sarah's headmistress described her as a very sensitive teacher, and Sarah spoke with obvious pleasure of the other mathematical event that had stirred her. She had greatly enjoyed teaching math to a group of children: "I felt that what I was doing had a sort of depth to it and wasn't a superficial thing. The children had time, and I had time to understand what they knew, or what they had already experienced. I was able to give them that experience over a period of time in a small group setting. In fact I did manage to look at the sort of concept formation much more than..." Sarah trailed off. When I asked why, she said, "Yes I know, I suddenly felt embarrassed. It always embarrasses me to be successful. I prefer people to have no expectations of me." This linked back to her remarks about games, and it is a general characteristic of Sarah (and of a great many other people). It does not derive from the area of math but will be particularly inhibiting in that area. More than other subjects, there are clear goals and expectations, with success or failure often clearly demonstrated.

We discussed briefly whether math had to be "relevant." It is not exactly easy to think of an everyday situation where Ramanujan's observation about 1729 would be helpful! Yet it had caught the interest both of Sarah and another teacher. She explained, "It's what has connections for you." And this is the point. It matters as much or more that the information fits into our minds comfortably as that it has a relationship with the actual world.

At this stage Sarah did not know of the reaction of others and the word "panic" had not been mentioned. The following passage between us reveals a number of the recurrent themes of time pressure, demands, expectations, all accentuated by past experience.

**Laurie:** What are the factors of 12?

**Sarah:** Sorry...6. 1, 2, 3, 4, and 6.

**Laurie:** Add them.

(This command, given reasonably quietly was accompanied by a flip of the hand toward her, a slightly imperative gesture.)

**Sarah:** Sorry, what did I say? 1, 6, 3, 4...did I forget 2?

I asked her about the effect.

**Sarah:** Do it, do it, there's a right answer. "Do it," you see? You say it quickly, I have to answer quickly.

The fairly calm presentation she had been offering had broken into a sort of shattered flight (the image of the Picasso *Weeping Woman* came into mind).

**Sarah:** Who? Me? Yes. At the sudden demand. You see, of course I can add that up. Of course I knew what the factors were, but as I mentioned before the sudden pressure of the expectation to do it quickly — immediately I can't.

**Laurie:** How would you describe the feeling?

**Sarah:** Panic. Having panic at this level is stupid really. Yes, panic in the mind, it was almost a panic in the mind with those figures dropping away. You know I had to keep recording them to be able to add them up.

Sarah also saw the situation as a competitive one between us, with the scale heavily weighted on my side. She felt, a curious perception, that to be wrong under pressure was a humiliation.

**Laurie:** Did you ever do mental arithmetic at school?

**Sarah:** That was my worst thing, definitely my worst thing.

The value of having mature and responsible adults who can talk in this way about what they feel is manifest. Whether such feelings are widespread or whether relatively few suffer them (at least to this extent), no child could tell us with such clarity of his or her feelings. Nor could one recreate for them in this way the feelings that they were then expected to describe! Following the mental arithmetic line, we tried to see if sufficient preparation would make it possible.

**Laurie:** I'm going to give you a couple of numbers that I want you to add together, and they are not numbers where you will know the answer automatically. You've got to receive the information, settle it in your mind, decode how you're going to do it, and then do it. And if I said 87 and 15? Now can you do that all right?

**Sarah:** [*very quickly*] 102.

But the next time it did not work.

**Sarah:** $15 \times 12 \ldots 300 \ldots$ no $\ldots$ see, I can feel myself, it's happening to me so I can feel myself under pressure you see, my mind is going $\ldots$ I know you $\ldots$

**Laurie:** There's no hurry.

**Sarah:** I know that, but I can still feel it.

We moved off to a spatial problem and I gave her a sliding block puzzle (see appendix A). Block A has to be maneuvered to the middle at the top. There was some hesitation when I watched her; she did it rapidly when I turned to something else.

Sarah recorded her own views on panic:

> In your paper on panic there seemed to be no very precise difference described by the group between *panic* in the *mind* and an emotional feeling in the stomach, sweating, numbing, etc. I feel these as two very distinct things. With me, the mind itself is thrown into a confusion and cannot make the necessary connections. I am not necessarily sweating or stomach churning but I am trying desperately to calm the mind so it will perform the necessary switchboard connections to get the right message across to me (the one I have asked for). Stop! Perhaps this is the crux of the panic. I haven't asked for the right one, I haven't made the right

demand of my brain and the brain knows it and consequently, because of all previous input and store of information it rebels.

Is this an *input-output* dilemma? At the time of making the demand I could not consciously (or anyway immediately) recall all the information already stored over the years. I might make a demand which is not compatible with the information stored. This in turn may be caused by my misinterpreting the demand made on me which I then pass on to my brain in a confused state. It may be the phrasing of the demand that throws the switchboard in confusion, trying to plug into a nonexistent hole!

Why am I making this distinction between me and my brain? Am I really talking about my *emotions* and my brain? The one paralyzing the other.

(This was a crucial observation in terms of the model of chapter 9.)

Finding the next perfect number above 6 went well, and Sarah thought it "fun": "It's more like a puzzle; you can work through. Not a snap answer. Here was something I could do—keep on working through." Similarly the work with a cube went well, to such a degree that after her evident pleasure at seeing that when one painted the outside of a three-by-three-by-three cube one of the small cubes remained unpainted, she moved on to examine larger cubes and discovered that not till one reached ten by ten by ten did the unpainted exceed the painted. This desire to explore indicated a real feel for the subject. Only when flustered did she fail, or when my manner threw her into a state of uncertainty. Faced with the problem of cutting up a three-by-three-by-three cube into unit cubes she said, "It's a new problem to me; I have nothing to measure it against. No, I can't do it, I don't want to do it." She then calmed herself:

**Sarah:** I believe that four is right but I think maybe six and I don't want to be wrong. Why should it matter? Now all I want is for you to tell me what it is. It irritates me that I am now in the situation where you know what it is and I don't know what it is.

**Laurie:** So the balance is down your side?

**Sarah:** Absolutely—I don't want to do it.

(Situation 5 in chapter 7 is relevant.)

In the event she did work on it and asked other people for their views (on the basis of the common belief that people's opinions on matters of fact are important). The majority voted for four cuts. When eventually it was shown to be six she said, "Oh God, isn't that funny? And I was convinced because other people had said it. Bloody hell— I'm flabbergasted. That gives me confidence." This feeling of confidence generated by the fact that others too could be wrong was increased when, after a lot of successful progress, she was unable to understand a point — nor could I: "You mean you can't immediately see it?" she asked delightedly. When later I managed to write $25 = 13 + 13$ she was even more pleased.

Another problem concerned the planning of team tennis tournaments. Sarah was able to solve it rapidly when she remembered that she had been successful in similar work during her time as a photographer, when she had to arrange timetables (note Ruth Eagle's point on p. 52 above): "If I hadn't made the connection I wouldn't have been able to do it."

The issue of control, mentioned by two previous people, was also important to Sarah: "I'm a great one for control." But she added that a sudden demand can break this control. She agreed that displaced anxieties (as discussed in chapter 7) could be "pushed into that area because it is a demanding area," and that the frenzied activity she sometimes showed was to avoid experiencing such demands. This was related to her classroom. She tried to create an atmosphere in which failing to respond was acceptable and in which the children understood her general approval of them; it then became easier for them to tolerate questions and cope with demands, though they would still have the feelings. One boy who reacted adversely came to her mind: "I think it's what happens to me; it all falls away in his mind."

Throughout I was concerned (as were they) that the reactions of the individuals were highly idiosyncratic, and in a large measure dependent also on my own personality. Naturally the effect of both could not be ignored, but the perception of similar reactions in the class was a valuable assurance.

The Wason problem, described elsewhere (chapter 11), started a downward trend in Sarah's confidence (and not only hers!). Her reaction is given in chapter 11 and she felt much "put down" by being taken through the problem. I managed to add to this (quite unintentionally) by giving her a CSE paper that "made me feel sick, physically and mentally." She did a number of questions but claimed that they were the easy ones (they were of the same difficulty as the others). When taken through some, she said she could not have done them by herself, and that this is what happened with kids.

**Laurie:** Does it have an anger element?

**Sarah:** No, I don't think so — hopelessness. My mind wouldn't hold anything.

This led into something later (chapter 7) characterized as concern with "world 1." She said she controlled panic outwardly but not inwardly; the energy goes into controlling appearance and one can

become too worried about what is going on outside. This was a very
helpful explanation. Nonetheless she was feeling fed up and had lost
enthusiasm: "You're getting me to do math just to see the reaction.
You're interested in the psychology of learning—you're not teaching
me any math." The latter comment may have been true in fact at that
time—though not in intention. Sarah also stated that I was naive to
expect negative feelings to be easily moved: "They go too deep." A
memory did surface. A friend of hers and she got their 11 + results
and her friend went to phone her mother. Sarah remembered standing
by the booth while her friend was telling her mother she had passed.
Sarah hadn't, "and that was quite a potent memory."

We drew some graphs. Sarah was quick and accurate and seemed
to be enjoying the work again. Meanwhile, the children in her class
were cube building, an activity that spread through them with many
becoming very involved. Inevitably we ran into problems in plotting
some graphs with negative numbers, and the same problem of
"acceptance" that nearly everyone found with operations between
negative numbers. It is odd how central an issue "a minus times a
minus is a plus" became. Sarah remembered but did not accept it:
"Forced to accept something, when you don't want to, the whole of
you revolts against it, emotional, authority things, you've never really
assimilated it." The strength of this sort of remark lies behind some of
the more speculative interpretations of chapter 13. As with the others,
a variety of approaches to directed numbers resulted generally in
more, not less, confusion, though the appreciation and depreciation
analogy was more acceptable. On the whole an operation with negative
numbers has "something alien about it."

Again, a topic with which no interpretation with actuality was
attempted—indices—proved more, not less, acceptable and she enjoyed
doing a number of questions on them. These were developed as a form
of internal and arbitrary agreement, starting with $5 \times 5 \times 5$ being
represented as $5^3$.

We returned later to her apparent desire not to succeed, which she
associated with promoting expectations in others that she could not
meet. With some who felt this, the origin eventually came out; with
Sarah it did not. Whether the demands or expectations were originally
related to math or to something else, they certainly became associated
with it and, as she said, it was "almost as though I can't bear to be
right." This was apparent most strongly in quick demands for answers,
quite strongly in responding to explanations, but was much lessened
when she involved herself in an exploration, as with the cubes, or a
puzzle, where it was clearly right when finished—and not a response
to someone.

Sarah was quick again with geometrical work (though she would deny it) and although upset during one particular session owing to a classroom situation she advanced quite rapidly. As with the others I had a great desire to continue, for all could certainly perform well at O-level standard, and it would have been good to prove this to them.

A more detailed description of the manner of working with individuals appears in the case study of Elaine (chapter 6). Those readers who would like to continue the descriptive rather than the more analytic approach could read that chapter now. Others may like to move toward a crystallization of at least some of the issues, and read this last study almost as an appendix.

# Chapter Six
# Elaine

Some readers of this chapter will identify with a sympathetic character having the same problem as themselves. Certainly two such people who have read it claim, probably prematurely, that it removed their fear of math. At the very least it should prove therapeutic for some.

Others will wish to read it as an example of a particular method of tackling the problem. Were it presented in less detail the style would not in fact be apparent, and the emotional climate would not come through. The dozen interviews were originally transcribed verbatim. This produces a very great deal of writing. Though there has been a considerable reduction in the verbiage, there are times when the discussion as presented may seem rambling, personal, or perhaps rather too "cozy." After considerable thought, I decided that if it were cut any further it would in fact not convey exactly what we were about.

Those likely to identify with Elaine should not find the style irritating. If more objective readers feel there are digressions and irrelevancies, I would at least ask that they consider whether their approach may not still be too strongly fixed in a cognitive rather than an affective mode.

Elaine is a very successful person. At the age of twenty she gained an honors degree in English, and in her thirties she became headmistress of a girls' grammar school, which she later led into an amalgamation with another school to form a comprehensive. In doing so she drew on her own confidence as a teacher, working with the more difficult groups of girls at the second school in the period leading up to the schools' joining. At the time of these interviews, well into her forties, she was a divisional inspector for the Inner London Education Authority. Her age is emphasized to bring out the length of time during which she suffered from one area of deep insecurity that greatly colored her view of herself. She could not do long division. You may well think I am seeking to draw humor from this, but it is not so. For her, the inability to deal with simple arithmetic calculations was an intensely serious matter. It was not helped by the fact that no one took it at all seriously. Elaine is a rather extreme case, and there may be few like her, but the doubts and fears that she expresses will touch chords in many people.

Elaine was one of three people, all women, who helped me enormously in understanding the problems that people may face in the subject; not simply those posed by the fact that some parts of mathematics, even at school level, are quite hard to understand, but also the strength of the emotional forces that may render a powerful mind ineffective in that one area.

The mathematical material used with the three people who afforded me "in-depth" interviews was very similar to that used in the group, but the interviews were not heavily structured; I felt the need to follow where the answers led. Nor was I as neutral as many people might feel proper in such an investigation — the subjects were of such a quality that they could and did regularly resist interpretations or opinions with which they did not agree. When I did feed something to them for comment I also noted if the reply showed weak or strong agreement.

The analysis of what I was told and my speculations about the way things might be are recorded elsewhere in the book. In pursuing a study of Elaine, it seemed more sensible to follow the chronological order of our interviews and to let the main ideas emerge from the transcript with occasional comments and clarification.

When I started these interviews I had known Elaine for perhaps ten or twelve years, not particularly well, though I had taken an interest in her reactions to work on curriculum analysis which I had devised. Initially I had wondered if her fear of numbers was slightly affected, but I had soon rejected the notion. The readiness with which she became one of my guinea pigs was very pleasing. The bulk of the interviews were held in the Christmas term 1977.

## First Interview

We talked at Elaine's home, setting aside an hour and talking with a tape recorder on. Important issues arose from the beginning.

**Laurie:** What I want to get at especially with you is this terrific anxiety.

**Elaine:** Yes.

**Laurie:** Do you feel that at this moment?

**Elaine:** No, because I've made a conscious effort not to, because I was preparing for you coming, I thought, "Now I am not going to get in a state about this, I am not going to get nervous about something as irrational as this." But I was also thinking how people boast about not being any good at math. Now I've never felt like that, Laurie, I've always felt ashamed; it's always worried me. I've always felt it was a worse weakness than in fact it is. I have honestly thought, "How can I lay claim to intelligence when I can't add up a row of figures?"

We moved on to discuss Elaine's background with parents who "decided when I was born that I was going to university," and the growing problem of a math pass, without which matriculation exemption was not possible. Elaine did not take math, but by taking biology she managed with "two distinctions, four credits, and a pass" to finally gain university entry, still without math. In fact after the end of her fourth year of secondary school she had done no math:

Well, because I got in such a state. The math mistress still said, "I think she could do it." I had got into such a state about it I really was having sleepless nights, so it was decided it would be better if I didn't take it.

The only time I ever passed a math examination was in my fourth year when the math teacher was ill for a whole term and the English teacher (I don't know how she was able to do it) took us for math. My results suddenly shot up.

Elaine had not liked her math teacher, but this was not by any means standard among those to whom I have talked, and in fact the teacher adopted a very sensible point of view. In retrospect, Elaine felt:

No, I think she quite liked me and I think she really did want to help me, because she did try to build up my confidence. She used to say, "You do see the theory of it, it's only the arithmetic that's letting you down; it doesn't matter, even if you get the arithmetic wrong." She said, "It won't matter as long as in School Certificate the examiner can see that you understand the working." It was no use, I still got terribly overwrought about it.

Some others had remembered with painful clarity episodes in which they had been exposed and humiliated, but Elaine remembered just one:

And I knew she was going to do that. If it was wrong she would make me go through it again until I got it right and she used to say...she guessed this was happening...the only time she ever put me down in public, I remember, was when she read out the whole class's — we had fortnightly marks — she read out the whole class's average for the year and then their exam result. My average for the year was something like 70 and my exam result was something like 36 and she said, "Obviously then, your father is doing your homework," and I remember smarting from it because it wasn't strictly true.


Time pressure does seem a very important issue (and is discussed at length elsewhere) and I was sorry afterwards that I had introduced the topic rather than hoping it might arise from Elaine.

Laurie: Do you see math as associated with getting a thing done in a certain time?

Elaine: I hadn't thought of that, Laurie, yes, I think I do. Because even now, I was doing a timetable analysis last week in my own home and I found myself getting worked up again. "I've got to get the sums right. I must do it to time," and I thought "Why?" And at home there isn't even a bell going to go.

Laurie: So the time is somehow being built into the math.

Elaine: Yes, I think the worst moments of my school career were mental arithmetic tests, which had to be done to time, and my father to try to teach me my tables. Quite often he would, before I went to bed, jump through tables ...quick, quick 7 × 7 ...

Laurie: But if somebody rushed you about something else, I mean often in the job you'd be doing something that's important, there'd be a very urgent call from somebody else, there's a parent on the —

Elaine: I find that stimulating.

Laurie: And you're under time pressure then, aren't you?


Once she had thought more closely about it, the significance began to emerge, and again, slightly overpressing on my part, we clarified this and led on to the matter of authority figures.

Laurie: So that I mean, supposing I were to give you a math problem within your competence, and I said to you, "Do those whenever you like, and perhaps I'll see you in three week's time," where there is obviously no time thing, you would still feel pressured by time?

Elaine: Yes, slightly.

Laurie: Even if they're the sort of thing that in fact would take you say twenty minutes and you had three weeks to do them in...

Elaine: Because I would begin to build up such a dread about them, Laurie, that I would do them as soon as you'd gone because I would rather do that than get worried about them. But it wouldn't be as bad a pressure as if you said, "Now I'll just go and read the paper and do them while I'm doing it," that would make me — really bring me near to tears and I don't cry easily — the feeling that I'd got to do it within even twenty minutes even if it was something really you knew I could do in five.

**Laurie:** And my presence would make a great deal of difference one way or the other?

**Elaine:** Yes, it would, though I'm fond of you. It's not *your* presence as such, it's the presence of the authority figure in the math subject.

The pressure on Elaine from an early age was extremely heavy. We were talking about her first going to school.

**Elaine:** Yes, just five, I think I went on my fifth birthday, but before I went to it my father had taught me to read and I remember sitting in my high chair with a little thing where my dinner plate usually was with long sheets of foolscap and before I was let out of my high chair I had to put my numbers from 1 to 100, and I remember putting them distinctly and how they went downwards because I couldn't keep a proper line.

**Laurie:** Was there the same pressure about learning to read? There would have been surely.

**Elaine:** Yes. Oddly enough I was thinking about that before you were coming. I remember this feeling of pressure and it was hard and I didn't like the book, I remember the book now — it had a black cover — and how I wished I could go out to play and my mother standing beside my father and saying, "You've got to. Avril across the way can read."

And then, going back still further:

**Elaine:** I am conscious of my high chair and not liking doing those figures. I was three.

**Laurie:** As early as that?

**Elaine:** Yes, but then on the other hand I wasn't all that keen on learning to read either. At school I forged ahead with the reading and that became pleasurable and something rewarding because I was praised for it and I found that I enjoyed reading as well, but I was a bit uneasy about math in my very first form. I remember reaching a crisis point and I really recognized that I didn't like sums as we called them then.

**Laurie:** Five years old, first form was that?

**Elaine:** No. For the very first form yes, it was called kindergarten. The next one was transition and the next one was called the first form; that would be when I was seven and that I realized that I didn't like and could not do sums. And the following year after that when I was eight I remember starting long division and that — I never mastered it. Terrified me.

Part of my rationale for talking to adults rather than children about issues that must eventually be dealt with in the classroom was that I could induce, though hopefully not at too stressful a level, some of the feelings that I was concerned to study.

**Laurie:** If somebody snaps things at you what happens, do you go into a fog? Freeze?

**Elaine:** I feel my throat tighten.

**Laurie:** [*sharply*] 7 × 8.

**Elaine:** Yes, that's right, my throat tightens and then I calm myself and I think, "I know that 7 × 7 is 49, all I have to do is add 7 — it's 56." Oh, I suppose I would say 56 in the end without working it forwards or backwards but that's how my father used to try to teach me . . .

But the aim throughout her schooling was not the pleasure of the study, or any value or purpose in it. Elaine represents one of the extreme cases of a state I have called "Situation 4" in chapter 7, in which the interpersonal and not the subject is completely dominant. The next comment is one of the saddest that can be imagined.

**Elaine:** Oh, no, it was simply to please my father or my teacher. But that was, as far as I was concerned, what school was about. You went through meaningless hoops and they had meaning for me because I pleased somebody, my mother stopped crying and my father was pleased.

**Laurie:** And that was the total purpose of the operation.

**Elaine:** Yes.

We tried together to find areas that did interest Elaine that had some mathematical content. She takes great pleasure in arranging, sorting, and ordering things and had not seen this as at all related to mathematical thinking. In a later interview we discussed operational research and the role that math had to play in problems of a sort that might well interest her. But the most directly relevant problem that came up was school timetabling, an activity that headmasters/mistresses will often delegate to someone who knows some math, on the grounds that it will suit his or her type of thinking.

**Laurie:** You like timetabling.

**Elaine:** Oh, yes, yes, that's a very positive pleasure to me.

**Laurie:** The actual arranging of the small squares, not just devising of the curriculum?

**Elaine:** Both, I find both intensely satisfying, but the actual labeling of the small squares I find...um...I was going to say an almost, but it is, a physical satisfaction, I get a physical glow that is pleasurable to me as I do it. And occasionally I'll stay home for one day to do it because I get so many interruptions at school. And when I wake in the morning I think, "I can do the timetable *all day.*"

Later, on timetabling being a mathematical type exercise:

**Elaine:** Would you say that timetabling was?

**Laurie:** Oh yes.

**Elaine:** I always think that it can't possibly have any relationship with math because I enjoy doing it and do it well.

For much of the rest of this interview we became much more discursive, talking of the Greeks' contribution to our culture, and particularly their mathematics, of the concept of infinity and the disciplined emotion she found in certain poetry. All had some connection with our study, but to contain and order it is more than can be attempted at the moment. There were two specific passages of interest near the end, the first not easy to interpret.

**Elaine:** One of my earliest memories of all, and one that was very clear to me because I think it must have been my first abstract thought, oddly is connected with number. My father was lifting me up to ring the dinner gong in my grandparents' home and I was feeling particularly happy because something had reminded me that it was my birthday soon and I was going to be four. And as I stretched my hand up to reach the bell rope, for some reason I thought, "Four years ago there was no me," and I found that stopped me being happy because I realize now it was the beginning of my first intimation of death.

**Laurie:** Yes, of nonexistence.

**Elaine:** But I remember thinking four years because there was a month to go yet, so that four years ago there was no me, three and a half years there was.

**Laurie:** Do you have a problem with negative numbers?

**Elaine:** *Oh yes,* I've never mastered those.

**Laurie:** You see that's the same statement...

Elaine: You mean as the...yes.

Laurie: The idea before I was born is one of the strongest sort of ways of thinking about negative numbers, isn't it? Because zero is when we started, isn't it?

Elaine: But I remember that so vividly because — what can have put it into a little girl's mind? Something must have been said that made me think of it, it was the most powerful thought I'd ever had, I think it's my earliest memory.

Laurie: Well, essential thing, building up identity, isn't it?

Elaine: Yes.

Laurie: To think you didn't have an identity once is shattering.

Elaine: Yes.

At the very end, impelled no doubt by a feeling that I wasn't really getting down to work, I returned to some rather bread-and-butter math, and again it would have been better not to press but to explore more slowly.

Laurie: If you take the first few numbers there, 1, 4, 9, 16, how big are the gaps?

Elaine: 3.

Laurie: 4 and 9?

Elaine: 5.

Laurie: 9 and 16?

Elaine: Oh, 7 — now you see I've started worrying.

Laurie: What I want to do with anxiety is edge in on it. If you go into it and then I detach you from it if possible. Because you can't learn about what it is until you actually get at it. Well, on the other hand if you get it too strongly it finishes you, you get screwed up. The first gap was 3 and the second gap was 5 and the next one was 7 and between 16 and 25 the gap is 9.

Elaine: Oh! Yes, I don't think that has ever been pointed out to me. It may have been...

Laurie: The gaps are just the odd numbers.

Elaine: I never grasped that...

Laurie: And so if you add up the odd numbers you get the squares, and nobody has ever mentioned it to you?

Elaine: No, not that I remember.

The issues that come out in these early interviews with Elaine and others remained important throughout my investigation, though perspectives shifted. Each of the many hares that started here ran well and led through paths along which we have already made some advances, only to suggest much more to be done.

# Second Interview

By this time I had discussed panic at some length with the group and Elaine gave me further valuable insights into it. Initially I returned with her to the issue of time, and the feeling some people had that there was such a mountain of material in math that it could never be dealt with. I asked if that rang a bell for her.

> No, it doesn't really, Laurie — when I tried to think back to it, it was always that dreadful numbing panic. I remember distinctly in one exam knowing that I knew *how* to do a problem or whatever it was and being quite paralyzed so that I could not remember what — I think it was seven sevens, so I remember writing down seven sevens and adding them up and getting stuck two thirds of the way up. You know, thinking, "I'm not going to get beaten by this, I can work out what seven sevens are," and yet I couldn't because of this *awful* panic. When I came out of the exam I don't think I would have been able to say $7 \times 7 = 49$, but I would have been able to add up seven sevens. It's the hysteria that I think about, because the homework was often easy — it's linked with exams certainly.

It was encouraging that Elaine did in fact sweep away a suggestion of mine, since the danger of feeding in material that is too readily accepted is ever present.

In her reply she was clearly remembering vividly the emotions of that time, and the fact that they are so remembered is possibly one indication of their intensity. We went on to discuss the physical symptoms and arrived at the surprising conclusion, mentioned in the opening chapter, that they were very similar to those she felt concerning a much more serious issue — the much-delayed return of her husband, Stephen, from abroad and her intense fears for his safety. Panic would seem to be a response to an attack of some sort, either directly on oneself or on a person deeply involved with oneself. The question of how one's ability at math could relate in any way to personal worth is strange, but the following passage explores it in some depth.

**Laurie:** Now the math thing, does that threaten part of you in any way?

**Elaine:** [*long pause*] Self-respect?

**Laurie:** Yes. You mentioned in the first interview you felt shamed.

**Elaine:** Oh yes.

**Laurie:** Now shame is another strong emotion isn't it?

Elaine: Yes.

Laurie: Now, what does shame mean? In relation to self?

Elaine: Inferiority. Disgrace. A low opinion of you in other people's eyes.

Laurie: So perhaps the threat was of diminishing you in others' eyes. Am I...I'm leading you again, aren't I?

Elaine: I don't think it was in others'. It's somehow in my own. Because if I, when I'm adding up the AUR [*Alternative Use of Resources, an ILEA scheme concerned with allocation of money*] I have to do it very, very slowly to get it right and I'm ashamed— nobody cares tuppence how long it took to add up the AUR, nobody is interested.

Laurie: Nobody is going to ask you.

Elaine: No, I should tell them and they'll laugh and just ask "Yes, what was the result?"

Laurie: You'll feel impelled to tell them.

Elaine: Oh, yes, oh yes, puritan.

Laurie: "I must be seen for how bad I am"?

Elaine: Yes, certainly. You see I always think people think too well of me and it is important to me that they shouldn't like me for things that I believe I do not possess and they therefore must not think that I am intelligent or nice or the things that people tend to think I am. I have to go out of my way to prove that, while I'm quite intelligent, I'm not *very* intelligent; whereas yes, I've got a kind nature, I'm capable of very unpleasant things and *therefore if they think I'm a good head it is important that they know that I can't add up*. That's putting it rather crudely, that is exactly what I feel, as far as language can convey it that's what I feel.

Laurie: Don't you see that sometimes other people understand all that, don't necessarily agree with your assessment of yourself and like you for that particular—

Elaine: Yes, and then that comes round, I know it sounds absurd, that makes me all the angrier that I can't get it into their heads...

Laurie: That you're not as you seem...

Elaine: That's right. Then I think, "Damn it, they're thinking I'm nice because I'm doing it." I don't know if that's related to math...

Laurie: Don't suppose it is, no. Well, in a sense it is because if math demonstrates to you—to your satisfaction—that you're not intelligent...

Elaine: Yes, yes.

**Laurie:** It's the thing that really confirms...that you're not intelligent.

**Elaine:** Yes, yes.

**Laurie:** It's not acceptable that I think you're intelligent.

**Elaine:** No, I feel that I'd fooled you.

**Laurie:** How could you if I'm that bright compared to you?

This obtruding of her inability to do math had been characteristic of Elaine since I had known her, and statements such as that italicized above, "Therefore if they think I'm a good head it is important that they know that I can't add up," were treated by most people with casual amusement because of the obvious imbalance of importance of the two issues. *Yet they were not out of balance to her.* Her failures in math were an essential and important part of her character.

The next passage is a very significant one. At a crucial stage, by a lucky chance, I dispel the panic as it is rising. The issues of time and authority, which we shall later see in connection with panic, are both present. The release of time pressure and the lack of crossness of an authority figure together trigger the change that will gradually take place.

**Laurie:** I'd like to see if you could do mental arithmetic in the sense of doing something in your head, but something that doesn't just involve recall. So supposing I asked you for instance what's $15 \times 12$?

**Elaine:** Oh, I couldn't possibly do it.

**Laurie:** Not in your head.

**Elaine:** No. I would have to say $12 \times 12 = 144$ and write it down and add on the others, oh I suppose the next step would be — *you don't mind how slow I am.* How many 12s did you say?

**Laurie:** 15.

**Elaine:** 15. [*mumbles*]...144, Oh I can't do it, I can't carry it in my head. I can't carry the, you know, the one on.

**Laurie:** What you are doing is visualizing the paper and pencil method.

**Elaine:** Yes, yes, I see exactly what I am doing.

**Laurie:** And that's what you believe mental arithmetic to be about.

**Elaine:** Well, I remember when I did mental arithmetic I knew that it shouldn't be. I knew it should be instant recall.

**Laurie:** No, no. Instant recall is for facts not for calculations. Supposing I said 87 and 15, try it.

**Elaine:** 102.

**Laurie:** How did you do it?

**Elaine:** Added 10 and then added 5.

**Laurie:** Now that isn't the way you were taught at school?

**Elaine:** No, no that's the way *I protected myself inadequately* but that's the way I taught myself to do it.

**Laurie:** It's the way everybody does it.

**Elaine:** Is it? *Oh...*

**Laurie:** If you say 87 and 15 — I say everyone — *most* people would say 87, 97, 102.

**Elaine:** Really you break it down still further because you say 3 and 2, don't you?

**Laurie:** Now return to the other one and you had...you'd got 144 and you'd got 36.

**Elaine:** Yes.

**Laurie:** And you proceeded to set it out in your mind, you tried to picture it...

**Elaine:** Instead of adding 44 and 36.

**Laurie:** Can you do that?

**Elaine:** 70? No that's...

**Laurie:** No hurry...

**Elaine:** 80.

**Laurie:** So what are $15 \times 12$?

**Elaine:** 180. Now I did that quite calmly. Now you know why I did it calmly, it's because you said in that nice voice, "No hurry." That was the key, I was beginning to get panicky...Now if you'd said "Don't worry," that wouldn't have mattered, but you said "No hurry." You said it in a kind way.

In fact, a great deal is said by Elaine in those last two lines about the mechanism of panic. The issue about my not being cross is pursued later in our series of interviews. It is interesting that Lynn was very tentative for a long time with me, because she expected me to show anger, and in fact had a dream in which I did so, which enabled her to think "So that's what he is really like."

We returned to the particular point about the mental arithmetic after a few minutes.

**Elaine:** ...because I felt just the very beginnings only, a ghost of the panic — and it went, linked with a confidence that you weren't going to think badly of me for being slow.

**Laurie:** No...Well, that's very ambivalent because you don't want me to think badly of you, but you want me to know how bad you are. And then accept you?

**Elaine:** Yes, *yes*, that's it exactly. That's what I want people to do.

By now we were near the end of this interview and I gave Elaine two puzzles. She seemed to welcome them, and admire their shape. (They are described under "Solid Block Puzzles" in appendix A.)

After this interview I felt I needed to check that my impressions of the progress matched Elaine's. I therefore established a routine whereby after each interview we put our comments on paper, independently, and then exchanged what we had written. These formed an interesting series of papers and illuminate further the changes in Elaine's attitude.

# Interviews 1 and 2: My Comments

In the first interview there was distinct hesitation about the home situation; it had to be negotiated. What is Stephen's attitude to the investigation? Might he be derisory? I felt a *prepared* openness on her part. Perhaps this was simply a settling of herself against possible anxiety.

Nonetheless, the openness seems quite remarkable. She exhibits confidence in asserting those areas where she is confident and those where she is not; a sort of second-level confidence. She dismissed the idea of confidentiality almost out of hand. Was the issue previously considered? Can she be so totally open about the exploration? Can strong anxiety exist without there being areas she will wish to avoid?

The switches from her marked competence in professional management skills to a willingness to adopt a pupil posture with apparent dependence occur so naturally that the difference in attitude implied might well pass unnoticed. How often and with whom is the second mood possible? In the first interview I talked too much and felt I was feeding answers in. In the question of time pressure, there may have been a lack of definition of which area of math occasioned it, or she may have accepted my interpretation too readily when in a dependent mood. By the next session her critical faculty had been at work and she retracted some earlier statements.

She has a perceptive and analytic mind, and since she will constantly review what has been said there will not, I think, be a problem. She will, naturally, think she has conned me into believing this of her, and that she is not *really* intelligent. Thereby she denies me my own perceptions!

The mathematical points will mainly be dealt with in the longer statements based on more people but there are three areas worth commenting upon.

First, the way in which she was able to weave in her feelings about 7 × 7 and her husband, Stephen, was extremely interesting. It is remarkable that feelings about math can be so clearly related to other situations that are evidently so much more important. Perhaps one might observe that intensity of feeling may *not* relate to importance of event as closely as we might initially believe. (See the fuller statement on panic in chapter 9.)

Second, the perception by both of us of the almost mechanical switching off of the "panic button" by a calm "No hurry" at a critical moment.

Third, the earlier remarks about visualization need to be explored to see if they are really the same as spatial perception. We may here have a parallel to rote recall and seeing relationships. It may for some be easy to achieve visual recall but it may not imply an ability to see relationships in space.

## Interview 2: Elaine's Comments

As this session was at school and I had had a busy and potentially upsetting morning I hadn't thought about the session at all, yet I ended it feeling happy and encouraged. I give a lift each evening to one of the math juniors and I found myself telling her about my success over a mental arithmetic sum. I remember first about the session the moment when I was just about to panic or give up over multiplying 15 × 12 and Laurie said *quietly* (that's important, I'm sure), "No hurry." On reflection I think the remark was so powerful because he had earlier stated, almost casually and in passing, "I think you're intelligent" — an assurance I always welcome from people whose intelligence I respect since my respect for the other people's intellect is invariably linked with a downgrading of my own — and because he had prodded me into talking about my marriage. My happiness with Stephen is the bedrock of *all* my happinesses, even unrelated ones, so unconsciously Laurie had made me marshal all my psychological antibodies for the arithmetical threat that followed. The following day in Sainsbury's (a grocery store), I made myself multiply 13p (the price of a tin I was buying and a *very* threatening number!) by 4, since I had 4 tins with me and I did it before the counter clerk's machine had! Normally I would have panicked away from it, as I'm afraid I still would have done had I selected 5 or 7 tins! But I am certain a small breakthrough has been achieved.

# Third Interview

At the beginning of each interview we now had a fair amount of material to pick back over. I gave Elaine transcripts of earlier sessions and we both had comments made by us after the last interview. On this occasion Elaine was full of things she wanted to tell me.

**Elaine:** Since I mastered adding up those rice puddings I've given myself a small sum each day. Not a challenging sum but one that was a little frightening and each time the panic has been a little less. Now every morning I bring a young math staff member (whom I mention in that report) to school and I was bringing her to school this morning and she was talking about something that she found difficult at school. And she said, "I just always panicked as soon as somebody said a certain... (I've forgotten what it is)," and I said, "That's just like me with $7 \times 8$, *I never know that it's 56.*" And I said, "Monica! I've never in my life known that before," and I haven't, Laurie.

**Laurie:** Isn't that wonderful!

**Elaine:** I couldn't get over it because I have always said $7 \times 7$ is 49 and I didn't have to say to her, "It's 56," *I knew* it was 56. Do you know I felt euphoric!

For someone who has never experienced anxiety of this sort there is an element of the ridiculous in some of these statements — and indeed there might be now for Elaine. But it is precisely this feeling that we must resist. It does indeed seem ridiculous, but if it is not so to the person, then any expressing of this is most unhelpful. To empathize with someone who is experiencing feelings one has not been through oneself is a difficult but necessary task.

We played with numbers for some while, and, though Elaine showed anxiety, she "reacted with far more strength," as she herself phrased it. I introduced the idea of factorizing numbers rather than finding products (as in the tables), because it was a new way of looking at things for Elaine and because there may be grounds for thinking that it is psychologically easier to break up a number (63 into 9 and 7) rather than remembering products ($9 \times 7 = ?$). She was cautious at this activity, advanced slowly, putting in stakes at every stage and claiming she could go no further. This is very common among individuals; the group activity helps urge people on.

**Laurie:** So if I said to you 36... would you give me any pairs you can think of that will multiply together to make it?

**Elaine:** Immediately I thought $6 \times 6$. But at that I'm stuck.

**Laurie:** That's the only one that comes?

**Elaine:** Yes, 3 × 12, no, I'm stuck again...twice 18...you see how slow it is?

**Laurie:** Not very.

**Elaine:** No, that's it.

**Laurie:** Well that's three of them out isn't it? Er, 9 × 4.

**Elaine:** Oh, yes, I wouldn't think of a 9 times, I'd shy away from 9.

**Laurie:** You didn't like the 9 times table.

**Elaine:** *No.*

**Laurie:** That was a nasty one, was it, the 9 times?

**Elaine:** *Yes.*

Many of those whom I spoke to disliked the 9 times table, and they seemed never to have been shown the simple pattern:

27    2 + 7 = 9
36    3 + 6 = 9
45    4 + 5 = 9
54    5 + 4 = 9

The sum of the digits is always 9 (up to 10 × 9). When I showed this to a friend named Sybil, she said, in her strong Australian accent, and putting weight on every syllable, "It's un-be-lie-va-ble!"

The work on factorizing went well and Elaine was visibly gaining in confidence, though she again mentioned that percentages and long division loomed large. She described how she managed to see a shortcut on a percentage question but failed to get the answer because of the arithmetic. This gave me a clue that, if the number barrier could be further broken down, then an approach in math might quickly yield good results — and so it later proved in long division.

We briefly discussed her father, about whom I made further inquiries, but he did not seem especially relevant. In view of the effects she describes after this third interview we both looked carefully at the transcript but could find no real starting point for her subsequent turbulent emotions. We both remembered that after the interview we did further discuss her parents (not recorded on tape) and this may have contained the matter that later disturbed her.

At the end of the interview we started on the cube (see appendix A), which eventually yielded much of interest. Foolishly I started in by asking her to see a three-inch cube and imagine it cut into one-inch cubes, rather than stabilizing a simple cube originally. Her opening remark is of importance later.

Laurie: I don't want to tell you how many cuts because that's one of the things I want to ask. Can you see how many cubes there would be?

Elaine: *I can see there would be two cuts down and four across*, I can't see how many cubes there should be.

Laurie: You are prepared often to say something you see immediately and then you say, "But I can't do any more." You repeatedly do that as a stake point—say "Can't go beyond there." Sometimes if I leave you, you *do* go beyond there, and you want to stake out what you're not prepared to go beyond...

Elaine: Yes. I think that I want to make clear that I'm incompetent at that stage.

Laurie: That's right. Now in fact...this is not recall, it's not really mathematics, it's seeing how many are there. There's a small bit of counting involved but it's a question of whether you can hold the thing in your mind.

Elaine: Yes.

Laurie: Can you try and do it or does it...does it frighten you, does it worry you?

Elaine: It worries, it doesn't frighten me. No, it's not panic, it's a feeling I can't imagine it. What I can't imagine is the depth.

Laurie: OK. So calm down and get the cube in the mind; that's the unbroken-up cube. Let's take it in simpler stages than that. I rushed rather straight into it. Can you see how many faces there are on that cube? Prowl round it and look at it.

Elaine: Six?

Laurie: Yes.

Elaine: I had to go round it.

Laurie: That's what I wanted.

Elaine: I had to walk round it and look under it and over it.

Laurie: There isn't another mechanism; that is, I'm asking you to hold a visualization and then observe it, I'm not asking you to do a problem-solving thing exactly. Now, next, how many corners are there, can you go round and count those?

Elaine: Eight.

Laurie: Yes, can you count how many edges there are?

Elaine: Eight, aren't there, let me go round again.

Laurie: You're hurrying too much. Look round it, stand it on the ground, make it bigger so you can get your arms round it.

**Elaine:** By the edge you mean that bit there. Now I've got aware of that, it is a form of cube. (Points to object on desk.)

**Laurie:** I wondered whether you would and I mean I thought, that's very good, I thought "I don't want to draw her attention to it."

**Elaine:** I saw you thinking that.

**Laurie:** You saw me thinking that, yes.

**Elaine:** And I tried to join in by not looking at it and I thought if I look down that will be cheating, I shan't do it properly, I must tell Laurie, let me see, 1, 2, 3, 4, 5, 6...well that is 8 isn't it...it's 12!

The interview finishes on a rather odd note, with Elaine's saying: "Do you know, as you're talking I'm finding it remarkable that you're not cross with me." This links back with an earlier statement, but it might be possible to read more into it. Is Authority always cross? But, of course, we are not into psychoanalysis.

## Interview 3: My Notes

*Immensely* pleased. She felt, rightly, that she had made an enormous breakthrough (though she minimized it). Had actually done some mental arithmetic problems. Four tins at 13p! Not easy. Also had responded to $7 \times 8$ without having to creep up on it from $7 \times 7$.

Part of the problem has been the difference in the way Elaine has perceived it, and others' attitudes to it. People see her incompetence in calculation as a minor (even endearing) eccentricity. They, rightly in the abstract, attach little importance to it. But *she* feels it very important—and can convince no one it is. They feel she *could* do it anyway if she wanted. Two levels of *could*. Evidently she has the potential and intellectual equipment for this low-level task. But no one has accepted the degree to which emotion can block the cognitive process, and that this in fact is why she could *not*. By expressing the fact that *the* task is trivial, they have not accepted that *her* task is not. It may be that she needs to articulate this to Stephen.

I am hopeful that tackling it now for herself she will resolve this area quite quickly and with enormous relief. It is in fact *very* important.

She tackled the problems of visualizing a cube very well and got to all the answers. Will go a further stage with this next week. She repeated her practice of stopping and saying she could go no further and then, when I did not comment, doing so. Eventually I mentioned her trick of setting a stake in the ground to hold on to the limit of how far she could get. This view was rapidly acknowledged and seemed to give another access of strength.

Returning to the beginning. She read my comments on the first two interviews, commented, "How perceptive...assessing," and exhibited some caution and withdrawal. I don't think the perceptions are necessarily accurate but they are exploratory and may, when she has considered them, allow new areas to open up

The "assessing" might have been a correction of "perceptive" and was certainly an ambivalent statement. Relating it to further comments she made about her father, who at the end of a day marked her for behavior (!), I think that she is concerned that it can lead to judging (which so many of my people seem to fear) rather than the intent, which she recognizes, of diagnosis and aid. Perhaps it is the habit I have of both engaging with people and observing the engagement—it does worry people.

Other important points, no doubt, but they will appear on the transcript.

# Interview 3: Elaine's Notes

A curious amalgam of extreme emotions after this interview. I drive home by myself without my usual companion feeling euphoric working my way through the 9 times table, first of all right through and then jumping about crowning my triumph with progressing from my new grasp of $7 \times 8$ to $7 \times 9$. I remember almost saying aloud, "Got you!" as if I'd literally pounced on an object. Yet about a quarter of a mile further on I discovered I was immersed in self-pity, reliving a scene I'd had with my mother, too painful for me to write down, when I was twelve. It had nothing to do with math, but it seemed to crystallize my mood of blaming my parents for my arithmetical paralysis.

I regularly phone my parents on a Friday evening, so I tried to discuss my interviews with Laurie with my father, but couldn't get far as I realized *he* was as vulnerable as I am on the matter. He blamed my teachers, saying interestingly that my very first one worked with him over my difficulties. This is interesting, as I don't remember having any difficulties with *her*, only with her successor, whom my father found more hostile. He also said that when I was four and he was teaching me numbers and reading, I had more difficulty with reading, being unable to recognize *it*, although I identified *its*. He wrote sentences for me to copy, apparently, until I mastered the difficulty, yet reading developed into English—the only area in which I've *known* I was able. Why did math end up the bogey subject?

I played with the easier puzzle that evening (the cubical wood-block puzzle)—the one I thought pretty—and reassembled it with interest, taking twenty minutes. I felt no anxiety or fear with it as I found myself thinking, "But it's nothing to do with math, it doesn't involve tables." Stephen then came home and I found myself telling him quite excitedly of my session with Laurie, once again feeling happy about it. I was particularly happy about the cube problem as I had found it daunting, but *not*, at last, panic making.

However, the self-pity and accusatory feeling toward my parents recurred all weekend, churning up unpleasant memories. I was dress making, so my mind was free, and, in trying to order my thought and control the unpleasant emotions I was experiencing, I observed the following statements and questions were in my mind:

> Tables are soon not going to frighten me any more and they're not an important part of math anyway.

> If I overcome my feelings of inferiority over math how am I going to "stop feeling superior"?

> I've *wasted* years of my life over a chimera! It really doesn't matter whether I can add up or not.

> Stephen is nothing like my father, yet I've transferred some of my filial attitudes to him.

# Interview 3: Elaine's General Observations  •

1. Towards the end of the session I found myself wanting to grip Laurie's arm and say in an almost groveling burst of emotion, "Thank you, *thank* you, for not being cross!" Yet I don't remember anyone actually ever being so — more puzzled than cross.
2. Difference in my vocabulary between fear and panic. Fear is controllable. It can't be obliterated, but it prompts action and can sometimes sharpen intellect. Panic inhibits rationality completely. It is entirely a gut feeling and shatters both intellect and personality.
3. I find the "pupil posture" easy and the publicizing of my difficulties acceptable "because of my driving urge to make people see me with all my weaknesses and then accept me," as Laurie summed it up for me in an earlier interview.
4. When my father was helping me with my homework, he would ask me arithmetical questions and if I didn't answer them more or less at once would answer for me. This, on reflection, I realize is why I "put my stake in the ground." I want to break the tension of waiting for Laurie/my father/my teacher to supply me with the answer. I used to feel it as a dreadful tension too, very near panic. But my father loved me! And my teacher certainly didn't dislike me. It was their puzzlement and disappointment that worried and panicked

me — somehow I had got to be as good as my parents wanted me to be. What a terrible weapon love is!

5. I cannot overestimate the sensation of relief and security I feel when I remember that I now *know* that $7 \times 8 = 56$. I've got it for good, only brain damage can take it away — the thought recurs to me now and again with almost physical warmth. This is not exaggeration, yet I realize many of my friends would find it laughable. Yet I know equally well that Laurie knows exactly how I feel. Am I attaching gurulike qualities to him because he's breaking down a painful barrier?

6. I obviously have a tinge of the "mountain" attitude towards math, as I feel the area of difficulty in tables has shrunk to the negligible. Laurie reinforced this by writing it down as a diagram. Diagrams usually set off panic immediately.

7. I have just reread all the material so far. I find I now understand exactly what squares are and how they are spaced out by odd numbers. When I read that part before I skimmed over it as it threatened me. There can be no doubt about it — I am growing calmer and getting nearer controlling figures as I can do words. I sometimes use the wrong word — so what? Soon I shall say, I sometimes slip up in arithmetic — so what? But not quite yet.

# Fourth Interview

Naturally, we were both a bit shaken and surprised at the consequences of our third interview, and the question of psychotherapy continued to concern me in all the individual interviews, particularly with the other two people I was interviewing "in depth." I was, however, in regular touch with Richard Skemp, who was experienced in psychotherapy. With Elaine, the matter was quickly cleared, as the following passages indicate.

**Elaine:** Quite, quite, so I suppose my trust in you gets reinforced by every example you give me of the fact that you are taking it *seriously*, that you understand, I don't think I've ever met anybody who took it seriously. They always thought it was...But what puzzles me is why was I *so* grateful, pathetically, grovelingly grateful to you for not being cross. When searching my memory, I can't remember anyone ever being cross. Stephen, when I discussed it with him, said. "But they must certainly have said, 'Oh, *come on* Elaine, you *can* do it,' and that was enough to make you feel — "

**Laurie:** Yes, but you said the strongest thing that your parents could hit you with was disapproval.

Elaine: Disappointment.

Laurie: Or disappointment, so that nobody was cross but they all expressed disappointment and they didn't understand and that was what was bugging you really, the understanding. As for why you are pathetically grateful, I've got some concerns that I shall talk...I'm seeing Richard [*Skemp*] on Tuesday and one of the things of which I'm becoming aware that I hadn't really expected is how interwoven it is with many deep and personal things and so you are getting into what is technically a therapy session.

Elaine: Oh, yes, hence my violent reactions...

Laurie: And my concern is that, well I did talk to him briefly about it, because he, before he went into the psychology of learning, was a psychotherapist for a while and I personally have serious concerns about mucking about with people's lives. I've got a very ambivalent reaction to the Grubb style [*I had had experience of group dynamics in work with the Grubb Institute and had run a course, which they helped devise, in which Elaine had participated*] although I'm sort of fascinated by it on the one hand; it's got a sort of power, seductive...

Elaine: You're playing, not God, you're playing Satan with people's lives.

Laurie: Well, you can be immensely affective and that's a thing I worry about here and the level of disturbance, say about your parents, I have induced is a concern.

Elaine: I think I can cope with it, Laurie, I obviously thought that through because I thought, "If this is going to attack my personality I'll tell Laurie I can't go on with it," and then I thought, say about Wednesday, "I really am sufficiently integrated and firm to be able to meet it and deal with it and perhaps it's as well that I *should* meet it and deal with it."

Laurie: It's that, while I am the right person to deal with the mathematical side of it I can't claim competence in the other area which will constantly evoke—

Elaine: Yes, but perhaps it will get better.

Laurie: The one attitude one can take of course that you're responsible as much as I and you can cut out any time.

Elaine: Yes, yes, oh I'm conscious of that...

Laurie: So perhaps it needn't worry us too much.

Elaine: I don't think so, and of course I have always been aware of this feeling toward my parents; in fact I occasionally have dreams about it still, but the math is only one aspect of it, and we're concentrating on my father because he was the math one. In fact my conflicts with my mother were *far* greater, but they didn't impinge on math.

Elaine had been successful with the nine-piece cube problem (see appendix A) though Stephen had come in unexpectedly and given her a little (unnecessary!) help at the end. This led us into an interesting discussion on her ability to be cross, which related to the earlier work on the expectation of others being cross, but led us further away from the math.

The "Passalong" problems (see appendix A) seemed to me to bear some resemblance to processes involved in timetabling and I felt Elaine would enjoy them. They could be handled and were not three-dimensional. I gave the puzzle to her and explained it. As we were discussing it, I led back into the question of time, which was becoming important in my thinking. It may be that again, I was overpressing my opinion, but Elaine, though very accommodating to what one says, will resist if she does not agree and will return later to the issue if she feels she may have agreed too readily.

Laurie: You don't find it worrying, not even with me here?

Elaine: Well, then I feel that I'm going to take too long and that it might take an hour.

Laurie: Well...

Elaine: It's more worrying with you here, but it isn't *very* worrying.

Laurie: It isn't very worrying...I'm still pursuing, and haven't written anything about the time pressure. You accepted it the first time, went back on it rather the second —

Elaine: It's an element, isn't it?

Laurie: — then specified it, on the third occasion, I think, as being related to mental arithmetic where it was obviously presented to you as a time thing.

Elaine: And with my parents of course, that was when I felt the panic worst.

Laurie: But every now and then it *seems* that when somebody starts on a mathematical type thing or puzzle, there is a feeling that it must be done in a certain time.

Elaine: I timed myself with that puzzle, you see [*the nine-piece cube*].

Laurie: Twenty minutes, yes...

Elaine: And I felt, I remember thinking, "It's nearly twenty minutes, surely I ought to have done it more quickly than this."

**Laurie:** Because there are people who wouldn't be able to do it all. Lots of people wouldn't be able to do it at all. You had no idea how long it should take.

**Elaine:** There isn't a *should*, is there? Rationally I know perfectly well there isn't a *should*.

**Laurie:** It will be different lengths of time for different people.

And, shortly after, Elaine commented: "Oh, I would go on doing it even if it took me days, once I'd started doing it. Oh yes, I can't bear anything unfinished, that's another element of the panic in math because I can't get to the end..."

We finished the session on a discussion of goal seeking related to Skemp's 1979 work on intelligence, discussing the distinction between reaching goals and the specific sort of pleasure that the puzzles afforded because something was manifestly made complete. There is a curious pleasure in this. The desire Stephen had to say where the last piece went, and the way in which a latecomer to a jigsaw may want to help with the last section (only to be firmly rejected by those who have worked from the beginning on it) are examples of this satisfaction. It is distinct from that of simply reaching a goal.

## My Letter to Elaine after the Fourth Interview

Dear Elaine,

Great progress, I feel, and extremely interesting. I don't want to know your comments until I have written mine, so here they are. I will give Richard Skemp a complete rundown on the exercise so far, but he will need to think it through before we get a reaction.

Meanwhile there was a *difficult* problem I promised you. Richard was unsuccessful with this! What is the effect of an avowedly difficult problem on your desire to complete? It does *not* require anything you do not know, but it is hard to see.

Take the cube again and this time you can use a drawing or actual bricks if you like (though it would be cleverer not to do so!). You have a saw and are going to cut it into its 27 individual cubes. The first question (not too easy but not the hard one) is "How many cuts do we need to produce the 27 pieces?"

Now for the hard bit. Once you are sure of the first answer, can feel it and see it, can you now do it in less cuts if after every cut you can rearrange the pieces before the next cut?

Spend time *stabilizing* the problem (like walking round the cube) and do not seek to hasten the problem.

See you Thursday,

Love, Laurie

## Fourth Session: My Notes

A good deal to comment upon, particularly related to Elaine's reaction to the third session. A good deal of stuff had been churned up about her parents which she did not get sorted out until Wednesday.

I am concerned about the psychotherapy we seem to be into. There are two slightly different aspects. One is the problem of intrusion into areas properly private to her. Her own clear understanding of this will mean, however, that she will feel free to avoid certain questions or to state openly that an area is private—and this will embarrass neither of us.

The other is the disturbance unforeseen in intensity—like that with her parents. She again asserts her own responsibility, but I cannot thereby completely disclaim my own, particularly because of her feelings of gratitude.

As far as her parents are concerned they are elderly (eighty and seventy-six) and I think she has to resolve something about her relationships with them. The (avowedly) therapeutic nature of our interviews clearly induced this examination, for which she was very ready.

I have some concern that in the fourth session I attached weight to her husband's intervention in doing a puzzle (see transcript) and I asked her to think about it.

But apart from my concerns, why should our entry through doubts about $8 \times 7$ lead into such areas? Have anxiety states been transferred there at some time? Did she feel that her inability to learn her tables, with the consequent disappointment of her parents (an immensely powerful sanction in her case), made her feel that she was not returning their love? Yet the strength of feeling in math is totally genuine and significant, however it got there.

The release in this area is irreversible and seems to have been achieved with such ease. She will work, casually, in her own time at number and spatial relationships, and she will I believe develop a strong interest in them. There are various technical and psychological tricks to tell her, which will help in the solution of problems, but the process may not need much help from me.

Obviously, on the face of it, what has been done is beneficial, but there is a small query in my mind. Elaine has been strong in all areas except this. She wonders in her notes to the third session what the effect of removing it will be and so do I. It may not exactly be a cherished weakness, since she was shamed by it, but she did regard it as a significant feature of her personality, even though others did not treat it seriously. There must always be speculation about altering something that has been there a long time.

Elaine is what I would regard as an extreme example of Richard Skemp's goal-seeking organism! She expressly sees life as a series of goals, minor or major, to be achieved.

This is associated with another math/psychology area I must examine: the desire to *complete* things. Elaine says she will *not* give up something once started, though in math she has not been able to achieve this. She tackled a Brian Willsher puzzle [see appendix A for a discussion of wood-block puzzles], which she did in the good time of twenty minutes (she decided to time it), but what will the effect now be of giving her a problem she can't do? Completing is not the same as seeking goals.

During the interview I talked too much and was seduced into didacticism by her "pupil posture." That is not to say that I believe these sessions should involve my saying little; there is active teaching to be done.

A last comment, on my use of the third person for Elaine. This was probably a desire to objectivity, and hence these read as if written for Richard; but the questions posed are also for Elaine.

## Fourth Session: Elaine's Notes

In most ways this session was one of taking stock. We had both been a little worried by the strong disturbance I had experienced psychologically after last week's session, but I am now convinced that the emotions I experienced are controllable. Indeed I feel that it is possible that they were the last fling of the ambivalent feelings I have entertained toward my parents all my life. After these sessions with Laurie I feel that I can control my mathematical attainment and also can accept the fears and insecurities my parents gave me as a stage of my development that is now past but that eventually proved an asset; e.g., because I know what fear of a subject is like, I am an understanding teacher. I think this is now behind us and that it need not be raised again.

This belief comes because at the end of the session I was impatient with myself for having talked at length of past insecurities and found myself regretting that we hadn't continued work on cubes as Laurie's notes on our last session suggested. When I read that observation initially I felt a shadow of nervousness (I'm choosing words with great care—it wasn't panic), but in our conversation Laurie mentioned almost in passing that some people would not have been able to perform the tasks of cube visualization he had set me. I was astonished (the word is not too strong). On reflection, this was the moment when I switched from negative thinking ("I am not going to panic about this task") to positive ("I'm going to enjoy this"). Laurie picked this up in my reaction to the puzzle he gave me and assumed correctly that it reminded me of timetabling, but at last I am beginning to put the label math in areas where I now see it belongs and am breaking down my numerical-centered concept of the subject.

An appropriate metaphor for what Laurie has induced in my mind would be a surge of cleansing, revitalizing water breaking down an ugly, prohibiting wall. The wall in my mind is crumbling, but since I am now psychologically confident in the areas most important to me it isn't harming me. Perhaps even ten years ago these sessions would have come to soon.

## Fifth Interview

Elaine was obviously full of herself, and for once managed to talk more than I did! She had enjoyed the 25-piece problem (the wood-block problem) and had succeeded not only in completing it, but in overcoming the time bogey.

**Laurie:** That's the wooden-block puzzle and the "Passalong."

**Elaine:** And in my systematic goal-setting way I would like to do *that* but *that* is what I must do first because I was given it first. Isn't it funny how you set yourself these goals? So I undid it and I mixed it very, very thoroughly and I very soon became completely absorbed by it. Halfway through the phone rang and I dealt with it, I've forgotten what it was now, all the time I was thinking, "I want to get back to that." Only half my mind was on the phone call and I had no desire to time myself. I didn't consciously not, I just forgot about timing myself. [*She had moved on to a Passalong problem and, with not much time available, got stuck.*] Well, let me finish telling you. I thought without any panic and without any inferiority, "I'm tired, it's the end of the day, I've been overdoing it, I'll leave that for a moment." By Tuesday and then all through Wednesday I was quite extraordinarily happy. You know how sometimes you have a mood of perfect contentment, you feel, "How lucky I am. Everything in my world is perfect." It's a mood that everybody gets occasionally then conversely you can get a mood of acute depression often for no real reason either, but I had it and I'm certain it was to do with profound satisfaction having done that puzzle. It wasn't triumph, it wasn't a feeling "I've mastered math," which is the euphoria that I'd had earlier over 7 × 7. It was a feeling of calm satisfaction, completion of a task, the mastery of something. I think it was a feeling of completion; it wasn't euphoric, it was calm and wholly pleasurable. Anyway, the next evening I got your letter, the question about the cube. [*I am not sure why I had written to Elaine offering the much harder problem, but the effect was apparently dramatic.*] Now I noted that I kept warning you in my comments that I'm not better yet and I can see I'm not, because when I read your letter I had total panic. "I can't do that, what's it all about, what's 27, I don't know what 27 means—I can't do it." And I put it down and I ran away from it—almost literally—I walked very hurriedly away from it. Then I had to do some cooking, and I was also doing a set of keep-fit exercises that I do three times a week that last forty minutes. Now I've noticed before that those exercises have a calming effect upon me. They last for forty minutes and after ten minutes I suddenly found that that cube was in my mind, because like dress making, physical action leaves your mind relatively free. And I found that although I was doing quite a complicated set of exercises, I thought, "I know perfectly well what that cube looks like." I didn't have any need to be frightened and I visualized it. I continued through this set of exercises, visualizing the cube calmly (in your words stabilizing it). I then started counting how many divisions it took—how many cuts. And first of all I thought "I can't do it," and it was almost literally as if I were holding an image and the image shook slightly and I thought, "Don't be silly, I've done it before, I can do it again." They quite suddenly I saw it, the image came into focus quite sharply and I saw there were four cuts. There was no question about it and I thought I'm nearly ready to consider the problem. And I finished my exercises and I had a meal. Then I went and read your letter again without any panic at all and I thought—I laughed in fact when you said it would be clever to do it in your mind, I laughed. Now I wouldn't have laughed some time ago; I would have thought, "Yes it would be clever and I can't do it on paper but I'll try it" and thought it doesn't matter whether I do it in my mind or do it on paper, but I'll try it in my mind. And in my mind I cut a third off and I moved it round to its adjacent side and I cut another third off and I put them in a line and I cut them all in half and I thought, "I've done it and it's only three cuts." That's when I went to ring you and you weren't there—because I wanted to, if possible, have done it in my mind. I came back and couldn't find anything to cut up so I cut up an apple and realized that I hadn't done it, because I'd been thinking flat. I thought, "Damn it, I've phoned him and said that I've done it so now I've got to do it." You see, here we go again, I have got to sit here until I have justified making a claim like that. But it wasn't panic.

**Laurie:** I didn't know which problem it was, I thought it was probably this one or the Passalong.

**Elaine:** I of course had expected you to realize that I'd got your letter so I was excited, in the nice sense of the word, because I thought — I must admit there was an element that this was going to please you — it would give you pleasure by having done it. It was also I wanted it to be right. I really didn't know whether it was right or not and hence of course I found that it was wrong. But interestingly I wasn't shattered by it being wrong and I didn't feel that mattered a bit, not a bit. I worked all the evening on it, I always go to bed early about 9:30 and when Stephen is away, I usually go about 9 and I didn't go to bed until 10:10. I thought this is silly, I'm going to stay up all night because I can't tell you how many cubes I'd thrown on the floor by this time but I still wasn't really frightened. I went to bed —

**Laurie:** Obsessed.

**Elaine:** Obsessed; it was exactly like the timetable.

When finally stuck on this, she left it without tension, as I describe in chapter 7 (Situation 1), and moved back to a Passalong problem she had spent twenty minutes on before:

**Elaine:** And I spent I guess about twenty minutes or half an hour not being able to do it so clearly, having done, tried to do, the cube. Not having solved that one had nevertheless somehow sharpened my perception of shapes in some way, because I saw immediately how to do that lot as a whole. I started to do it and I thought, "Oh, it's just a pattern; do the same pattern with each side and there they all are." And I think I did it in, again, I quite forgot about time, but I guess I did it in four minutes.

As the investigation went on, I had been writing short papers on aspects that arose. One of these, "Approaching a Problem," discussed the value of emphasizing the receiving and stabilizing of the information provided. Even people rather anxious about the whole process were willing to do just that if there was an assurance they need not go further. Elaine comments.

**Elaine:** Yes, except one more thing I want to remember. I found your paper on tackling a problem eventually very useful, because the language of stabilizing and the three stages you described were enormously reassuring to me. But again when I first began to read it—and I think I read it on Saturday morning or Friday evening when some activity like going shopping or cooking a meal was in process and I hadn't really time—flung me into a total panic, the first page. Just couldn't go on reading. So I left.

**Laurie:** But it wasn't mathematical language.

**Elaine:** Yes, there was just a little bit. I can't find it at the moment. When I turned back and looked at it twenty-four hours later, again it was the same as going away from the cube and coming back. I was perfectly calm and I thought, "All that is there is just one mathematical jargon word, there, that I don't understand and it doesn't matter that I don't understand because it's not central to what the paper's about," and I read the paper through and found it immensely helpful.

I explained to Elaine now that if cutting the cube naturally, it would take six cuts. This is the first level at which many people experience difficulty in the graded problem. She had thought it was four, and so did other people I asked. When I had first offered this problem to Elaine, at the end of the third interview, she had remarked: "I can see there would be two cuts down and four across." This is slightly ambiguous but may mean that she did originally see it. It is slightly worrying if immediate perceptions can be correct and well-thought-out ones wrong, but this is a point made also by Lynn. She felt she sometimes jumped to a correct conclusion and moved from it if asked to justify it.

When I explained the six cuts I had in front of us the nine-piece cube as a model to work on. Elaine soon saw that there were six cuts. I then went on to explain why it could not be done in less. This I felt she did not fully grasp, partly because she was remembering a dream where I had said to her, "It can't be done." This had worried her slightly, in that she had felt I might have misled her. "Can you do it in less?" had carried the implication to her that it was possible. Not so for a mathematician, of course. We discussed and agreed on the language of implication.

I then reverted to numbers, and started on some factorization; it proved too rushed, we did not have the time.

## Fifth Interview: My Comments

A very detailed analysis by Elaine of her reaction to the various spatial problems I set her. They were:

1. A nine-piece Brian Willsher cube.
2. A twenty-five-piece Brian Willsher block.
3. Passalong—more difficult problems.
4. Cutting a cube by saw.

She has now largely controlled her panic by the use of the reflective intelligence. My letter caused her panic by giving her (impersonally) the fourth problem, but her mind was not prepared to receive information. It was on household matters, and not therefore brought to calm by higher-order faculties. Later she read this letter and "Approaching a Problem" without panic, though she had to subdue it first.

The switch in attitude in a mathematical activity from panic to obsessive pleasure is very interesting. The mind is really working as if you can switch it from one emotion to another at the other end of the scale. Interesting and a bit frightening.

Elaine derived deep satisfaction from finishing three of the puzzles, but also gained considerable satisfaction from her attempts on the cube, albeit eventually uncompleted. She was then prepared to admit defeat, but had enjoyed the struggle. I really do want a further serious and long discussion with Richard on goals—since there *can* be satisfaction in the attempt, even with a heavily goal-directed person like Elaine.

A mathematical comment. In visualizing, Elaine sees the vertical and not the horizontal(?). When she dismantled the cube originally in her mind to find the twenty-seven pieces, she did it on three walls (significant?). She placed the curved-block puzzle pieces vertical at first, though they do not all easily stand up. She saw the vertical sawcuts in the cube and not the horizontal. Though we say in the tape we are seeing it "flat," we are in fact looking at the vertical cuts through the flat top surface.

Ambivalence of *can* or *cannot* (e.g. her own "Can't do it"). She assumed if I asked whether it could be cut by less than six saw cuts that it *could*. Soon recognized the failure in communication here, but it was a language inhibition (which we shall examine) to the solution.

The pleasure of retaining a problem in one's mind to play with when one wishes, without *demands* for completion or any time limit, offers a breakthrough to learning. It is an almost casual handling of a problem. "I control it, and not it me" is the type of feeling.

This is related of course to the very general question of time pressure, which I must tackle.

Elaine thinks of herself, correctly, as disciplined, and that involves routine. She had difficulty in *not* watching *The Rockford Files* because she normally did so, but the puzzle was more interesting. Has she never learned to play? Am I teaching her that?

Two things I was worried about, so I had to ring her the next day. She was abashed when I told her she was wrong about four cuts and I had wished to avoid it by using material and getting her to do it. A small issue — no harm done because of the recognized difficulty of the problem.

When I commented that Passalong (not the other two actually) was like timetabling I sensed that she almost felt "That's why I can do it — but it is not *real* math." The converse is true; both are mathematical activities.

A comment on her comments. Did she always use figures when numbers came up in a piece of writing?

## Fifth Interview: Elaine's Comments

This session was quite different from any of the others as it carried no unpleasant or disturbing overtones. I looked forward to it as I was happy about my success with the wooden puzzles and wanted to know the result of the cube problem Laurie had set me. When I grasped that I had failed to visualize the cube accurately I had no sense of humiliation nor any feeling of having disappointed my teacher. I *did* feel a blockage about imagining the cuts in the cube and made a mental note to show it to myself in concrete terms as soon as possible. I noticed, from the transcript, that I had in our last session visualized the cuts correctly and while this surprised me, it also reassured me. The next day, on the way to County Hall for an interview that I thought was absorbing my thoughts, an image of the cube, correctly cut, appeared suddenly and with apparent irrelevance in my mind.

During the rest of the session I felt intellectually stretched but not daunted and there was no conscious panic in my mind. I did however feel an emotional tremor when I got the wrong number of threes and wanted to push their image away to be thought of later. Obviously Laurie's paper on the three stages of tackling a problem is exactly how I used to tackle literary essays at college. After I had been given the essay title I would spend the days in the library reading the relevant books then on the way home would think about the material and begin to rearrange it in the light of the essay question, which I always found highly absorbing. Then after about ten days I would write the essay without notes or a plan. I don't remember often having to redraft the subsequent result, but I used to be exasperated when my fellow students said I could write essays without preparation. Laurie's paper has helped me to adopt this process with all its reassuring associations of success and confidence to the problems he has set me.

Another significant feature of the session, I feel, is that I felt no emotion toward Laurie of subservience or groveling gratitude — he was simply a person I like and feel confident with feeding me intellectual problems. It was the problems that preoccupied me.

Afterwards I had no violent reaction of either pleasure or pain, such as I experienced in earlier sessions, and drove home with my mind occupied with other matters that had happened during the day as well as our discussion.

Another symptom of my increasing sense of proportion is, I believe, as follows. At my first interview for my new post the CI [Chief Inspector of ILEA] asked me what doubts or fears I had about it. I mentioned two and then wanted to add, "And I can't do arithmetic so that work involving that will be difficult or impossible for me." I didn't say it because it seemed such a shameful thing to say. I remembered that incident when I was preparing my mind for the second interview and found that I now found the reaction I had had ludicrous. At last I saw my predicament as other people have always seen it, yet I know I shall always remember what I used to feel like. So I *haven't* "wasted years of my life on a chimera"! QED.

## Sixth Interview

This discussion was rather wide ranging, and there are few extracts that can be quoted in isolation. We started on the question of "play" (which Elaine had never done) and the emphasis that I placed on this feeling; that math, even when serious, can be a sort of contemplative play. This is one of the areas that needs, and has not yet had, further investigation.

We briefly returned to the question of authority, and Elaine managed to sum up, very crisply, a number of feelings.

Laurie: It being released in that manner, did it have to be released by an obvious authority figure?

Elaine: Yes, I think so.

Laurie: So that somebody else who might be more skilled in the therapeutic thing —

Elaine: It wouldn't have been the same.

Laurie: — wouldn't have been able to do it because of not having the position in the subject?

Elaine: That's right. I think that's why it is so successful, because you were the supreme math figure, you can't go higher in the authority fear structure than an inspector in charge of all the mathematics. And you didn't get cross with me. And you didn't think badly of

me. And so, I think that's why all that awfulness came out. I
regressed totally one little bit of my mind and started building it
up again. In fact, I found myself thinking, "Wish I could go to
classes in arithmetic and math and sit in with the first years."

For a while we continued with our spatial concepts. The three-by-
three-by-three cube is in fact a very satisfactory model for three-
dimensional work. From the center cube we can move out one in any
direction and thus, with the minimum of complication, deal with all
the directions we are likely to need. We explored this by asking what
was immediately above or "one down and one to the left," in her
school and her home. In both she had a clear picture of the relative
positions of different rooms, although her house was one to which she
had only recently moved. I have found that for some people a wall, or
more especially a ceiling or a floor, completely block out for them
what is beyond.

Then came Elaine's central question for this interview:

Can I ask you something that's been in my mind as a result of reading
your comments? I suddenly thought, "I don't know what mathematics is!"
I always thought I knew what it was: it was tables. I know that sounds
incredibly childish, but in my mind that's what I thought math was. A
towering wall that was tables. Anything beyond it was far too esoteric for
me to grasp. I could accept that I had heard people talking about elegance,
and I could see that it had an affinity with poetry and music and abstract
thought but it was blocked for me. Now recently I've been asking myself,
what is math? Now what is it, Laurie?

Not easy. Unfortunately it is also something seldom even attempted
in many people's mathematical education, and for many people it
matters. All my subjects had very unhelpful impressions of what math
is about, and correcting these views proved to be an important part of
the whole operation. A subsidiary question was why I thought that
timetabling was connected with math. This proved easier to deal with
through a discussion of the development of operational research. On
the main issue I managed to convey some ideas to her that helped her
shift to new standpoints.

# Sixth Interview: My Comments

Before reading Elaine's comments, it is necessary to know that I had
by then written a first theoretical attempt on the cognitive-affective
interaction, which Elaine had read. Unwittingly, I had used the terms
*Intelligence A* and *Intelligence B*, which had already been used with

other meanings in psychology. These now correspond to delta 2 and delta 3 in the present theory (see chapter 7).

Characterized by a lack of concern and no detectable anxiety. Elaine was cheerful, busily sorting things out and then settling for a chat. Quite keen to tell me what she had been doing, but without anxiety.

The significant question she asked, which I had listed in my preparatory notes, concerned the nature of mathematics, which she now realized was not *the tables*. Also why I should think that timetabling was a part of mathematics. The second question was fairly easy and I attempted the first. The significance in the first lay in her wanting to start at the beginning again; that about timetabling a stake-post in the area.

She asked questions genuinely for information (like train times!) and did not adopt the pupil posture!

The impression really is that a major problem has been solved — though we both cannot really credit it. She does not know much more mathematics — but will be able to explore it without difficulty.

## Sixth Interview: Elaine's Comments

[This commentary was written on 6th November as considerable domestic "goal setting" filled half-term and I was at Stoke d'Abernon (a residential teachers' center) for three days of the following week. Laurie's notes on the interview are at school so my comments cannot be enlarged by reference to them.]

My recollection of this interview is that all through it I was trying to reform my picture of math, and though I am only just beginning to be able to do this, the process is in no way painful as breaking a habit can be. My old view is very hard to dislodge, and when I read Laurie's report on cognitive-affective interaction I recognized exactly what is happening in my own mind. Preparing myself for Laurie's "lesson" as I only half-jokingly call it to my secretarial and my math staff. Delta 2/Intelligence A had worried that he was going to make me move on to long division, the next hurdle I fell over after tables had thoroughly reinforced my sense of failure. Delta 3/Intelligence B pointed out that long division was so terrifying (of all my math lessons it's the one I remember with most distress — I had to stand out at the front with two other girls who couldn't do it and they always sat in the two bottom desks after fortnightly marks were read out (!!) while I was always in one of the first three desks) because it used tables, and those no longer frightened me. But their interaction made me muse on what math *was*, if it wasn't tables and everything that followed from them. I therefore asked Laurie this almost as soon as we'd settled, but as a genuine perplexity, not as a child's red herring. His answer touched on two areas that give me and always have from childhood given me profound pleasure, namely Greek civilization and astronomy. I found geometry less appalling than arithmetic or algebra, because the names Pythagoras and Archimedes echoed pleasure. I found a sense of wonder in myself when Laurie connected for me the intellectual games of slave-tended aristocrats with actual laws of physics discovered centuries later. Instead of continuing to try to pull "math" back into shape, I found on reflection when I began to write this that I have started again with a whole new intellectual joy like my middle-aged discovery of bird watching.

As soon as I returned from half term I asked Radha [the head of mathematics at my school] for Book I of SMP (School Mathematics Project, Cambridge University Press) to teach myself this new interest and her pleasure at my request reinforced my new positive attitude. I don't want to succeed any more as the word seems irrelevant — only to comprehend, without any sense of shame that some people can comprehend more quickly or more fully than I do. A proof of this is that I play with my math puzzle in Stephen's presence and together with him and the fact that we've only solved two of the tasks doesn't worry me at all.

I think this sharp dichotomy, this starting again, is delta 3/Intelligence B's answer to delta 2/Intelligence A, which will never, I think, be totally free of ugly association when suddenly confronted with a test of numeracy. At Stoke d'Abernon the course leader referred to some curriculum analysis he had provided us with and said collectively to us: "Now I'm simply not going to accept that you can't do this or understand it. *It is a task well within the capacity of any fourth-year junior child provided the child is in Band one.*" The italicized words are exactly what he said because they burned and fragmented my delta 2/Intelligence A totally. "I'm not fit to be a head — I can't compete with a child — I *know* I'm not in Band one — I should never have been given a First," all reverberated through me followed disappointingly by, "I'll get out of doing it somehow — I won't do it — I *can't.*" This was said in the morning and it was only as I was preparing for bed that night that delta 3/Intelligence B introduced the subject to my mind and calmed it. Then I found myself thinking rather impatiently, "Does he really think we like not being able to do something easy?" Significantly *we*, no longer *I*. I sat down on the edge of the bed and opened SMP Book I, noticing with a feeling of relief "(Metric)" on the cover. When new pence came in I was relieved — a fresh start! I read only the first half page, but it restored me completely — it didn't ask for tables but for solutions to a number of problems that seemed part of the world in which I'm an efficient figure. I closed the book now I had restored my so recent confidence and haven't done any more in this field yet, but look forward to it as a treat in the next holidays.

Finally I discover I can now use a calculator. Stephen gave me one yeas ago to try to sidetrack my terrors, but I was too frightened to the numbers on it to use it. This weekend for a massive set of forms I have to complete for school, I've used it and found delight in it, yet the tiny sums I didn't use it for I did far more quickly than ever before.

During our interview Laurie urged me not to forget exactly what my difficulties used to be and I hope as I progress with my new interest I may remember the stages at which once again I failed. One powerful factor the SMP book reminded me of is the matching covers of successive textbooks — Durrell's *Algebra* was the same dangerous red in every stage and was the only book I've ever hated!

## Seventh Interview: My Comments

[Although we both found this interview interesting, much of it was concerned with the theorizing dealt with elsewhere in this book. Therefore, none of the interview is transcribed here. Nonetheless, our comments are worth recording.]

Intellectual kinship in perceptions of authority relationships, etc. — amusing how we checked it out, knowing it would match.

Felt generally this session that I was more discursive than I should have been and explored my own attitudes at too great a length. This was evident early on, where I stopped her pursuing what her blockages in math were, but she returned to it and we got all we could at this stage. Nonetheless, a very interesting session, with points to follow up, very broad and general in nature and we will need to move closer in on some points — particularly the analytic and gestalt approaches.

My concern at her losing the memory of her early problems was not well founded. In fact removing the "tables" barrier will reveal the lesser successive problems, which I think will be triggered when we touch new areas of math (none this time, oddly, except an interest in area, to which I need to return).

There was a worry that she could still be thrust back into her earlier state. I do *not* think this is possible. Panic feelings can still be induced, but delta 2 now knows that this problem can be handled! This because it has once been done with a very substantial barrier. This does *not* imply that she will necessarily cope with math problems. I think the extended attack on the difficult cube problem was the critical point because it showed things could be tackled and there could be interest even in failure. Elaine made a very substantial point about coping with mathematical material when it is subsidiary to the main aim. Seen as unimportant, it becomes easy to deal with.

Yes, it is that the insights now achieved into the problems of learning cannot be forgotten. So...

Amusing again, the return to the question of letting me know that she is not as good as she has appeared to be (in connection with spatial perception).

Related to this, the belief that she is slower than everyone else in doing some mathematical problems. Some evidence that she *is* slow, but there is a tendency for her to compare herself with the quickest of the other people engaged upon it. Very pleased at her reaction to Report No. 5 (on cognitive-affective reactions). Really seen as fitting her own perception. Only doubt—in identifying with some of the feelings, has she properly exercised her critical faculty?

I must pursue the idea of relationships, which has so central a position in math. This arose from the remarks about the relationship between time allowed to subjects in the school and the allowance structure.

Also must pursue (too much to follow!) the points about certainty of knowledge discussed with Lynn and Sarah.

And some math—talk about computation.

## Seventh Interview: Elaine's Comments

An interesting session totally free of anxiety, but leaving me baffled in my search for why I was always unable to cope with math. I think I now have arithmetic (I am deliberately downgrading it with no capital a!) related properly to math as a facilitating agent only. This I feel was only completely clarified for me when I read Laurie's comments on this interview and when I told him of someone pointing out to me that I add up figures when I work on the timetable. I had made a dichotomy here—the analysis I did for the staff after completing each timetable, was, in my eyes, arithmetic, because I found it hard to grasp, whereas totting up to see I'd allocated the correct number of periods to each department was so obviously necessary and so easy (no one has more than seven periods in a year!) that Intelligence A knew it wasn't arithmetic (or in this case Arithmetic!).

So where is the broken valve or whatever that has stopped me operating mathematically? Partly because I am grateful to Laurie personally and partly because I altruistically want to help with his research as a necessary and long-term constructive operation, I worry away at this whenever I have a few moments available. I've tried to see a pattern in my other failure areas: e.g., I can't judge distance accurately, although my sight is excellent; I have little sense of direction; linguists tell me that while I am not tone deaf I have what they call "a lazy ear" that sometimes distinguishes tones, but usually can't; I could never understand scansion and completed an English degree and two years research into medieval poetry without any comprehension of it at all. Counting syllables was involved so I suspect a connection, yet can't see what it is.

Laurie blocked me in this pursuit by saying he shared some of these weaknesses to some degree so I tried again from the other end working out my intellectual strengths. These are emotional empathy with the moods of people and words; an ability to grasp meaning in quite convoluted or compressed language; and diligence. The last two seem to me to apply to math, so why did they fail to operate?

I was left wondering if I just simply have no mathematical ability, yet Laurie says he sees rudiments of it in me and I agree with the examples he has given me. I keep returning to the timetable, which was never a dutiful chore—it was the intellectual excitement of the year for me. That sounds ironic, but it is simple truth. I often found it baffling and hard, but I enjoyed it deeply—it was the ultimate in goal seeking and goal realization in sequence. Just like math, damn it— what *did* go wrong?

# Eighth Interview

It may be that for the last two interviews we had been avoiding the issue of long division, which looked so large, but it may be that they were simply a necessary preparation, in particular the downgrading in importance of computation to its proper level. This session we really began to hit the numbers! After a trip through the meaning of logarithms (and how few know) and some other early calculating devices we "did" long division. The transcript is of great interest here, for I appear to be (and perhaps am) in a complete muddle at some stages. Naturally I was working with pen and paper and the incoherence was somewhat moderated by what I was doing there. In fact the explanation at the conceptual level was direct and simple, and my muddle over routine in fact proved reassuring.

Laurie: If you wanted to divide something like 345—let's say we were going to divide it by 10 which of course we could do in a much simpler way, what really what you do is you take off 10—335, and then you take off another 10—325, and every time you did it you'd make a mark and you'd end up with 34 of these marks and you'd land up with 5 left over.

**Elaine:** Do you know, I've never thought through that that's what division is.

**Laurie:** You'd never thought that division was repeated subtraction?

**Elaine:** Never. I thought that multiplication was adding but I have never thought. That's why long division has always defeated me because I hadn't known what I was doing. Do you follow?

**Laurie:** Yes, I do. You're just taking the number away as many times as you can.

**Elaine:** I had never known what division was in that strictly accurate sense.

**Laurie:** There is another meaning of division, but I'll leave that for the moment because I'll do the taking away one. Of the four rules, that is more or less an inverse of that — that is repeated back and that is repeated — so the whole four signs are related.

**Elaine:** Yes, yes, I got those two because they're positive but I never got that one.

**Laurie:** That's interesting, isn't it? And the most elementary algorithm would be this. You know how many times can I take that away? Then people would say, "Christ, I don't want to be taking this away like that, I know what, let's set it out as though it was a long-division sum. I know that the 340, well I know that I'm going to take 300 lots away first and we get 30 there" — right? Now really what we're doing is we're saying, oh Gawd, I'll get it right in a minute — hang on — I can't remember how to do it myself...

**Elaine:** Very reassuring.

**Laurie:** Um, I think they have curious rules for doing this — let me do it in my own commonsense way. The first thought is, look at that 3 and the 10 has to go into it 3 times, it's really 10 going into 300 isn't it? And that's obviously going to go in 30 times. Three 10s are 30, well they're not 30 they're 300 really, it's crazy they should call it 30, it's really taking 300 off. So instead of saying I'm going to keep on taking 10s away, they're saying, "Hell, let's take a lot more of them away first, let's take 300 away first because we know —" so we take 300 away and we got a 4 left over and you bring down the 5.

**Elaine:** Yes.

**Laurie:** But the next thing you do is say instead of taking 10, 10, 10 away, let's take four lots of 10 because that's 40 and that leaves 5 over so you've got 34 and 5 remainder. So all it is doing is taking away as many lots away as you can; just to do this repeated subtraction in great chunks.

**Elaine:** I see, how surprising I never understood it.

**Laurie:** Well, it's because when it's presented as something more difficult—supposing you've got 29 into 345.

**Elaine:** Now that is frightening.

**Laurie:** Well, um, the thing is I could take 29, 29, 29—do repeated subtractions and you could do it that way, couldn't you? How many subtractions would I have to do until I got a number less than 29, so that would be the simplest algorithm. Now the next simplest algorithm is to say—

**Elaine:** You've no idea how reassuring that is to me, that there is a way to do it, however long. . . . well it's what you said, it's the first stake I put in, if all else fails I can do it that way. Yes, go on.

**Laurie:** This says that 29 into 34 goes once. You know it's the language they use that is wrong. It's not 29 into 34, it's saying that 10 lots of 29 will make 290, right—so why not take 290 away because you know that's 10 lots of 29 anyway at the beginning.

**Elaine:** I remember being puzzled by not—I wouldn't have put it as precisely as that—that is why we ignored the 5 and why we could and how it all worked out anyway.

**Laurie:** We hang on to it, we don't lose it, but the biggest chunk we can take away, 290, it leaves you 55 doesn't it? Now you then have to estimate really, it's not exactly the tables, you have to know whether that goes in once or twice, well in fact it only goes in once and you take it away, 26 left over so it's 11 times with 26 remainder and all that is, is taking away the biggest chunk away you can at first.

**Elaine:** Yes, I see.

**Laurie:** You see, what I've done is take 30 lots of 10 away in that column which is taking 300 away leaving me with still 45 left. I've jumped all those stages down to 45.

**Elaine:** Why didn't I see that. I wasn't a fool; I suppose again it's just emotional blockage. I was too frightened to think about it.

**Laurie:** Yes, I would think that. A big proportion of people who could do long division (which in itself is not a large proportion of the population) did not know why it worked.

**Elaine:** Really?

**Laurie:** Yes, I really think so. I mean if they hammer away in the schools now they're obsessed with the routine. You know how muddled I am about routines—it doesn't matter because I know what it's about you see.

We moved on to a more difficult one, and suddenly. Elaine exclaimed, "I did that in my mind before you did it, I understand!" The final bastion falls!

We left numbers and the rest of the interview was spent on some rather high-flown stuff about the contributions of Kepler and Newton, and to something on non-Euclidean geometries.

## Epilogue

There is much else, but let us leave it at this climactic point. The change in *attitude*. It may be that not much math was learned, but the tables and long division, with their symbolic importance, were mastered.

Later in the summer term, after several months in her new job, Elaine faced a situation, totally unconnected with mathematics, in which she felt some uncertainty. She suddenly thought, "I expect I can't do long division any more." When she got home, she found that she could, and was settled again.

# Section Two

# Theoretical
# Considerations

# Chapter Seven

## Reason Blocked by Emotion

As the year proceeded, it became clearer when things were going to be successful and when emotions were induced that stopped progress dead in its tracks. In some senses, the latter situation was the object of my study; it interested me and I wished to analyze it. Certainly a pattern began to form, each category backed by remembered statements and reactions, but the way in which it fell out was in itself a puzzle for my own mind. The particular analysis formed in my mind at three o'clock one morning, was written at speed once I rose at about eight o'clock, and has not been amended. Whether that be good or bad it is difficult to say. If any situation makes particular sense for you then perhaps something has been achieved.

## Situation 1

We start with the basic model, which is shown in figure 7−1. Delta (which I have adopted to signify reason) engages on a piece of mathematics, either to understand something or to solve a problem. The feedback, indicating approaching success or failure, induces emotions. These in turn improve or diminish performance. In general, a feedback that success is likely is pleasurable and the thrust of reason is improved by that emotion being played back on to delta. A feedback indicating likely failure produces feelings of frustration. These will mostly diminish performance, though sometimes an effort of will may remove the obstacle. (This latter statement needs further examination.)

Most classroom math sets tasks, often with very clearly defined goals; whether they have been reached or not is seldom in doubt. Some more modern developments in the subject present it, very properly, as an investigatory subject, but in the past the emphasis has been on questions with single answers−right or wrong. This clarity

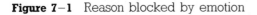

**Figure 7-1**   Reason blocked by emotion

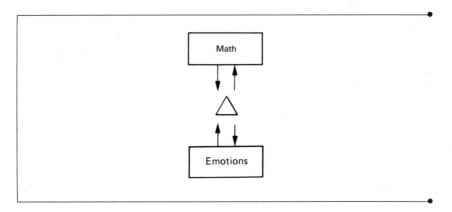

tends to enhance the sharpness of emotional response. There is a nakedness about the success or failure in reaching a goal that evokes clearly defined emotions whose nature one cannot disguise to oneself. A piece of writing may be good, bad, or indifferent, but this fact is not always as abundantly clear to oneself as is the result of an attempt upon a mathematical problem. There seems to be no obvious reason why pleasure from success should have less force than frustration and disappointment at failure, but the evidence is that more people end up anxious about math than enthusiastic.

This leads us to a conclusion widely accepted in many quarters that in teaching we should try to ensure a high success rate and arrange problems so that students will seldom fail. There are some reservations to be made about this approach, although in general it is a sound principle. Many teachers claim, perfectly correctly, that the class enjoys doing repetitive work of a sort at which they are competent, such as columns of addition. The class, however, is engaged in occupational therapy, not learning, and one might have supposed the latter to be the primary task of an educational institution! The circuit in the diagram is being pursued painlessly, with mild pleasure at the continued success, but no development of mathematical knowledge. On a number of occasions my customers denied themselves pleasure on the grounds that the material was too simple.

Goals must not be too simply achieved. The pleasure arising from the process does depend on the difficulties overcome. It is even possible to gain considerable pleasure from a lengthy attack on a problem with many avenues explored but the goal of a solution not achieved:

I sat down and spent about twenty minutes on it and then I thought quite calmly, with no sense of humiliation and certainly not sadness or despair, I'm blocked. I've gone down so many blind alleys and I'm not going to be able to do this. I must ask Laurie what the trick is. Once he tells me the trick I'll have got it. Just like 7 × 8. I'll never again forget it because I've explored so many blind alleys.

Failure must be handled sensitively, however. The early realization of this is the essence of good teaching. The central problem becomes the adjustment of the level of difficulty for a particular individual at a particular time.

# Situation 2

The first situation assumes that we are approaching a task for the first time, or at least with limited previous experience. The emotional reactions are then assumed to be largely related to the task at hand. We are, of course, seldom faced with work that is unconnected with previous experience, though sometimes it is possible to create learning environments in which a "fresh start" is made. But the reactions to the task are related to its difficulty.

We can, and many people do, arrive at a state where this is not so. If we have had a considerable amount of experience, strongly charged with emotion, it may well lead to a position where this previous experience, and not the present task, will be the main determinant of what happens. It might have been positive enough to produce great drive and determination in both learning and problem solving. Unfortunately, the more common experience is reiterated failure, and people for whom this is true find there is a great inertia in even considering a problem.

It is worth analyzing three stages in approaching a problem. The first stage is well described in Krutetskii (1971). It is the receiving, sorting, and imprinting of the information. This is a *still* occupation of the mind, which does not have to go anywhere, do anything, or carry out a search. The second stage involves a search in the memory for relevant facts and tools for attacking the problem. Generally the tools or methods of approach are more significant than the facts, though some of the latter need to be known. The process requires judgment as to what might be relevant or not. It can still be seen as preparatory, and not as the actual attack, though both it and the first stage are quite essential. The third stage may go hand in hand with the second but appears to be a distinct activity. It is what most people would refer to as "thinking," and involves a move from present knowledge to some

new goal. This may be reached by careful construction of new conclusions from our initial information and remembered tools and/or by
insightful and intuitive leaps. It is more active and demanding than
the first two stages.

To people who are in the situation I am describing, the mere
suggestion of a math problem produces feelings of anxiety and an
unwillingness even to enter the area. This is demonstrated by an
inability to receive and *stabilize* information about a problem.

I had asked Sarah to find any whole numbers that went exactly
into 12 (factors). She started them, cautiously, but at a demand from
me (introducing other elements into the situation), "the numbers
toppled out of my mind." Within the group there were regularly
demands like this: "What was it you said, Laurie? I've forgotten the
problem."

This is apparent with people who are in fact trying to be cooperative. With those who are not even willing, the reaction is to
claim that the facts, however few, cannot be remembered. If in a
position to do so, the person may say that the whole thing is too
boring and that they have something better to do. Some children
nowadays may indeed say this—many more think it.

Briefly, a violent reaction from the emotions, rather like a depth
charge, completely ruins the reasoning process. This phenomenon is
diagrammed in figure 7−2. Here the feedback is not connected with
possible difficulties in reaching goals experienced by reason once
engaged on the work. The message that it is math that confronts us
conveys such expectations of failure and general unpleasantness that
no start is made.

Taking terminology from the medical field, situation 1 is "normal"
in that everyone should expect to feel emotion when attempting a
problem; situation 2 is "pathological" in that it is completely dysfunc-
tional. Repeated efforts to encourage the person to make further
attempts may well result in further failures and a reinforcement of the
emotional inability to tackle math. The process simply becomes
counterproductive. Teachers know of pupils whose ability at math
seems less when they leave secondary school than when they entered
it. This raises serious questions.

An adult who has developed this distaste for math and who feels
that knowledge of it is not particularly relevant to the conduct of his
or her life has a perfect right to refuse to think about it. It may be a
wrong view in the event, and it may shut off areas that could be
enlightening, but it is a decision a responsible adult can properly
make. Some would extend this right of decision to those of school age.
Here I would sharply disagree with views expressed by Skemp (1979).
I fully accept that the best learning situation is one where the learner

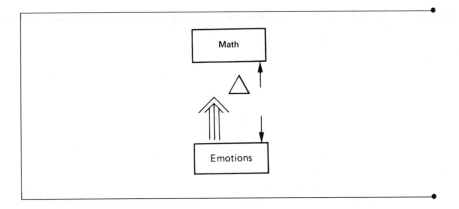

**Figure 7-2**  Violent blocking emotions stemming from previous negative
experience

freely enters into it and engages in genuinely cooperative activity with
the teacher, and I have been fortunate in experiencing it with many
individuals. I regard it as naive and idealistic, however, to believe that
it can be in any way a basis for the mass education of the whole
population. That is not to say that all children must pursue compulsory
math until the age of sixteen — but total freedom of choice cannot be
theirs, and we should expect the vast majority to be taught math to the
age of sixteen.

The evidence from my subjects is that they spent much of their
secondary school life learning no math and becoming increasingly
bewildered, anxious, and frustrated about it. The answer is not to opt
out, but to seek remedies, conscious that they will not be universally
successful. Some of these ideas will be expanded at greater length
later, but it is worth indicating some guidelines.

The first and most obvious suggestion is not to allow people to
reach situation 2, and this is explained in situation 1. We must provide
people with a high level of success and a level of failure that they can
tolerate. On the whole, our primary schools are very effective in this,
and the most likely stage of breakdown is at the beginning of secondary
school. In part this derives from the attitude, explicit or implicit,
prevalent in some secondary schools that their previous experience is
of little consequence. Only now are they getting down to "real" work.
Once this real work has afforded a certain amount of failure and the
previous success is disregarded, we are well on the downward slope.
Clearly past success should be treasured and past failure regarded as

of little importance. This is a sensible maxim for all stages where a fresh start is being made—be it a new school, a new teacher, or the beginning of a new session.

How then to escape from the situation, once in it? One of the most helpful starts comes from the idea of stages in approaching a problem, and I found it very useful in the group sessions. It was suggested that everyone simply tackle the first stage—no more. The information should be *received* and *stabilized.* When this is seen as the goal, emotional disturbance is minimized and the task does not appear demanding. There is a certain sleight-of-hand involved in that the students believe they are not actually being asked to do the problem (they are not being asked to complete it) while the teacher has over-come the refusal even to approach the problem and recognizes that the first stage is a genuine part of the process. The teacher establishes a position where the students know what the problem is and are then allowed to rest. The second stage can be conducted by discussion along the lines of "What might possibly be useful here?" With certain well-chosen problems the statement together with a discussion of tools for attack achieves a position where the answer is suddenly apparent—and a success is recorded to tilt the balance slightly from unrelieved failure. There was a very favorable response from most of my subjects to the "staging" approach. Rosita commented that, when attempting some homework in the evening, she would feel the paral-ysis to which she was accustomed and would say to herself, "Now just receive the information and stabilize it." There is, I believe, something about the very use of the word stabilize, since in stabilizing the information, one does in fact stabilize the mind.

Two other guidelines more relevant in later situations are worth mentioning. One is the request that the process be started with full attention but *slowly.* The other is that the answer can be checked by internal means or by an external method not involving reference to the teacher. The rationale of this is that it is not only failure that matters but its exposure to judgment.

Another route that may help someone to return to mathematical activity is somewhat devious. Some activities that many mathema-ticians might consider to have a mathematical element are not in fact so labeled. Elaine happens to get intense pleasure from timetabling for a large school, and she was most surprised to find that I felt it had a large mathematical element—not in the calculations involved so much as in the ordering, arranging, and assertions of priority. She was fairly resistant to any classification that put timetabling (which she could do) with math (which she couldn't). If, however, it could be established and believed that she had had success in a mathematical type of operation, the certainty of failure is dented a little. Sarah enjoyed fitting together wood-block puzzles, and because she enjoyed them and was successful with them she refused to acknowledge that the perception and matching of shape had any mathematical connection. The thought that it was what geometry was about was not accepted. Yet it could be a way through.

In some senses, whatever the difficulty, the recognition of it by the teacher is the most important step. It is all too easy to believe that if one explains once more and gets the pupil to make yet a further assault on a problem, the breakthrough will be achieved. The pressure to achieve this and the anxiety of the teacher convey themselves all too readily and frustrate the desired end. Stop and recognize what may be happening and respond sensitively through some of the modes suggested and attitudes may be changed.

Is there a chance that one can shift one's own attitudes without the help of a sensitive teacher? Certainly there is. We all have the capacity to reflect upon our past experiences and actions; this reflective intelligence is one of the most powerful weapons we have. It is the teacher in the mind. Reading, understanding, and recognizing emotional blockages in ourselves can lead us far on the way to their removal. Know thyself.

To recapitulate the first two situations. Success or failure in cognitive tasks brings about emotional response which in turn affects the performance of reason. Success that comes too easily does not have long-term payoff, but the level of failure must be carefully monitored so that it can be tolerated. Repeated failure can lead from the normal situation described into a pathological situation where problems cannot be tackled irrespective of their difficulty. Remediation is then more difficult but should be attempted, certainly while the student is in full-time education. The attempted remedy may come from a teacher or from the student's own reflective intelligence.

The assumption of the analysis so far is that it is the cognitive difficulty of the math that starts the process and that we are throughout concerned purely with math and with success or failure in it. Our further situations will indicate that other matters may intrude themselves.

## Situation 3

The emotions may directly help or hinder our attack upon a problem; they may also deflect us from a particular task. Their role in ensuring survival is very important and the alarm bells sounded at the approach of danger allow our reason to plan for its avoidance. At times, however, they attempt to assert priorities which should not always be regarded.

One evening Sarah arrived for her weekly interview and was obviously disturbed about an incident at school. One of her class had got into trouble of some sort and lied to his mother about it. Sarah had been involved in the whole affair and had counseled the child to explain it to his mother. This the child had done at the end of school, but Sarah was uncertain about what the mother's reaction was going to be. She felt a sense of responsibility and guilt and could not settle to the work that I had intended we might do. Most sensitive teachers would observe such a disturbance in a pupil; it is often wrongly assumed of adults that *they* can put such matters aside and get on with the task in hand. There was nothing Sarah could do about the matter; there was no action or preparation that would affect the situation the next morning, when she would learn how things worked out. She understood this rationally, was concerned to be helpful and not to waste my time (as she felt she was doing), but could not settle to doing some math. Naturally the matter had to be talked through, explained to me, and sorted out. That does not mean it was resolved; there was no chance of that until the morning. The statement of the problem, the organization involved in making the statement, and the listing of possible eventualities made it more tidy, but we did not really get down to the math. In a one-to-one situation, we know that the distraction has occurred and can try to allay the emotional turbulence and seek to press on with our task. How often in a class is this missed through no fault of the teacher?

One evening at the group Sue arrived late, having been involved in the purchase of a house. She was clearly unable to think of anything else. Here the emotions were entirely pleasurable but equally demanding. We were supposed to be working on negative numbers. The connection is not immediately obvious, but a discussion of appreciation and depreciation in value, forward or backward in time, yielded us a very satisfactory way to model directed numbers.

There is no need to labor the point. It is a commonplace that other concerns may deflect us from what we should be doing. This is diagrammatically represented in figure 7–3. The effect of the emotions is to swing direction and prevent delta from tackling the math. (At this stage in the development of the argument, this diagram may appear very simple, but this style of representation will be very useful later.) There is of course nothing unique about math in this situation, but since it occurs in math lessons as much as in others we should list it. We also should think what, if anything, we should do about it, and examine the different levels of distracting concern.

It is interesting that the importance of the other matter may not be the main criterion in determining the degree of distraction. A very weighty concern, such as the loss of someone close, a deep emotional

**Figure 7-3**   Direction deflected by emotions

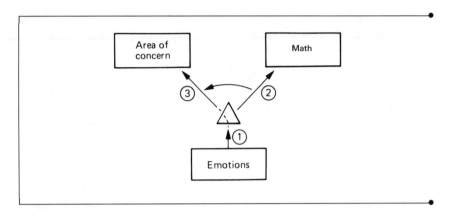

involvement, or major issues in one's career, may demand to be thought about to the exclusion of some less important cognitive task that presents itself—and that may be a sensible thing to do. However, if the thinking and plan making we feel obliged to do become evidently fruitless, a switch to unrelated tasks (such as math) may in fact prove a therapeutic diversion. Some people in such circumstances may think very hard about a math problem to avoid further thoughts about their deeper concern.

Middle-level concerns such as these can prove very difficult. Either the teacher or one's own reflective intelligence must allow the problem to be worked through to a stage where it can be left, and the attention then directed to the learning or problem-solving activity. The ability to compartmentalize and thrust aside such a distraction at a certain stage is one that we should seek to develop. That does not imply that the moment a new task presents itself we can put aside other matters, but we do need to recognize when something is tidïed to an extent where we can leave it and engage the full attention on the new task.

There is, I believe, a special feature of math here, though others may claim that their fields of interest have the same quality—that is, that it is best tackled with deep and undivided attention, even if that can be given only for a short time. The benefit of this in comparison with more half-hearted attempts over a much longer period is considerable, although this does not deny the importance of the periods of gestation in between, when the subconscious works upon material.

The implication of this is that people whose general lifestyle or job situation affords a variety of these middle-range concerns sometimes become accustomed to them all overlapping and rarely give full attention to one. It may be a perfectly satisfactory way of operating in many areas, but it is unhelpful in the study of math or indeed of anything requiring undivided attention. The mind becomes absorbed in the input from many different problems and develops a second-order worry: that they may be forgotten. Once the reason is engaged on simply ticking over all those things that have to be done it is not available for proper work. Most of the people I have interviewed are in fact very busy, yet it is significant that some always claim to be and others do not. The more effective workers are able to compartmentalize and undertake to think of one thing for a specific period of time. This is a matter of almost conscious training of oneself, but many do not even recognize the problem. As regards the business of spending all one's time monitoring those things that have to be done (without actual working on them), the simplest solution is to externalize them. For myself, when I find my mind flitting over jobs to be done and simply trying to keep track of them, I list them on paper and feel a sense of satisfaction as if they were actually done! My inner workings have lost the sense of tension developed in the interplay between reason and emotion.

Essentially minor matters may produce an emotional interference with our reasoning process, which on the face of it is not at all reasonable (and why should it be?). The other day I read my mail at home and intended to bring it to the office to sort out, but I could not find it as I was leaving home. This minor concern was aggravated by the fact that it had included a check I wished to deposit. I did not really believe I had lost it, but the thought was nevertheless worrying. The episode returned to consciousness several times during the day and at other times occasioned a slight restiveness, which lowered my level of concentration. A variety of minor issues such as this are constantly with us ("Will I be able to park when I get there?" "Did I shut the upstairs window?" "Why does the bank think it has so little of my money?") and often they can be below the conscious level. Our emotions feed on worry (mild anxiety), and this input into delta makes it less effective than it should be. Occasionally when they are below the level of consciousness they can be seen for the trivia they are by bringing them to mind, and then perhaps making a note of them on paper, thus removing them from inside us.

A last brief example of deflection. The expectation of some event, pleasurable or otherwise, will readily interfere with our concentration on the matter in hand. If we are sitting in our office, happily working, but with the expectation of someone's arriving at eleven o'clock, we might experience minor impediments in the smooth flow of thought as the hour approaches and more serious ones if the caller is decidedly late. This is not easy to avoid. Perhaps calm contemplative thought is possible only for an aristocrat in a slave-based culture that does not greatly concern itself with time.

# Situation 4

The first two situations described emphasized the nature of the subject and the effect of success or failure on it. Much (probably most) of our emotional response to a subject, however, derives from interpersonal relationships connected with it. It is well known that pupils' choice of subjects is dictated as much by who is teaching what as by proper educational reasons. While many teachers might feel this to be wrong, they still assert the primacy of the relationship of teacher to taught in the classroom. Accepting that there is a basis of truth in this, there are some dangers to be avoided. The central one is that teacher approval rather than learning satisfaction is sought, and this is a serious deviation from what education should be about. It may result in the subject becoming almost an irrelevance.

Marie reflected on her state of mind when posed a mathematical problem by me: "You see, I've still got this, if I use this word 'eagerness' again, still trying to show that I can do it. It's partly wanting to be right, it's partly wanting to be the bright girl, it's partly wanting to show off, it's...and I think at the same time as the show-off part, the display part, there is also the fear part, that if you do it, and do it in a hurry it will be over and done with." Many of the problems of satisfaction and dissatisfaction are summed up in this statement. Both Lynn and Sarah in early sessions with me exhibited the anxious side of this polarization of feelings and manifested on a number of occasions the offering up of answers at random in the hope that the question (and questioner) could be disposed of.

The balance between eagerness to respond, usually seen by teachers as a positive feature, and the fearful anxiety that can be produced by an expectation of quick response is an important issue. Evidence from the subjects of this present study suggests that there is in fact a much higher level of anxiety among students than many teachers would credit, and that this is true even when the relationships are particularly good.

Time pressure and constant questioning need to be examined at some length elsewhere, but the response sought by questioning is an important emotional feature of the classroom. The sight of another human being trying to attract your attention has obvious satisfactions and we need not be surprised that this form of response is sought and the structure of the lesson designed to give it. That is not to say it is necessarily bad, though one has reservations when the teacher appears to be trying to satisfy strong emotional needs in this manner, for then it is a deviation from the primary task. In such situations pupil response gives teacher satisfaction and teacher approval gives pupil satisfaction. This is independent of the content, wherein at least some of the satisfaction should lie! The subject gets left out. The pupils' performance becomes too heavily dependent on the teacher. If this teacher is a powerfully affection-seeking personality, he or she may achieve good results, which cannot, however, be sustained with a new teacher of different style.

Mathematics is a largely contemplative and exploratory subject and the extent to which it can be an inner private pursuit is not always understood. It cannot be pursued without considerable input, but the satisfactions should lie in success in pursuing it, not in a teacher telling you it is right. The authority lies in the subject, and the fundamental aim of the operation is that the student should learn, understand, and actually do math. Satisfaction in the teaching/learning process should be strongly related to the primary task. It should not hinge on personal factors largely independent of the material. In figure 7–4 we diagrammatically show emotional response, which affects our cognitive performance, as dependent on who is there rather than on what we are doing. The main message is to avoid the situation described, but it is not easy.

A number of my subjects so lacked any confidence that they could ever be right that they remained dependent upon my agreement that they were in fact right. Though it seemed (and this was largely subjective) that they became less concerned with my *approval*, they still needed my *agreement*. My insistence that both the satisfaction and the

**Figure 7–4**  Emotional response dependent on who rather than what

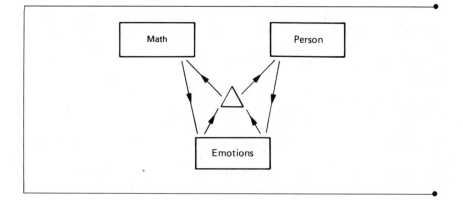

certainty of correctness could lie in the subject was not accepted. Lynn was given a series of problems involving visualizing a three-by-three-by-three cube like the one shown in figure 7−5 (see appendix A for the complete series of questions). It was a series graded in increasing difficulty, and the answers, since they were strongly visual, were satisfying when reached. The question Lynn reached was, if the outside is painted black how many small cubes have no faces painted? Once the answer is seen it should be evident that it is correct. Lynn did reach it; she found it interesting and discussed it with a mathematician friend. When I asked if she felt that she would defend the answer, she said that her reply to anyone who questioned it would be: "Two people that I know, who are better at math than you, agree that I am right." Yet she claimed to feel certain of the answer.

A more successful attempt, with Sarah, involved a wood-block puzzle (appendix A has a more detailed discussion of wood-block puzzles). A cuboid of wood is cut two ways with a bandsaw in wavy lines, providing, in the case mentioned, some thirty pieces. It is rather like a three-dimensional jigsaw (see figure 7−6). The block is dismantled and the problem is to reassemble it. The matching of shapes involved is a worthwhile geometrical exercise, and involves an appreciation of simple curves. The value of such a puzzle (indeed of many puzzles) is that when they are done, there is certainty that the solutions are right. Sarah gained satisfaction from doing it and had no need to refer to me to confirm that her solution was correct (though she was pleased to tell me she had done it). She decided that as she could do it, however, it must be (a) "very easy" and (b) "not connected with math"!

**Figure 7−5** Perspective drawing of a segmented cube

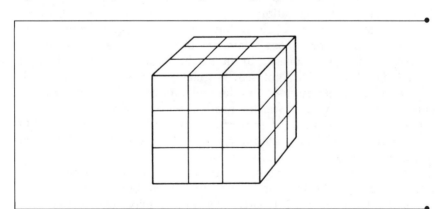

**Figure 7-6** Perspective drawing of a three-dimensional jigsaw puzzle

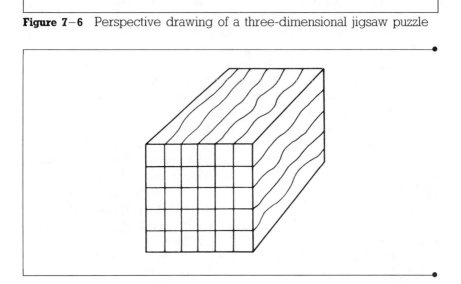

If you are really sure that you cannot do math there are many ways of refusing to admit that you might. Difficult though it may be to achieve, it is necessary that people experience pleasure at doing math for itself and feel content about the rightness of what they do by way of the material itself, not from teacher agreement. Only in that way can they carry through the periods of bad teaching they are likely to encounter.

# Situation 5

In some senses the situation we now describe could be subsumed under the last heading. Again we have emotional responses inhibiting the reason; these responses relate not directly to the task of doing math but to a person engaged in the teaching process. The distinction is that the student does not see the relationship simply as a pupil-teacher one, but is reminded of other encounters of an unhappy kind. One person I interviewed was the headmaster of a large comprehensive school. He was a man of powerful intellect, sensitive and highly perceptive. I arranged an interview at his school and expected to learn much from him; and so it proved. One of the most interesting ideas, described in the next section, started with him, but so also did an understanding of how a one-to-one discussion about math might be perceived by people with early unfortunate experiences. His own early schooldays were dominated by the arbitrary distribution of punishment. Although he was very able at English, and by diligence and punctuality managed to avoid many pitfalls, his weakness at math often put him in danger of a beating. Thus a one-to-one encounter about math, such as I had arranged with him, brought back the deep-seated fears of his childhood, and he acknowledged after our talk that he had felt most anxious about it, though he knew me quite well, felt friendly, and in no rational sense should have found it difficult.

Talking about math seems to produce a more *demanding* situation than most. Perhaps it involves more questions being asked and more challenges being present. In several cases the interviews clearly brought back memories of early parental relationships. The parents may have been rather insistent about math, but the interviews clearly triggered off more general concerns about unresolved problems in this area, with the resulting difficulty of not being able to tackle any math until some of these problems were shifted. One particular interview led to a subject experiencing several days' disturbance, a disturbance that she was in fact well able to handle and that indeed it was perhaps appropriate to handle at that stage. With someone else we uncovered a serious and lengthy struggle with her mother, reinforced by an experience with a teacher at the top junior stage, of which mathematical encounters reminded her. Working through this led to some marked changes in attitude.

These were clear and specific cases, but I felt more generally that one-to-one interviews about math were often colored by other such encounters. Perhaps the dominant anxiety was related to authority, and we shall say more about this in situation 7. Certainly the reactions described already involved clear authority problems. With one other subject, the mere assumption of a teaching role on my part would sometimes make her bristle.

The interpersonal situation here, then, unlike that in situation 4, is seen as resembling some other interpersonal relationship of an unsatisfactory kind — so the math does not get done. This leads us on to our next situation with which it has certainly much in common. The distinction may prove to be a fine one.

## Situation 6

In the situation diagrammed in figure 7–7, anxiety that is in fact unrelated to math has become arbitrarily associated with that area. It is not the immediate interpersonal relationship that is wrongly interpreted but the whole of math. We have seen the effect of some deep-seated feelings about early relationships being transferred to the area

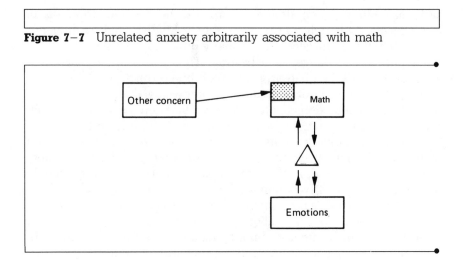

**Figure 7-7**   Unrelated anxiety arbitrarily associated with math

of math. Once that is done, the section labeled "math" in one's mind may be regularly used as a dumping ground for difficult and unresolved problems. A number of people have, curiously, expressed the view that the subject was all right until they had to do "problems." There were some very clearly defined memories of that section of the 11 + exam that dealt with problems, and the identification of math with problems in general may easily be made. As Sybil put it to me, very succinctly, "Category — problems."

A particular stumbling block for many of my subjects was the encounter with *x*, the unknown. It is perhaps unfortunate that a word like "unknown," with its built-in anxiety, should be attached so firmly in people's minds to *x*. It may also open the door to feelings about sex — regarded as mysterious at some stages — being stored in that area.

This may seem a little far fetched, but some signposts are there, and for those whose reaction to the subject is extreme it would be natural to suspect that a more sensitive issue than math might have become associated with it. Any approach to the "no go" region is strongly negated by the emotions, and the result is that the math ceases to grow. Such a situation may lie behind the many statements that "I can't do math" or that it is "boring." The use of this latter term is commonly a defense mechanism.

There is an interesting feature about math and our early experiences. It is the main substantial piece of explicit learning that stretches back into early childhood. It is true that language also does so, but it is doubtful if it is seen as either so contained or so developmental. In math we have a structured subject, seen as of considerable importance, stretching back as a ladder to the past within each human personality.

If I speak to someone about learning to count, I expect this to have happened at say four to five years old; if of quadratic equations, at about fourteen. Experiences contemporaneous with this, and particularly those with a heavy emotional charge, may then surface into the consciousness. Touching on mathematical experience does therefore release other memories, as I have found with a number of people. Memories that people may wish to suppress because of the unpleasant emotions associated with them may in fact be associated, purely in time and in no other way, with some piece of math. If that too gets blanked out, it is a problem, math being a subject that is built up piece by piece. Attempts to explain it later may then be seen as threatening to the area that is not to be thought about.

So there are special reasons why unrelated anxieties may be attached to math. It is not easy to indicate a cure. I could offer (at an exorbitant fee and with no guarantee of success) weekly sessions for anyone who wants to get sorted out, or you could try a psychiatrist who unlike me may know some psychology but no math.

# Situation 7

When we extend the model we shall need to include several types of delta (see chapter 8) and to suggest links with Freudian theory (see chapter 13), though the general trend of this study does not depend upon Freudian interpretations. At this stage we might, following Skemp, introduce the superego without reference to the ego and id. Briefly we may say that the superego operates as a powerful punitive mechanism in all areas associated with authority, questions of right and wrong, and with personal worth. It is the image of authority built in the mind.

Math is seen by many as involving just those issues of interest to the superego. It is seen as important. Of the early dropouts interviewed for a Schools Council document, some 92−93 percent believed math to be important. (The proportions believing it to be interesting were much less.) It is both supported by all sorts of authority figures and carries considerable authority of its own. It is seen as concerned with questions of right and wrong (rather than with correctness or incorrectness), with all their heavy moral implications. This is a semantic error from which it is difficult to escape. Furthermore, schools have often made, by implication at least, the quite unjustified connection, math = intelligence = value as a person.

Many of those I interviewed felt personally diminished by failure in math and this is a quite intolerable thing to do to a person. Schools of course are bound to have aims and purposes to which they attribute moral virtue. If the climate is such that intellectual quality is much to be desired, and that mathematical ability can establish it, then the effect on those demonstrably incompetent at math is very unfortunate. Failure in math becomes peculiarly significant, and the emotional effects of working at it are accordingly enhanced.

Some of the fault, and therefore some of the remedy, may lie in the ideas that people are given as to the nature of the subject. When I have described it to people as an activity of a contemplative nature, with material available at all levels of difficulty, which is amusing and interesting to explore, which involves little remembering, and which, while of central importance to many aspects of our present technological society, is not of great significance in everyday transactions, the reactions are almost always of surprise. Often it is not because they have been incorrectly told what math is about, for it has never been discussed. They have nonetheless abstracted a view of its nature from the arid exercises that they have been asked to perform. There is an urgent need to talk about the subject at large and in conceptual terms, in order that techniques may be seen in their proper perspective. (See chapter 13, under "Attitudes toward Math.")

Above all, we should not induce guilt in those who have found math difficult.

Perhaps we could further categorize situations in which mathematics and emotion interact or, alternatively, combine those situations in which the distinctions may seem small. It is always a problem to decide how far to separate and distinguish, and one can always argue that it should be done differently. Clearly people will sometimes find themselves in more than one of the situations listed. I would claim, however, that my analysis derives from what people said of themselves, and that some at least accept that a "situation" properly describes how they feel.

Finally, let us review the situations, each with a brief description.

1. The standard Skemp situation with emotional response to success and failure in tackling each problem.
2. A "pathological" reaction to repeated failure that stops the student before he or she starts.
3. Emotional distractions of various levels, which prevent reason from applying itself to the problem in hand.
4. An overemphasis on teacher approval rather than on the subject's internal interest.
5. False interpretations of the interpersonal relationship in a teacher-pupil situation.
6. Transferred anxieties from areas unrelated to math.
7. The superego in action.

# Chapter Eight
# Mind Divided

We have separated reason and emotion in our analysis but agreed that their interaction allows neither to operate untrammeled. We must examine further the way our reason functions and the precise emotions generated by particular situations. In this chapter I hope to categorize our cognitive activities in a way that will then lead to an interpretation of panic, and of how it arises through math.

## Working in Three Worlds

We may begin with an important categorization by Karl Popper (1973) who distinguishes between three worlds. The first is the external physical world, which we recognize through our senses and whose existence we do not question. The second is that mental world within ourselves. World 3 is the world of statements — those utterances, in whatever form, that we have externalized. Although such categories may often seem arbitrary, Popper's three worlds certainly have immediate appeal in their simplicity and should help us in our present theorizing about learning, for which of course they were not specifically designed. Mindful, therefore, of the Buddha's instruction not to believe anything "on the mere authority of a teacher, myself or any other," and of the fact that we are using the ideas in a different context, let us see where they lead.

The concept of three worlds gives rise to a number of philosophical problems, some of which may be important in our thinking. Much of the material in world 2 (our minds) arises from objects in world 1 (the physical world). Certainly that accords with our belief that model making is of central importance in an intelligent organism. It may be that a world 2 may not start without input from world 1, but it is certainly possible to conceive of things in our minds that do not exist in the actual world, and this too may be of particular importance in defining intelligence.

Lest this be thought too philosophical and detached from what goes on in the classroom, let me point to the ever-present public discussion about the purposes of studying math. Some assert that what it is really about is giving change in the shops and knowing how many beans make five. Others (more sensible) argue that it has more extensive purposes. In our present terminology, those in the first group are asserting that only model making that is directly relevant to everyday transactions (and those at the lowest level at that) is important. They are asserting the primacy of those parts of world 2 whose connections with world 1 are most evident. The others are effectively saying that world 2 operations are central to our intelligence and our capacity to survive in and to control our environment. Hence they are valuable in themselves.

In fact, the first view, that our main aim is just to learn how to cope with the real world, would be a recipe for making no progress whatsoever. For the individual, it denies him the flexibility that he will need to meet new challenges in a world where constant retraining will be the rule rather than the exception. It is the teacher's task to expand the student's world 2 as far as possible, not to limit it to those activities for getting through a day in world 1.

We do seem to be capable of developing material in our minds that has no analogue in the actual world, and much of math may appear to be of that sort. It is at the root of many of the complaints from generations of children: "But what is the *use* of it?" Once they are interested in something, however, its relevance to the actual world is not questioned, and conversely, problems that do have direct relevance, such as income tax and reading gas meters, do not always enthrall. You will remember the question. "Do the prime numbers go on for ever?" Among those I spoke to, this was agreed to have intrinsic interest, though it can hardly be said to be of much practical value.

We can now present some of the interactions we discussed earlier in terms of three worlds.

# A First Division

In the situation diagrammed in figure 8−1, someone in world 1 (generally a teacher) thrusts some mathematical material into the student's world 2, with the demand that it be worked upon. The student emits a world 3 package for the teacher to pour scorn upon! It is the student's experiences with *world 1* that occasion anxiety.

We can use the distinction between world 1 and world 2 to create

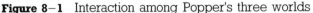

**Figure 8-1**  Interaction among Popper's three worlds

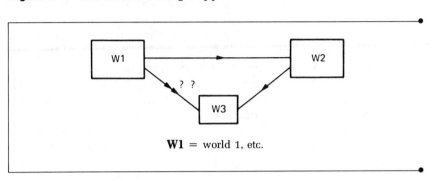

$\mathbf{W1}$ = world 1, etc.

distinctions between different deltas. We have so far used one single delta to represent reason, as distinct from emotion, and will now concern ourselves with what reason is operating upon (its *operand*). It is natural to separate the occasions when the operand is world 1 and when it is world 2, thus locking our present theory into a well-established one. Clearly we could seek to classify types of reason on the basis of activity rather than the material dealt with. We may indeed use this method later, but the primary distinction is now assumed to rest on the operand. We shall call reason, when operating in world 1 (through the sensorimotor system), *delta 1*; and when it is operating internally, *delta 2*. It is useful to move a stage further and separate these two conceptually as we did with reason and emotion. Instead of a single delta engaged at different time on different material we have two separate deltas, neither of which can exist independently.

The justification for this lies in the undoubted fact that we can think about two things at one time (or at least during pretty short periods of time) and that it seems easier to do so when they are respectively internal and external matters.

I once drove Richard Skemp through London and conducted a complicated discussion on this very matter of deltas. I must modestly admit to a high degree of competence in driving a car in London conditions, and my sense of social responsibility is enhanced on those days when, as a magistrate, I have spent the morning on the bench taking other people's driving licenses away! So I regard it as important that my intelligence is engaged upon the task of driving. My delta 1 does this driving since it is an engagement with world 1. It is perfectly possible for my delta 2, however, to be engaged in theorizing *at the same time*. We shall develop this situation later, but for the moment let the example illustrate the virtue of regarding delta 1 and delta 2 as separate, although, as we shall argue later, not independent.

The way in which delta 1 operates is a central feature of Skemp's theory of intelligence and we need to give some explanation of it. In so doing, and in the ensuing discussion on the deltas, the reader may detect differences of approach and assumptions between Skemp and me. We recognize these and do not feel that they are in any way incompatible. He starts with a model that owes much to cybernetics and has analogues in thermostats and stabilizing devices. His director-system delta contacts the environment through sensors and has a comparator that records the relationship of our present state to our goal state (where we want to get to). This has similarities with the way in which a thermostat must record both the present temperature and that which it is desired to reach. Though at first this may seem a somewhat mechanistic interpretation of our processes, it is in the question of the way in which goals are chosen and reached that we differ from such devices. To determine where we are and where we should be we often need mental models, sometimes referred to as schemas, on which we plot these positions (see figure 8–2). The comparator records the present state and the desired goal on the map or schema we have in our mind. It would be wrong to think of schemas simply as maps, though it is a useful picture. In solving mathematical problems, for instance, we have an end in view, a present position, and the need to plan a route. In fact these geographic analogies are deeply woven into the language we use.

**Figure 8–2**   Skemp's model of delta 1 operation

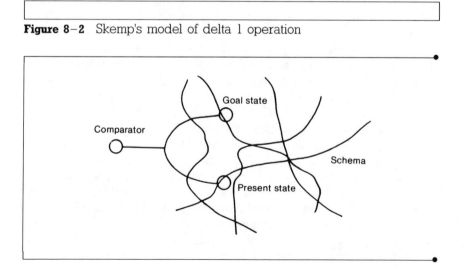

Our ability to achieve goals depends on two features: (a) the quality of the schemas we have, and (b) our skill in making plans to get between points in them. This gives us a clue to a distinction, not to be pursued at length here, between learning and problem solving. Learning is mostly related to schema building, and problem solving to planning — and they are distinct.

If we are to relate delta 1 to world 1 and delta 2 to world 2 as I have proposed, then the two important activities I have defined, building schemas and planning to reach goals, are both seen as being done by delta 2. Their quality will affect how we relate to the outside world through delta 1, whose activity is therefore dependent on delta 2. There is mutual dependence. Delta 1 will feed information about this outside world (and how well it has been coped with) back to delta 2, and the quality of this information is important.

Let us return to the example about the journey through London. Over the years, through traveling a great deal in London and through looking at maps (world 3 information) I have within myself, under the action of delta 2, built up some maps (and also an understanding of how to read maps). I have also had the advantage of sensory input through delta 1 concerning various landmarks. As I set out for my destination, delta 2 sorts out the map, makes a plan, and, as it were, slots it into delta 1. If the journey is a very routine one, the plan is lying ready to hand for delta 1. We now drive with delta 1 in charge. It not only deals with that particular goal, but from experience of many traffic situations conducts the car past various dangers in some safety. It has the quite sophisticated task of manipulating the car, a task that seems incredibly difficult when one first learns to drive. It must monitor the sensorimotor system and generally direct operations. While it has routine situations and properly devised plans it seems that it goes on functioning leaving delta 2 to think of other things if it chooses. Situations can arise in which a new plan is needed. *That* is a delta 2 function. Suppose we meet a new No Entry sign, a common experience in London. We, as we say, have to "think" about it. This terminology denotes that delta 2 is being set to work to devise a new plan. In the time it does so, delta 1 and delta 2 are dealing with the same problem (getting to the destination) and there is some danger that the car is driven less well. A more drastic example might be the sight of a lorry bearing down on us on the wrong side of the road. Again delta 1 does not cope without a plan from delta 2 for which it asks in some haste!

Mathematics is a delta 2 activity, though it is delta 1 that has to receive information and questions from the teacher and provide suitable responses, with consequent anxiety. A number of my subjects had come to believe that math was a collection of incomprehensible routines. Their delta 2s offered these routines more or less at random for delta 1 to convey to me. They seldom fitted the problem!

Though delta 1 always deals with the actual world it may operate at different levels and have different reactions. Some are so primitive and instinctual that they are hardly reasoned at all, resulting from basic "wired-in" drives (our mouths may water at the sight of appetizing food). They follow the stimulus-response pattern though they can be seen as goal directed and are common to all animals. We *do* operate in this manner but we also operate in others.

At the next level we may act in a fairly automatic way, but the process is learned and not instinctual. When the telephone rings I reach out to answer it. When a child runs into the path of my car, my foot hits the brake. In neither case is any "thinking" involved. Delta 2 does not play a part. Automatic responses are made — and in the second case the immediacy is of great importance. The plan on which delta 1 acts is a routine one but *not* an instinctual, "wired-in" one. The routine has had to be learned at some time, and *at that time* delta 2 had been engaged in making it. Consider a golfer who has over the years developed a smooth, full swing as he drives the ball. Ask him to think about how he does it *while you are playing him* and you may find to your satisfaction that it deteriorates! It has become one of delta 1's automatic routines, and you have effectively asked his delta 2 to reexamine it. Thus we may describe "gamesmanship" as an attempt to persuade one's opponent to use delta 2 to replan his game instead of letting delta 1 actually play it. How then do we learn and improve? We do so by letting delta 2 work on our schemas for hitting a golf ball or driving a car while we are not actually doing them, or at least when just at practice. Generally speaking, restructuring of a schema will result in initially poorer performance and then, when the new schema is properly integrated, in an improvement, taking the performance above the original level.

This particular level of operation of delta 1 — the automatic response — is valuable in the realm of skills. Strongly structured teaching followed by the reinforcement of constant practice may well make a good golfer or car driver. It will not make anyone better than good. For that, their own thought processes (delta 2) have got to work on the problem.

Two serious mistakes had been made in the mathematical education of many of my subjects. The first was the belief that skills in math could be learned in the fashion just described. The second was that math was composed mostly of skills. This led to several behavioral features that were very widespread. The first was a feeling of being overwhelmed by sheer volume of material. So many different (and apparently unrelated) routines had been attempted that a feeling of chaos was created. The second was a strongly held belief that immediate response (as in braking a car) was required. This derived from the assumption that the subject was about automatic routines. The result of this was that plans were offered up in the hope that they might chance to be relevant. Perhaps the most important result was that they were simply unable to believe that their minds (delta 2) could really work effectively on the material, since they had never been encouraged to do so. The contemplative and exploratory aspects of math were greeted with puzzlement.

For our immediate survival, delta 1 does need a number of automatic responses, routines once worked out and regularly reexamined, but ready to hand. Those people best equipped in dealing with world 1 have, however, spent a good deal of time letting their delta 2 work on their world 2 models of world 1.

At this level therefore, the functioning of delta 1 has long-term dependence on delta 2, though it does not need it for immediate reactions. Confronted with unfamiliar situations, however, the dependence is much greater. Unfamiliar material must be entered through delta 1, into world 2 where delta 2 can relate it to the schemas it already has, and try both to build it in and make plans for any actions delta 1 may need to take. This is what we call learning! By extending our schemas and improving our planning methods we make ourselves more adept in dealing with our problems. We extend our personalities and become larger people. That might well be thought to be one of the aims of education; it is denied by the sort of process that my subjects have experienced.

We therefore find delta 1, defined by the fact that it is concerned with world 1, exhibiting three different levels of activity:

1. Instinctual, "wired-in" routines related to basic drives.
2. Automatic responses, once learned and considered, but now available for immediate issues.
3. Responses to new situations where the material needs to be entered into world 2 for delta 2 to integrate it and create new plans.

Mathematics should go on largely in world 2 and is therefore a matter for delta 2. I have already emphasized the two important functions of delta 2 in making models and plans, but we have so far been mainly concerned with those it makes to enable delta 1 to function better. Yet a lot of what goes on in one's inner world is not direct and practical preparation for our activities in the outside world. Some of our planning and model building turns out later to be of value, but for purposes and occasions that were not foreseen. This is very evident in the history of mathematics, in which the theories of conic sections developed by the Greeks were ready to hand for Kepler and Newton in describing planetary motion. Similarly, Einstein found the tensor calculus ready for his thinking on the nature of the universe. This collective thinking that precedes, sometimes by centuries, an important use for these concepts is paralleled in the individual. We all regularly play through scenes for future situations that we believe may arise; few of them do arise, but we learn how we might and could behave through this practice. A childhood interest in mechanical objects, both practical and theoretical, prepares us for future needs. Play, properly understood and organized, is the basis for future success in many areas. The mind is seldom inactive or should seldom be inactive. The quality of our future behavior may depend on the nature of present delta 2 activities.

It does not automatically follow that delta 2 has the same sort of structure as delta 1, and there must be essential differences. They both, however, have *operands* (material on which they work), and they both have to use plans based on mental models. Delta 2 creates these for both delta 1 and itself; an essential difference. Both, however, are concerned with present states and goal states, so the diagram of the comparator is appropriate for both. Indeed the comparator is a totally essential feature, for the whole basis of our theory of the cognitive-affective interaction lies on the feedback to the emotions from the comparator. The emotions generated by success or failure of the reason depend upon this feedback. The emphasis on the penetration of reason by emotion applies not only to delta 1 but also to delta 2. Here too there are differences, however, and they relate to a number of the situations described in chapter 7.

## Teaching and Learning Math

The essential part of mathematics is within the mind. Some of it models the outside world, but much is a creation of the human intellect, built on various assumptions and tested for internal consistency but not needing to be tested, as scientific theories are, in world 1. It is therefore delta 2 that must do the math, and we might expect our emotional reactions to the subject to relate to how it is succeeding or failing. Bertrand Russell's intense delight when he first encountered the works of Euclid were part of the interaction between his delta 2 and his emotions. This is also so in the first situation of chapter 7, the basic model. Here the director-system postulated was in fact delta 1. When we assert that what we are doing is math, then we clearly are dealing with delta 2, but through its performance we experience frustration or elation as we fail or succeed, and the same model is clearly appropriate.

It would seem likely, however, that the deepest anxieties are generated through contact with the external world; even if we later withdraw within ourselves we still experience them very strongly. It is through these bruising contacts with the outside world, rather than through the intrinsic nature of the subject, that so many have suffered, and this is the evidence of all my subjects.

Our second situation, where repeated failure results in an unwillingness even to try, is seen now less in terms of the fact that there has been repeated failure, as that it has been repeatedly and adversely commented upon. Judgment (an awesome word) has been made upon one's attempts, and they (and by implication oneself) have been found wanting.

Our third, fourth, and fifth situations, as described in the last chapter, are all avowedly to do with interpersonal situations, and with world 1 rather than world 2. In our sixth situation, a most interesting one, anxieties apparently unrelated to math have been classified there, thus rendering the area unapproachable because of the discomfort in considering these anxieties. These fears, too, are usually related to the outside world and are not purely internal matters. The last situation, with our speculative excursion into the superego, we shall leave for the moment, only because we shall later have more to say about it.

In the diagram shown in figure 8–3, we have both delta 1 and delta 2 getting emotional kickbacks from their tasks. But in general, unless you happen to be Bertrand Russell, those from delta 1 are stronger, whether pleasurable or unpleasurable. The essential feature of most of the people with whom I worked was that they didn't really

**Figure 8–3**   Joint delta 1 and delta 2 reactions

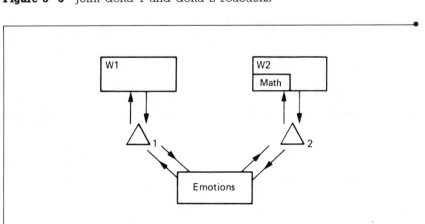

get delta 2 to work and were experiencing the world 1 concerns and deriving their fears and anxieties from the interaction of delta 1 with the emotions. My aims, seen in theoretical terms, were to get them to experience pleasurable emotions through delta 2 activity to replace negative ones of their delta 1 activity. This lay behind the emphasis put on the "authority of the subject" and the use of materials such as puzzles where it was evident that they were correct when complete. The very privacy of the occupation was of great value.

There is another interesting aside. One of the group said that in her limited experience those who claimed skill and interest in math were sometimes inadequate in their personal relationships. Without accepting this (for mathematicians are lively, cheerful, lovable people), it would be possible for someone who correctly saw the subject as an internal matter to retreat to such a pursuit if he generally was getting a rough ride through this contacts with the outer world.

We can express our concern about whether mathematical activity genuinely takes place in a different way by looking at it from the teacher's point of view. Teachers are aware of input to their students, since they supply it through books, materials, and their own explanations. A very great deal of attention has been paid to the question of input. If any teacher wants to discover the best way of presenting subtraction, there is a great deal of information on the subject, with detail on method, why it works, what material is available, and comparisons between main approaches such as "equal addition" and "decomposition." Many publications from the main organizations of math teachers have contributed a great deal to this sort of work, at many levels of difficulty, and much of it is valuable.

The output from students is achieved either by asking them questions to test their understanding, or by getting them to solve problems related to the work, the assumption being that if they get them right, they understand the work.

Between input and output is the real activity that we should be interested in — that of doing math. The output — on which the teacher judges — has to be considered with care, not least because it *is* an output, with all the disturbances that this might involve because of the external world. It is sometimes rather shattering for the teacher's *amour propre* to discover what the student really thought. In the group I tried to play a somewhat passive role, but constantly found myself yielding to desires to explain rather than let people work things out. We had been working on graphs of straight lines, and so we had to use a small amount of mathematics. The cognoscenti will know that the equation $y = 2x + 5$ can be expressed in graphical terms as shown in figure 8–4. (We were not at this stage using negative numbers.)

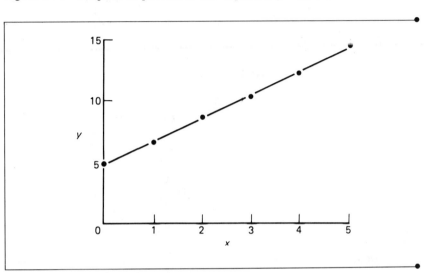

**Figure 8–4** Graphic depiction of the equation $y = 2x + 5$

They could all "do" this sort of graph. Then I found out from Rosita *how* she understood it. Her schooling had left her with the belief that everything in math depended on fixed rules, which had to be learned and memorized. By this stage she knew intellectually that this was not so, but her long entrenchment in a certain pattern of behavior in math had not yet been shifted. She attached (and I don't know why) special significance to the *first* point, by which she meant when $x = 1$: "You go two along the x axis, but it is really upwards (because Laurie says so). Then you go five and put a cross. This gives the first point. Then you go up in twos." She got her graphs right this way! We teased out, together, something of what it meant, and revealed that others in the group had had similar misunderstandings. The expression 2x and the statement $x = 2$ were not always distinguished; I had not realized that. For several of them 2x meant "go in the x direction." For Rosita, the starting point was always (1,0) and this would have landed her at (3,0). But at some time in discussing the labeling of the axes as x and y I had said it was pure convention that y was up and x across. This allowed Rosita to believe that 2x (which meant 2 along x) could be used in the other direction because I said so. The whole business was very sobering for me.

Weary of rectangles, let us express this thought in a diagram using a triangle (see figure 8–5). Using other triangles, our deltas, we have

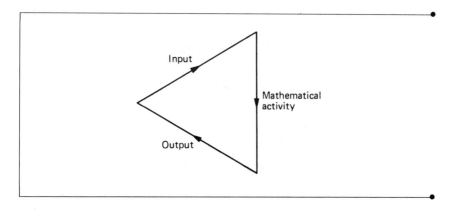

**Figure 8–5**   Attention to mathematical activity deflected by concern with input and output

delta 1 dealing with input and output and delta 2 with mathematical activity. The teacher tends perhaps to emphasize "input" while the student's concern (particularly if he or she is anxious about the subject) is with "output," and both could afford to pay more attention to the mathematical activity. The teacher must allow time for it and the student has to learn to enjoy it. Few do either.

## More about Delta 2

Before we go any further, let us collect up the various functions of delta 2. We have already seen that they come under two main headings: model building, or the formation of schemas; and plan making. We can now specify slightly further. We are faced throughout our lives with a colossal input of information. This has to be selected, sorted, classified, and made available for retrieval. It is a librarian's job, and that is one of delta 2's functions. These processes are emphasized in math in schools, in which children are encouraged to regard sorting as an important aim in itself. It is also, because of the learning processes that accompany it, important in early language development. Chomsky (1965) has suggested that the basic structures of language relate to common cognitive structures in human beings. At this level our brains, language, and mathematics show common patterns.

In performing this task effectively, relational methods must be used, rather as a librarian needs schemas in order to classify. We develop schemas to link together our pieces of knowledge, forming extensive networks. It is true that some factual knowledge does not lend itself to such schemas (often because of its arbitrary nature). Some may have to be learned by rote but there is much less of this than is commonly believed. There also appear to be limits to how much can be remembered in this way. Assertions that young children can remember facts acquired in this way may well be true, but they may seriously inhibit later learning. The ability to retrieve is clearly enhanced by learning material in a way that is schematic and emphasizes relational links (see Skemp 1971).

In the group we tried not to move on until all members felt they had genuinely "understood," in some satisfying way. There was disappointment when the work was not always remembered after a week or two. At first I was worried about this, believing that deep understanding should mean that it is not lost. There were examples where this was so. Lynn remarked of a piece of geometry, "I've got that now; I shall not forget it." The more general picture, however, was that knowledge did sink out of mind but that it was much easier to retrieve with a little help if it had been well understood.

Ausubel (1978) claims that this process, which he calls "reception learning," is an active one, rather than the passive one it is sometimes believed to be. This is certainly so. Delta 2 has to work over the material to fit it in and to integrate it with what is already there. Active "working" results in better schemas. Nonetheless, there are activities of delta 2 that are perhaps more demanding and creative. Building new constructions from existing material (a typical mathematical task) and solving problems are both more active. It seems (a purely subjective impression) that some people have great reserves of knowledge, but may not necessarily have great power in attacking problems, while others, with less information available, appear to be very effective in tackling new problems or building new structures. Both are delta 2 activities. The second, more creative aspect, relates to plan making and may hinge upon the range of methods of attack that have been developed.

In chapter 7 (situation 2) I referred to the stages in tackling a problem; this analysis is less extensive than that by Krutetskii, but is not incompatible with it. Seen now in terms of our new concepts, when a problem is received it comes through our sensorimotor system and is passed by delta 1 through to delta 2. Many people are inhibited by anxiety even in accepting it, once it is recognized as math. Delta 1 clearly sees or hears it, but it is not taken in, and immediate claims are made that it wasn't heard, or can't be remembered. In fact delta 2 is having nothing to do with it, for it only leads to trouble! In our experiment we all tried to fool our delta 2s by asking people simply to accept and stabilize the information, nothing further being required.

The group, and my individual subjects, all worked at this and generally found it helpful. Once the information is into delta 2, it has a retrieval task—looking around to see what facts or methods might be useful. This has got to be calm and reflective, or it will not work. The third stage is more active and engages the creative building and planning aspects of delta 2. This task is tendered decidedly easier if sufficient time is given to the first two stages. They can give the room to think.

# Do We Go Further?

In making a model, as we are here, there is always at the back of one's mind a nagging question. "Is it really like that?" Of course the model does not match the complexity of the mind, and one could brush aside many models on the ground that they are too simplistic, but the two levels I have so far suggested, delta 1 and delta 2, do seem to relate well to world 1 and world 2, and they make distinctions that we are able to use in classroom terms. There is another step that has to be taken, although perhaps with less confidence. I am going to postulate a *delta 3*! In one way it spoils the pattern, for it does not relate to world 3. In chapter 13 we shall see how delta 2 will work on symbols, so that its input is in fact from world 1 and world 3 together, with its own additions built in world 2. But our new delta has for its operand delta 1 and delta 2. It is the "psychologist of the mind," which observes both our thoughts and behavior.

The power of reflection is significant. It is the way in which we learn and it has enabled us to advance at a much greater speed than the trial-and-error methods of evolution. When I become aware that I have been in danger several times in the last few weeks in driving around London, I reflect upon it. My delta 2 examines my schemas for driving, finds that there are certain specific situations where I have been braking too late, and makes new plans for delta 1. So I survive longer. Experience gained by our contacts with the external world has constantly to be reflected upon if we are to improve performance. Yet there are times when we become aware that we are *not* doing this, that we have not spent any time in contemplating what we are about. Our inner thoughts and planning may have deteriorated and ceased to get good results. At such times it may be necessary to stand aside from ourselves and view both our internal and external behavior with some objectivity. As before, we could simply say that this is an activity of one single reasoning function, but since I have chosen to divide aspects of our mind by means of the operand, the material on which they work, it is natural that when the processes themselves are considered we should assume another delta to do so. There is the obvious danger of going into an infinite regress, but it seems both sensible and possible to stop at delta 3.

In everyday experience, delta 3 is in operation when we stop and ask ourselves, "What am I fussing about?" — or, rather like Alice in Wonderland, carry on conversations in which it, as one inner voice, offers advice to the other. It can at best perform the task that a good teacher will do. It may well exercise judgment and assert priorities. The model to date allows the emotions to assert priorities; these must sometimes be overridden by a more detached and cognitive function.

**Figure 8–6**  Summary diagram of delta/world relationships

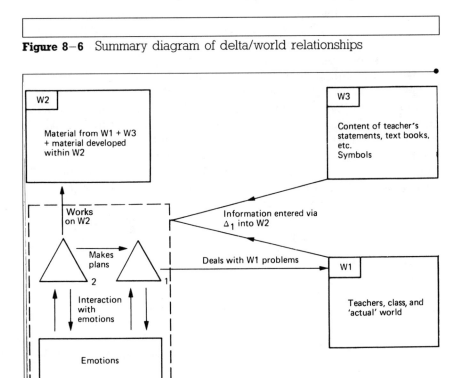

We can at this stage examine the full picture of how delta 1, delta 2, and delta 3 may be seen to relate to our three worlds, again by means of a diagram (see figure 8−6).

Both in history and in our individual development there has been a shifting emphasis on each of the deltas. It was the planning function of delta 2 that led to the improved ability of delta 1 to cope with the world and to establish mastery. Once that was done, we find great advances in abstract thinking, the manifestation of delta 2 in Greek civilization and the Renaissance. Great intellects have built extra-ordinary models of the universe itself, and we must stand in awe of their penetration. Yet it is only recently that we have really begun to study ourselves. Perhaps the growth of psychology implies that more delta 3s are at work. That is not to deny the many acute perceptions of the human condition over the centuries, but that it could be a defined corpus of knowledge is a new idea.

In our individual personal development delta 3 is the last to grow. Initially we must be concerned mainly with our senses and with coping with the outside world. As our delta 2 helps plan this process and we can cope, we enter into the phase of abstract thought, which may be at its best in our twenties. In our comfortable fifties we may not have the same cutting edge of intellect, but we may use our minds to better effect, because we have thought about how we function. We hope to have better judgment and to handle ourselves better; but only if our delta 3 has been at work. Through delta 3 we may aspire to the maxim "Know thyself."

# Chapter Nine
## Panic...and How to Cope

We have now extended the model considerably from that offered in chapter 2 as our starting point. We have seen that the emotions act to alert the director-systems (delta 1 and delta 2) to possible dangers. They direct the consciousness to the problem, and the deltas seek to avoid the danger, delta 1 taking routine evasive action or delta 2 forming a nonroutine but effective plan for delta 1. This is the normal process.

I will postulate that panic is a breakdown of this normal interaction between delta 1 and delta 2. There is a flicker of consciousness between the two deltas, and the system fouls up. The switching creates a neurotic situation with eventual paralysis (see figure 9-1). It matches with some accuracy the imagery in chapter 1 of "mind in chaos."

Under what conditions will this switching occur? The initial condition is that delta 1 perceives a threat of some sort, and that this is fed into the emotions. Consciousness is heightened in delta 1, and a

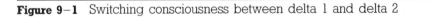

**Figure 9-1**  Switching consciousness between delta 1 and delta 2

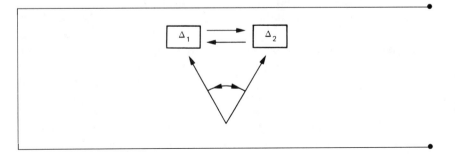

solution sought. If the threat is a minor one, such as bumping into another pedestrian while walking along, there is no problem. If our consciousness has been in delta 2, chewing over a math problem, it switches momentarily to delta 1, which then adopts a routine plan for avoiding the collision. We can then go back to thinking about our piece of mathematics. Even if we fail to do this, and collide with the other person, there is generally no serious penalty, no real *survival* issue.

If the threat is seen as more serious — and it is important to remember that it is the person's view of the seriousness that matters, not what an outside observer may think of the situation — then there are heavier demands from the emotions for a solution.

Suppose the teacher has asked you a question. This will be perceived differently by different people. We have Marie's reaction, mixed pleasure and fear (chapter 7), but we also have Barbara's (chapter 1): "Oh my God, I'm going to make a fool of myself — or be found out." The level of threat is different for different people — and for some there *are* survival issues.

There are then strong demands for a solution. If delta 1 has such a solution in its routine plans, then there is no difficulty. (The answer to the teacher's question may in fact be known.) When delta 1 has no such plan it calls upon delta 2 to formulate and provide one. If this is successfully done (the normal situation) that again finishes the issue. The pupil may not know the answer to the teacher's question, or even have a routine way of getting it, but he or she may nonetheless be able to think it through. It is only when delta 2 fails in its essential plan-making function that trouble may occur. It may fail (a) because it cannot make a plan; (b) because it cannot make a plan *in time*; or, at a slightly more sophisticated level, (c) because it has no *expectation* of being able to plan appropriately. Any of these three states, combined with a delta 1 (a) under a threat regarded as serious, and (b) without a routine plan, may result in the switching of the consciousness between delta 1 and delta 2, which develops to a flicker and produces the state we call *panic*.

It is perhaps characteristic of math that there are more occasions when *no plan at all* can be made than is true of other subjects. Faced with an English essay to write one's response may be very inadequate, but some attempt can be made, and something written. Faced with a problem involving a geometry theorem the response may be genuinely zero. Sarah, for instance, worked well and with considerable interest on a problem with the cubes of numbers and was willing to look for patterns. When faced with some work on geometry, however, she clearly did not enjoy the situation: "It is all right if I know where to start and what to do." She needed an initial plan, though once she had made a secure start she could then develop. The wood-block puzzles described in the section on Sarah (chapter 5) brought out the positive side of her statement. The aim was clear, and it was always possible to advance, even if slowly; she enjoyed them and was both persistent and successful with them.

Both the group and the individuals were given a set of problems set by Edward de Bono (see appendix A). Several people were interested in shape through their training in art, and it seemed possible that they might be able to do some. However, the characteristic of these problems was that they would not respond to routine plans, nor was it easy to devise any general plan of approach. People were deterred fairly quickly by "not knowing where to start."

In these cases the lack of plan did not involve panic, since no great pressure about doing the problems had been applied. As material for a panic-producing experiment, however, the de Bono problems might well rate high!

What sort of threat to delta 1 might be the starting point for panic? Obviously, heavy threats of the life-and-death sort might do so. Suppose someone were to loose a wild animal into my room and lock the door (a situation happily outside my experience), then my delta 1 certainly does not possess a routine plan for this. There would be an urgent demand on delta 2 to produce one, but as soon as the consciousness moved there in order to plan, the threat from world 1 might well cause the consciousness to move back to delta 1. It would more readily do so if delta 2 has no expectation of a solution. Once in delta 1, however, the only answer is to plan. The flicker of consciousness between the two begins.

A lesser, but still powerful, threat is that of exposure in a public situation as being inadequate or foolish. The classroom is one such public place. Before we return to the classroom, however, let us take a couple of more general cases. A famous actress once claimed that while she was playing highly emotional or tragic scenes she was also considering her shopping lists. This may well be. It provided an interesting example of the workings of the deltas. The original playing of the part would have required a good deal of working out by delta 2. From time to time (and *not* while performing) the part may need some reworking, but so firmly is it entrenched after a large number perform-ances that it is a routine, automatic response for delta 1. If for some reason (another actor giving the wrong cue, for instance) she attempted to move from the shopping lists to what she was saying, she might very well stumble and even dry up. If delta 2 had so far detached itself from the play as to be unable to plan, and with the public exposure as a very powerful pressure, we have a panic-producing situation.

Peter commented how easy it would be to panic in a public

position if not well prepared. Certainly in a lecture it is sensible to have the material well worked over beforehand to allow one to concentrate on presentation and audience. Again, an unexpected doubt in one's mind about what one is saying can jam up the activities. Question sessions at the end of a talk must have clear cooperation between the deltas, with delta 2 handling the nonroutine answering.

Certainly the public exposure that may have suffered in the classroom is an important cause of panic, and we shall pursue this point in chapter 11 in the particular context of being asked questions, but now we need to discuss a number of threats posed by authority in the classroom.

## Authority

We shall follow a categorization of authority given by Paterson (1966), which seems particularly useful in the classroom. He uses the three terms *structural*, *sapiential*, and *personal*. By *structural authority* is meant that which is derived purely and simply from position. The armed forces emphasize this form—a certain rank carries certain responsibilities, independent of the person holding it. When an officer is saluted it is explicitly stated, "You salute the uniform, not the man," for the uniform states the rank. Similarly the headship of a school is a recognized position held in turn by various people; there is a meaning and authority attaching to the post, whoever holds it. The teacher has this type of authority in the role as a teacher. This is not to say that different people may not handle this structural authority in different ways, and we indeed know this to be so. In part it hinges on the other forms of authority they have.

*Sapiential authority* is implied when we refer to someone being *the* authority on a particular subject. It is, naturally, an authority deriving from knowledge but it goes beyond this meaning (which usually refers to an academic field), to cover "know-how" in a wide range of fields. In all groups one finds that a particular person is always referred to for specialist knowledge, be it about Minoan civilization or the football pools. Teachers normally are expected to have this form of authority in their subject or in a band of education, and sometimes feel threatened when a pupil challenges it.

*Personal authority* is more difficult to define, but it recognizes that some people are more formidable than others or more likely to be paid attention to, even outside their official position and field of specialist knowledge. It does not depend on whether the person is extravert or introvert, charming or otherwise, but probably relates to qualities of independence and strength. It need not be virtuous. Some less than admirable characters in history may have had considerable personal authority. On balance the adult will carry more than the child.

Often the teacher will outweigh any of his or her charges in all of these forms of authority, and it is necessary that the teacher exercise them with care, for all of them can pose threats capable of generating negative emotions, if not panic. It may be through the *judgment* made by authority that the main threat comes. Few of us are immune to the judgments of others, particularly those in an authority relationship to us, and it seems to strike deep into questions of personal worth. This is discussed further in chapter 11.

There are threats more easily understood. In the classroom the teacher possesses, through his or her structural authority, those sanctions permitted by the school. In the case of several of my subjects this could involve severe corporal punishment, so the threat was considerable, However, much lesser sanctions, amounting to no more than disapproval expressed by the teacher *on behalf of the institution*, can be something one would strongly wish to avoid.

The sapiential authority of the teacher allows him or her to demonstrate features of the work that then appear simple and hence diminish the student who failed to see them. Some of my subjects had become so conditioned to appearing stupid that they did not like to be shown answers, and when they did achieve answers unaided they diminished themselves by saying how simple the question must have been.

Usually the teacher, simply by being an adult, also has greater personal authority, and when this is used wrongly to express scorn or to deride it can be very damaging.

So a number of aspects of a teacher's role — that it is a part of a controlling and custodial institution, that it explicitly involves greater sapiential authority, and that the teacher is an adult dealing with young people — all combine to produce a considerable weight of authority. This may not readily be recognized by a weak and inexperienced teacher trying to manage a tough class the last period on Friday, but even here the role remains and is recognized by the pupils even as they attack it. Unfortunately the teacher-pupil relationship is too often seen as one of conflict rather than cooperation, with the scales weighted for the teacher: "He knows and you don't." "He's right and you're wrong, and that's it."

There is an interesting feature of a subject like math. It can appear, when wrongly taught, as a system of rules. Its structure then may resemble that of an institution together with the rules that govern it. In an institution such as a school the students generally know the rules, whether reasonable or not, but in math they may not know them. A discussion I had with Richard Skemp is to the point:

**Skemp:** Those children who never really grasped the conceptual structure of mathematics are trying to make the symbols appear right without any underpinning of the significance of them.

**Buxton:** Yes. The common feeling would *not* be that they are capricious, but that they are — the Kafkaesque thing — subject to firmly authoritarian rules *which they do not know.*

**Skemp:** Absolutely — that's much better. And the panic is ...

**Buxton:** What is the rule we must obey?

We shall return to the authority issue later, for it would be incorrect to draw the conclusion that there should be no authority; we have seen the results of such a policy. The point made at the moment is that many people anxious about math see it in terms of unfortunate authority relationships, and that this pressure is certainly powerful enough to create the conditions for panic.

So we have in math *for some people* the image of a demanding authority asking for answers that are clear-cut right or wrong and on which judgments about them will be made. Couple this with a weak understanding of what the whole issue is about and we have a delta 1 under threat and a delta 2 unable to produce appropriate plans. That is why people panic about math!

# Time

The most stressful math situation recalled by my subjects was the mental arithmetic test. It is worth making the observation that working in the head is a valuable exercise, but not as directed by many teachers. The tests did not usually involve working things out, but consisted of recalling number facts *at speed*. The activity then was strongly teacher directed, with questions posed (and no other form of communication) whose answers were right or wrong and marked for a score.

The pressures created by time are very strong. Naturally a time limit on something that you are not bothered about doing anyway is irrelevant, but what a time pressure does when the initial condition of a threat is present is to enhance it considerably. I deliberately distinguished the failure of delta 2 to make a plan from its failure to make a plan *quickly enough*. This second condition in fact greatly extends those situations where panic may occur. No sooner is delta 2 about its planning task — and a task that *given time* may be well within its competence — than the external threat, or simply the time passed, is reassessed by delta 1, who then reemphasizes the urgency. The flicker of consciousness between the deltas begins. A student in time trouble in an examination or a chess master in similar difficulties may in fact waste time by looking at the clock too often.

Again, I do not suggest that time pressures are automatically bad. Some of us work better under time pressure—we all have deadlines to meet. Yet this is generally the case with tasks that we know how to do—even when hurried. It is the combination of a threat if we do not succeed, uncertainty about how to do the task or even what the task is, and an imposed urgency that together lead to panic.

Let us sum the whole thing up in another diagram, figure 9—2. At this stage we have a model for panic based upon the earlier model making of chapters 7 and 8. It is a speculation based upon what I was told by people who did panic. The speculations as they were developed were checked back with people to see that they fitted what they felt. As we said earlier, a model does not have a truth value, but it may prove helpful or otherwise in predicting or overcoming the occurrence of panic.

Some experimental work will prove relevant here, but first let me record an account of an experiment described by Skemp in his doctoral thesis (1959) which we would both now reinterpret in the light of the model. The thesis was on reflective intelligence, and his students were asked to do sorting processes of various complexity. They were given a number of cards with shapes of different sizes and colors on them (rather like Logiblocs) and were asked to sort first by one criterion, say shape. The tasks were gradually increased in difficulty until they were asked to change the criterion by which they sorted with every card. Richard Skemp meanwhile stood there with a stopwatch! He had observed as an interesting feature of this experiment that one student had reported "waves of panic." In view of our present analysis, it is hardly surprising. There was artificially introduced plan changing, which meant that delta 2 could not simply insert a routine

**Figure 9—2**  Diagram of panic

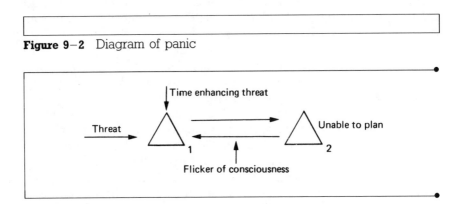

for delta 1 and let it get on with it. There was an authority figure standing there, parading the fact that he was exerting time pressure. It could have been designed to produce panic.

Now for an experiment designed to do just that. Near the beginning of chapter 1, I described some reactions from groups of people whom I had addressed about math, and the fairly regular offering of the word "panic." I decided to structure this more closely, to build in deliberately those pressures of authority and time, and to forecast a proportion who might feel panic. A description of one occasion will illustrate the sort of experimentation that is developing.

I had agreed to talk to a group of primary teachers—about twenty of them—on anxiety in math. Many of them held some responsibility for math in their schools and were nearing the end of an enjoyable six-week course under the guidance of an expert tutor who had in fact markedly shifted their attitudes and understanding of math in a very positive direction. My talk was on the last day but one. I had determined to "lean" on them with three sorts of authority and some time pressure.

I arrived on time. Some were a little late and I waited in silence, emanating but not stating my disapproval. I then stood, loomed over them, quelling someone who appeared to be about to speak and handed out some cards. It could be said that I have some peculiar advantage in this. I am a *very* large man and can appear (so I am told) somewhat forbidding. One of the teachers later said that she had whispered to her friend, "I bet he never had any trouble with his classes!" Clearly my personal authority had had some impact.

I then told them that it was near the end of their course and that as staff inspector for mathematics (my structural authority) I thought I should give them a test to see what they knew (sapiential), so that I could judge them. There would be a strict time limit—and I took my watch off and held it.

This process took very little time, yet presented all those pressures I had postulated might cause panic. It probably had to take a very short time, since given time to think they would surely detect that it was an act.

At this stage I asked them to stop, shut their eyes, get one word most appropriate to describe their feeling, and write it on the paper. I assured them that the results would be anonymous. When the papers were handed back I shuffled them and read the words back to them. Only two were really not affected in a negative way. One wrote "hilarity" having presumably seen through the game, and another "joy"—which I did not understand. The rest recorded various levels of concern, such as "nervous," "apprehensive," "fear," "anxiety," but three recorded "panic" and two others "terror" and "sweaty/palpitating," which the group felt were at a similar level. Further experiments of this sort show that as many as one in seven record "panic" under this sort of attack. This is a small beginning to the process of predicting the effect of given pressures in producing emotional reactions as highly specific as this. It is worth noting that in this experiment the task was not even stated. It was known to be math, and it clearly produced in some people a "situation 2" state as described in chapter 7. In terms of our model, delta 2 did not have the *expectation* of being able to do the task — even without seeing what it was.

By this stage we have devised a model based on observations made by people anxious about math, categorized some of the pressures that produce panic, and demonstrated that in artificially contrived situations based upon these speculations we can induce panic in a proportion of those present. It is a start.

# Avoiding Panic

We have two problems, prevention and cure. With what we now know, positive progress can be made on the first if teachers and parents take heed. Recovery from one's own bad situation is less easy, but there are very definite lines to pursue.

In the area of thought and feeling there is a close relationship between diagnosis and cure. If a teacher fully accepts what has been said and avoids the pressures described, the pupils may have a good mathematical experience; the avoidance of the errors is the solution of the problem. For the student being taught without this sensitivity, it is less easy to escape the pressures, even when they are recognized. Adults who would like to tackle, by themselves, the math they failed to cope with at school, have a good chance of success. Yet we should say more about what exactly one needs to do and offer some evidence that it works. Let us examine how teachers and parents can at least avoid inducing states of panic.

**Teacher authority.**   The feeling that the teacher and the subject both constitute external authorities to be placated is difficult to overcome. The teacher's authority has two aspects, often confused. In John Wilson's *An Introduction to Moral Education* (1967), an important distinction is made between "ground rules" on the one hand and the right to express what one wishes on the other. Freedom to discuss does *not* involve freedom to alter the *rules* of discussion. On the same principle a teacher should exercise authority in control and management of the class, but should not restrict thinking. Structural authority should be used to control behavior, not thought; to maintain the ground rules, not to stop pupils thinking. Perhaps the best example of a failure to understand this was given in chapter 3: "It was the whole school ethos. You get your figures in nice lines and you had vertical lines in the math books (which my handwriting didn't 'fit' anyway) and if you didn't do it, it was a mark of insolence and deviation and all sorts of things." Here, not only was the nature of math misunderstood, but not doing it correctly was seen as a behavior problem, an offense against structural authority, not as a sapiential failure. The teacher needs to retain structural authority and use it properly for control purposes, but the teacher must eventually seek to wean the pupil from this sapiential authority. If something is believed only on the authority of a teacher, it is not really believed. It must be made the student's own. In terms of our model, we are asking that delta 2 determine the rightness of a problem or piece of learning as often as possible, and that delta 1 should not have to submit it to an external judgment. This is a counsel of perfection; for much of the material and for much of the time it will be necessary to check in this way, but if the *intention* of internal checking is preserved, the right view of the subject is conveyed. We have seen that puzzle material often does not need external checking, but even in learned material, the knowledge can be made one's own. A number of instances reveal the pleasure this can give. With some simple geometry, we emphasized the matter of what was visually apparent. We worked at the angle sum of a triangle until the steps were not remembered, but the fact was seen, understood, and internalized. Once the mechanisms had been fully grasped and its validity accepted, external sapiential authority was no longer necessary. The work on the cube (see appendix A) again carries its own certainty, though early on Lynn was unable to accept this. A remark of Elaine's further expresses this idea: "I've got it for good, only brain damage can take it away." The knowledge was hers, no longer external.

Earlier in describing this policy, I used the term "authority of the subject." Once this is accepted, there is no *personal* pressure from outside. The authority pressures that lead to panic are essentially personal, and the removal of the (sapiental) authority from the teacher greatly reduces anxiety.

Two points, unrelated to each other, are worth making in this connection, for the whole issue here is of some importance. Popper (1973) elaborates the concepts of world 1, world 2, and world 3, which I have used in chapter 8. World 3 was the world of material created and uttered by us — of which math is an important part. Popper says:

> This autonomous part of world 3 is "real" in the sense that it can interact with world 2 and also, via world 2, with world 1. If one man or many men seek for a solution of an as yet unsolved mathematical problem then they are all, possibly in many different ways, influenced by this problem.

The success of their attempts to solve it will depend, at least partly, upon the existence or non-existence, in world 3, of a solution to the problem, and partly upon whether or not they are led by their thought processes to objectively true thought contents. This shows that the autonomous world 3 objects can have a strong causal influence upon world 2 processes. And if a newly discovered world 3 problem, with or without a solution, is published, then the causal influence extends even into world 1, by helping to set in motion the fingers of type-setters and even the wheels of printing machines.

For very simple reasons such as these I hold that world 3 is not only partly autonomous, but that its autonomous part is real, since it can act upon world 1, at least *via* world 2. And the situation is fundamentally the same for every scientific discovery and every technical invention. In all these cases, world 3 problems and theories play a major role. The problems may be discovered, and though the theories which are, say, about world 1, may be products of the human mind, they are *not merely* our constructs, for their truth or falsity depends largely upon their relation to world 1, a relation which, in all important cases, we cannot alter. It depends both upon the inner structure of world 3, and upon world 1, the latter of which, as I have suggested, is the very standard of reality.

This is what I now identify as "authority of the subject."

The second point is the attitude pupils seem to have to mechanical and electrical aids and specifically to such developments as micro-computers. These may be programmed to ask questions and to "teach" people. But they exert neither authority nor time pressures — and that is of great significance. Some pupils can work for much longer periods than anyone would expect when there is no *person* there. One hesitates to pursue this thought further!

There are some teachers who get trapped, as we said earlier (chapter 7, situation 4), into seeking affection in their intercommunication in the classroom. As a teacher one seeks for good relationships and hopes to like one's students as people, and it is a sad class where this is not so, yet the main satisfactions should relate to the task, and that task is learning or teaching. If the teacher has allowed his or her personal authority to be regarded as the main source of approval and disapproval, and hence of satisfaction or otherwise on the pupil's part, then he or she has done that pupil a disservice. The job is to make the work, not the relationship, enjoyable.

The conclusion of the last few paragraphs might well be that teachers have no role and that the best thing to do is to remove them! Not so. We have emphasized how teachers, by a wrong understanding of the types of authority they have and the way that they use them, can make authority seem a threat. The people we have studied have had bad mathematical experiences, and it is those we have been concentrating upon. They have been occasioned sometimes by bad teachers, and sometimes by quite good teachers who did not understand what was happening to those particular children. In no way does this deny the role of the truly inspirational teacher, whose enthusiasm *for the subject* infects others. But the enthusiasm is properly directed at the task. The great majority of teachers do a very good job, but an awareness that some pupils react negatively and a willingness to avoid those things that cause this reaction can only improve the situation.

**Parent authority.**   We have examined the danger of heavy pressure in math, and here parents as much as teachers need to exercise care. Children with their parents will sometimes complain that they feel under pressure; this is at least a healthy situation, and it is important that notice is taken and the complaint not simply brushed aside. Worse, however, is the situation in which the child accepts too readily the parents' view, bottles up the pressures imposed, and fails to resolve them with explicit statements. Several examples of this appear in this study.

It is in the area of authority that parents' attitude is crucial. In the development of beliefs about authority our parents are always with us, and if their authority attitudes are attached to one area of learning — and math is probably the most likely one — then those attitudes are very important. Throughout the study people spoke of being *judged*. That is what authority does, and it is a formidable action. Because in math things are classified as right and wrong, with all the moral overtones of this semantic confusion, judgment is more evident and to be feared than in other subjects (with the possible exception of reading, where the same emotional blockages occur). At least two of my subjects believed that authority would be *cross*. They had not experienced overt crossness (though others certainly had) but this crossness had been deduced from indications of disappointment or of wearisome reactions to their slowness to understand. These indications are strongly diminishing for a child.

**Time pressure.**   Let us now look at time pressure and how we can ease it. The most significant release obtained in the experiments was that of Elaine faced with the problem of 15 × 12, which she initially saw as well beyond her capabilities. I allowed her to take her time, was genuinely unhurried myself, and when her panic rose remarked, "No hurry." By good fortune and lucky timing this had a remarkable effect. She had always seen speed as an essential element of computation — certainly in my own schooldays it was so presented — and the suggestion that it was not was quite releasing. In our present terms her consciousness had begun to move back and forth between delta 1 and delta 2, her delta 1 assessing my attitudes and whether I was beginning to show impatience. My remark allowed her to remain within herself, to allow delta 1 to remain quiescent while delta 2 got on with the task successfully.

Lynn and Sarah both exhibited some characteristics similar to those of Elaine, feeling that quick responses were necessary, despite my insistence they were not. At times to relieve the strong pressure of a one-to-one situation I actually did something else, such as a drawing for the next piece of work, or even left the room. These were seen generally as subterfuges, I felt, and while that could have been one interpretation, it was intended simply as an attempt to reduce their feeling that I was waiting. If someone *is* waiting, then of course consciousness is constantly forced into delta 1. In the group, acceptance of waiting was achieved, but it may have been better to achieve more periods of silent internal working by everyone.

An example from an O-level paper used with individuals and the group illustrates the desire for quick, automatic response (which is not what math is about). The first part of the problem, which is all we need to look at, asked for the volume of a swimming pool with the dimensions shown in figure 9–3. It was deliberately not drawn to scale.

Lynn, certainly in the earlier stages with me, always sought to show a quick response, as she had presumably learned that this was proper in the pupil-teacher relationship. When I showed her transcripts of the previous session she read them with great rapidity and then looked up ready to start. If a quick response was not possible she was inclined to claim she couldn't do it. This was her reaction to the

**Figure 9–3** Dimensions for swimming pool problem

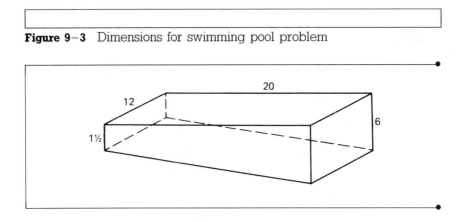

swimming pool question. She explained that she knew there must be some formula but couldn't remember it. When I explicitly asked her to consider ways of tackling the problem—not an immediate solution— she decided she could cut up the shape, and perhaps cope with the triangular bottom part. Another interpretation of this approach is that she was being pressed into stage two of problem solving. In either case it involved delta 2 activity.

In the group Sue arrived at the imaginative solution of turning the shape (the trapezium) over and putting it underneath (see figure 9–4). This gave her a shape she could handle, and the result merely involved halving. This sort of result can come about only through a "play" activity, shifting shapes about to see what might work. We seem to have three levels: (a) a routine plan—a formula for the particular shape; (b) a fairly standard strategy—cutting up—which had general applications; (c) an unusual schema for the particular problem.

The first is a delta 1 response; the others are for delta 2. The point is that (a) may be provided mainly for situations in which time is important, and if people think speed essential that is what they will look for. The other two are more useful mathematical activities and they should be given time. It is not enough that the teacher knows this. The student needs to know it.

There is an interesting point about apparent slowness to understand. Ideas in math, again more than elsewhere, seem immensely difficult before they are grasped, and sometimes easy to the point of triviality when they are understood. To the person who does understand, the one who does not appears stupid—yet the latter may take less time to reach understanding than the former originally took.

More than anyone the teacher tends to impose time pressures. The thought of a syllabus to get through and exams at the end imposes an

**Figure 9–4**  Swimming pool shape, turned underneath

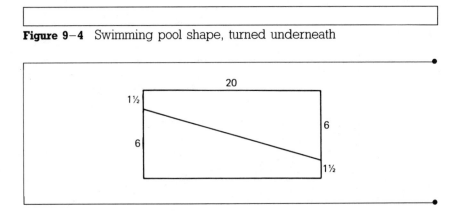

urgency, which is then conveyed to the pupils. On balance and in most situations this is counterproductive. The awareness of time prevents the mind relaxing into the work (and thereby doing it more quickly). The constant feeling of rush is further emphasized by the need to revise material learned only recently. This need derives from the fact that insufficient time was allowed originally; thus the urgency results in slower, not faster, progress.

The two crucial questions are time and authority, and this has been a continuing theme through this work. Both teachers and parents, quite unwittingly, and often before the child has gone to school, establish situations in which instant response is required. This cannot help people to learn math — at best it can train them for a life in TV quiz shows. It is widely believed that math should be done at speed, which is not the case. Unfortunately, this view is as widespread among teachers as among parents — so here it would be foolish to say, "Leave it to the professionals." The aim should be to concentrate one's undivided attention, internally and without interruption. In fact, this is the way to achieve the fastest speeds, irrelevant though this is. Making speed the avowed objective in fact defeats that objective. An interesting paradox.

# Remembering and Understanding

There is an important distinction between instrumental and relational understanding. Instrumental understanding is gained from learning rules and being able to apply them — and this has some value. Both the memory of the rules and the ability to apply them are soon forgotten, however, if not constantly practiced. Relational understanding implies an understanding of why the rules should be. It is deeper, less easily forgotten, and if forgotten more easily retrieved.

At this moment we are concerned with how we acquire knowledge in the classroom. It seems that there are two distinct approaches, and that at times we make a conscious choice as to which we shall employ. These activities are *remembering* and *understanding*. If I were to ask you to remember something you would, inside, do something different from what you would do if I asked you to try to understand something. The first gives instrumental, and the second relational, understanding; the second is unquestionably better in educational terms.

Why have we made this seeming digression? It is because it is at the root of a false solution to the anxiety problem that many pupils adopt. When under time pressure people switch from saying "I must think this through," to "Well, I'll just remember it." In the very short term, seeking just to remember will pay off. If I were taking an examination in routine calculation tomorrow I would memorize the rules, but if I needed to use them in the long term I would want to know why the methods worked. Memorizing cannot be sustained beyond a certain point. Some people I interviewed had sought to remember fifty geometry theorems — with some success — but they could not tackle a geometry rider. The method of escape from time pressure and the fear it induces may therefore be the adoption of a basically wrong way of learning.

Do we have evidence that the advice we have offered to teachers would work? Many teachers will have the answer in their own experience if they now submit it to scrutiny. I would offer two pieces of evidence: one the work with "my" group, the other the second half of the experiment with the group of teachers in whom I tried to instill panic.

**"My" group.** Throughout the work with my friends in the group, people who had not previously explored their feelings about math did so; they worked long and hard at a subject they had found distasteful, and they took their time to understand.

There certainly appeared to be a release for them in talking about how they felt and knowing that I was not going to be *cross* about it. Establishing that I was not going to be cross was less difficult in the experiment than it might be in the class, since it was their emotional reaction to the work that I was explicitly studying. This made it permissible for them to talk about it in a way that had not proved possible in class with even a sensitive teacher. It was not then seen as a proper part of what the lesson was about. A main theme of this book is that if it is not seen as an important part of the teaching/learning process in math, many people will suffer as a result.

The willingness to offer answers or ideas that they ordinarily might think would be treated with amusement or scorn was an important element. The fear of pressures or responses was removed, and the ethos that there was no hurry, that one must wait for understanding, was central to the work. Particularly useful was the idea described earlier of *stabilizing* the information at the start of a problem. There was great security in knowing that one only need sort out first what the problem was, not actually do it.

**The group of teachers.** More structural evidence, though not necessarily more convincing, came from the experiment with the group of twenty primary teachers on the six-week course. You will recall that they had expressed a range of negative emotions when I "came on strong" about giving them a test. The rest of the experiment had two stages. In the first I discussed exactly what I had done. I characterized the pressures that I had put upon them, as described earlier in this chapter, and explained the whole basis of that short experiment. In accepting this, they were also removing some of their own built-in fears, which were now explained, brought to the surface and shown for what they were. However we still needed to give them a positive experience in a piece of math, and for this I used the graded problem in the cube described in appendix A; but in doing so I removed explicitly the pressures that I had put in the first experiment and stated at the time that I was doing so.

They were asked to close their eyes and visualize a cube. They were asked to feel it, walk round it, examine it carefully, and *stabilize* it. The series of questions then started. They were asked to make sure they knew the answer but *not to check it out with me.* My approval was not necessary — the authority lay in the subject. After each question I left some time and asked those not finished to flap a hand — seen only by me for their eyes were shut. We waited every time until all had finished. I constantly assured them there was no hurry and that it was for them to do it.

At the end I asked them to describe their reactions. They were very much more positive. In particular, those who had expressed panic said how secure it felt and how pleased they were at getting the answers. The only displeasure was among those who felt frustrated at the delay when they had "got it" very quickly. No one felt the reactions that we had discussed and here sought successfully to avoid. Here at least were the beginnings of some good evidence.

There are two interesting points, not perhaps directly relevant, but worth recording. In the course of several group experiments of this type, I twice had it reported to me that a person did not like shutting his or her eyes, a fact that might be interesting to follow up, and, secondly, there was among some a very strong desire after the experiment to check their answers.

One group was happily engaged, eyes shut, on a later stage of the problem, when someone at the back blurted out the answer. The hostility this attracted had to be seen to be believed! When I met them the following week they had another go at him. There is no better proof that they enjoyed the work than their anger at having it snatched away from them.

## Antipanic Devices

So far, what we have said is largely for the teacher and parent; can we say anything specifically for the student? Since we have emphasized that it is important for knowledge and understanding to reside in the student without depending on the authority of a teacher, can we go further and suggest ways in which a person may control or at least influence his or her own learning processes?

Some advice is evident. Start afresh with a piece of math and see what you can make of it. Take it slowly, absorb it into your mind, and *contemplate* it. Let your mind *relax* into the work. There is no time limit, nor is there guilt in being slow to understand. Make the process an entirely *internal* operation. To master a small area of math may take considerable time; it cannot be read as prose. If you need help, ask someone to explain it — but remain in *control* of the process and do not allow memories of unequal encounters with your teachers to freeze your mind. Concentration and effort are necessary, however; math at any level cannot be mastered easily — but the process of mastery can be pleasant. The process of learning math and of solving mathematical problems is heavily dependent on a state of mind. Let us try to put that in terms of the model of chapter 8.

I have indicated that it is the ability to work with abstractions in the form of models that gave humans their dominance. We can *reflect* upon our experiences, and learn through this reflection to cope better with the world around us (world 1). This is an essentially different process from the *conditioning* that is at the basis of behaviorist theory. But we have seen that the reflection that leads to improved plan making by delta 2 (and to improved performance by delta 1) can be properly undertaken only when the consciousness is free to remain in delta 2 and that under some threats there is an uncertainty about which delta should be acting, resulting in a constant paralysis or panic.

It is for this that I postulated a delta 3. Defining different aspects of mind by the matters that they deal with (their operands), we have delta 1 dealing with the outside world (world 1), and delta 2 dealing with internal matters of the mind (world 2). We then suggested that if we wished to stand aside and consider how *we ourselves* were behaving (an experience we have all had) this involved a different operand and hence a different delta. The operand of delta 3 is the complex system of the other two deltas and the emotions.

If therefore we wish to be able to control malfunctions (such as panic) we need to reflect on how we operate. In a sense that is what much of this book is about. It may seem a "bootstrap" operation, but nonetheless that is what we must do. A growing realization of our own functioning will enable us to control our fears but will also assist our development. This is especially true in learning. Even as the functioning of delta 2 allows us through delta 1 to *do* things better, so the action of delta 3 will improve the whole system's capacity to learn and expand.

So the central message is to *reflect* upon how you are functioning when you are learning. It was through the process of asking people to say what was happening and what they felt, that they obtained some release in their ability to tackle math.

In this chapter I have offered a model for panic based on the more extensive theorizing of earlier chapters, analyzed the main pressures that caused it, suggested ways of avoiding it, and given such evidence as we can of the effectiveness of these ways. In a sense, that completes the discussion of panic as it relates to mathematics. No one would suggest that this, the first attempt to isolate this very specific problem, is going to be in any way a final word, but we can hope that it is a first benchmark.

# Chapter Ten

# In Denigration of Praise

The issue of authority, which is of such significance in the creation of panic, leads us also into the unexpected area suggested by the title of this chapter. The notion that we should praise our students for getting things right has moved from being an insight, to a state of plausibility, and finally to general acceptance. At one time, teachers offered much more blame than praise. As the serious ill effects of blame became apparent (as demonstrated earlier in this book), the balance shifted and the plausible notion that we should always praise and never blame was mooted, and even those who would not go this far believed that praise was an essential feature of teaching.

Once an idea has ceased to be questioned, we are on dangerous ground. It leads to a situation in which certain things may be said and others may not, according to the climate of the time. Such ideas should be made subject to critical examination, even if the result is simply to reinforce our belief in them.

In the argument here, I wish to make some clear restrictions; later the issue will be widened beyond these proposed limits to the general question of offering praise. Here we are not considering behavior in the moral sense, and we are only considering the teaching and learning of mathematics, not of other subjects. Naturally, if what is said here is seen to make sense, then we need to enter these other areas.

Conclusions reached about mathematics teaching may well not be valid elsewhere. The reason lies in the content of mathematics. It is not in itself value-laden, and it is emotion-free. By this I do not mean that society does not attach value to it, nor that people do not undergo powerful emotions in attempting to learn it. I mean that the statements of mathematics do not imply value judgments (certainly in the moral area), nor do they discuss emotional matters.

The issue is narrowed to this: if a student presents you with a correct mathematical response to a problem, should you offer praise?

My answer is "No." The reasoning behind this starts with authority aspects of the teacher-learner relationship. The classroom is heavy with authority issues, which as we have seen can be strongly counter-productive.

We have previously analyzed certain notions of authority, but it may help to recapitulate them. *Structural authority* derives from position, and its use is in management and control. The teacher needs to keep order in the class and has certain sanctions available to that end. *Sapiential authority* in its most powerful form is that of being an acknowledged "authority" on a subject. But we shall use it in the relative sense of the teacher being, we hope, more of an authority on mathematics than the class. *Personal authority* lies in the weight accorded to one's views by the world at large. Naturally, these aspects of authority can seldom be seen operating separately, but there are different balances.

Explicit understanding of the distinction between structural and sapiential authority would be helpful to both teacher and taught. Properly to control a class it is necessary on occasion to be assertive and not to permit discussion, despite those comfortable theories that say that no control is needed if students enjoy the work (they won't always!).

Yet in the area of knowledge, and especially in mathematics, it is wise to avoid constant statements as to what is right and what wrong. In mathematics, the authority lies within the subject and not with the teacher. I am not here referring to the weight and regard in which math is held by society. I am saying that questions of correctness and incorrectness are resolvable within the structure of math and are not matters determined by the teacher. Nor in most school math is there much room for interpretation, as there well may be in other subjects.

The problem is one of dependence, pupil upon teacher. The assertion of structural authority can lead, naturally but regrettably, to overdependence on the sapiential authority of the teacher. Ideally, the teacher should lead the student to a state of independence, so that they check within the mathematics whether they are right or wrong.

In passing, a society such as ours, which encourages boys to break rules and girls to conform, may well be the root of differences in the attitude of and toward the sexes later on. This is posited and developed in the last chapter of this book.

We are talking of aims and ideals. It would be absurd to suggest that young children will discover large ranges of mathematics for themselves. The teacher must organize the learning and must often say whether the results produced are correct or not. But in so doing, the aim must be to develop the child's ability to criticize his or her own work. The teacher must aim to wean.

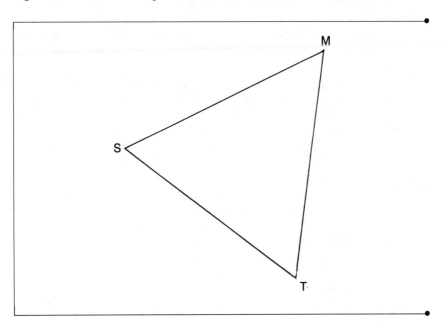

**Figure 10-1** Relationship between student, teacher, and math

In the diagram in figure 10-1 we have the teacher teaching math (TM), the student studying math (SM), and the reaction between teacher and taught (TS). The eventual aim should be to develop activity along SM and diminish it along the other lines.

Let us look at what are apparently good and bad aspects of the TS interaction. We are often faced with banal remarks such as "It's good teachers that we need." This reflects the view that the teacher is central and the subject secondary. When students are given a choice of subjects to pursue, they often are more influenced by the teacher than the subject. Not surprisingly, we all enjoy being admired by our pupils and are pleased that they choose our subject because of us. Should we be? If we have shown them how to enjoy the subject, perhaps. But we have all come across teachers who attract fierce allegiance from their classes, which then become very difficult to take over.

We have seen from reports from those whose early experiences in mathematics have been particularly bad that they emphasize feelings about their teachers first and about the subject only secondarily. It has been amply demonstrated that the use of authority pressures (with adverse judgments being made and blame being apportioned) coupled with time pressure can be totally destructive of a child's self-image. This self-image may be affected not only as far as ability at mathematics is concerned, but, as some of our subjects have shown, far beyond this, into unrelated areas.

The latter observation leads us naturally to the conclusion that one should praise rather than blame. Much of the evidence is in favor of praising.

First let us tackle the theoretical objection to doing so, then see whether there is an alternative that is more acceptable and more effective. The objection is that all ways in which the role of the teacher as a judgmental figure is emphasized need to be scrutinized. (This refers to sapiential matters, as indicated earlier.) Emphasizing the role directs attention, in our diagram (figure 10−1), along TS and not SM; that, fundamentally, is a deviation of aim. So praising is making the implicit statement "It is I who decides what is right and to whom you should attend." It does so quite as much as does blaming someone. From this point of view, therefore, the offering of praise or blame is equally inappropriate.

We are, of course, assuming throughout that the praise (or blame) is genuinely offered. We need not consider insincere remarks, nor even the casual and unconsidered "Well done, Johnnie!" We are talking of considered and meant praise, indicating that the work is indeed correct.

If we are to be sincere, then we must sometimes withhold praise. Will this not be interpreted as blame? It is clear that adverse criticism, however muted, may yet have a strong effect. A position where praise is offered or withheld can easily become indistinguishable from one where both praise and blame are used. If we seek to avoid adverse judgments, we must reconsider positive ones.

We now return to the main argument, for it may begin to seem that we are left with no observations to make in the classroom. This is not so. What we need to show, whether the work be correct or not, is interest. When a student does a piece of work we should be interested in how he or she did it. Of course, the interest must be genuine...but if you are not interested in how students think, you should not be teaching! And the interest is as great, or greater, when the work is incorrect. The more bizarre the thinking, the more fun! With praise there is a difficulty about withholding it; we need never withhold interest.

If we attempt to alter our practice in this way, there will be no immediate and evident change. Pupils used to praise will regard interest as praise. They are not the same, however, and in the long run the weaning of the pupil from a dependent mode will be more easily accomplished. Also, once the teacher's sapiential authority is no longer seen as carrying a moral element (as does structural authority), and the attention is firmly along the line SM rather than TS, then observations about correctness are less dangerous.

My position is that the response to mathematics teaching is as much emotional as cognitive. The most serious failures to learn are through emotional blockages, usually brought about by the teacher. Moving attention to the student's involvement with mathematics, rather than with the teacher, does not eliminate emotional factors. But the most negative effects, deriving from adverse judgments, will be avoided, and the pleasure at solving a problem will become an internal satisfaction, rather than a dependence on another's approval.

To sum up: Offering praise enhances the authority relationship and the dependence of those taught on the teacher. The positive emotional effects of an informed interest in what the pupil does, be it correct or incorrect, are less dependence inducing and lead more directly to educational advance.

# Section Three

## Emotional Considerations

# Chapter Eleven
## Emotional Responses

It has been a useful discipline to try to confine the issue of emotional responses to the specific reaction "panic," but we shall need to follow lines reaching beyond this. It is characteristic of this sort of work that any answers reached only open up more questions. On some of these we can make some clear statements; others need much more study, and some ideas may be regarded as highly speculative flights of imagination. The reader may decide which of the following sections fall into which category. The points discussed in this chapter may seem rather disjointed but they do form some sort of pattern. The chapter forms a fairly consecutive and cohesive whole, though each section could be read separately and could stand on its own to make its particular point.

## Asking Questions

The obvious way to find out whether someone has learned something is to ask questions about it. This is standard and largely unchallenged practice in many classrooms, but is worth trying to empathize with those at the receiving end and thereby recognize certain problems. There is no suggestion in what follows that any of the reactions to questioning I describe are universal, but neither are they unique to the particular people who comment. It would certainly be wrong to draw any implication that we should not ask questions, but we should recognize some possible consequences of doing so.

In the early preschool experience of many children, questions are mainly accusatory. "What are you doing out there?" is not a question to obtain information, but an implied demand that whatever the child is doing, he or she had better stop! Likewise, "Why did you do that?" is often rhetorical and a prelude to some form of punishment.

It is not difficult to see why many people view questions as hostile, for in adult life too this may be a correct interpretation. The mildest-mannered inquiry at a ticket office as to whether there have been any train cancellations may make the clerk bristle in preparation for (further) attacks.

Questioning can be strongly linked in some cases with authority relationships. The *right* to ask a certain type of question is often assumed to lie with the person of higher rank, and, as in the classroom, one's answer will lead to being *judged*. This can create quite serious tensions: "I always sat at the back of the class and prayed that I wouldn't be asked a question. There's a dim recollection of some pain associated with being asked a question, but it's too deep to come to mind."

A person in authority may welcome questions, provided they are couched in a suitably respectful and information-seeking style. Less welcome generally are those questions that seek to challenge either behavior or knowledge.

In the classroom the commonest response to being asked a question may be embarrassment, deriving from the exposure involved in a class situation. Perhaps many subjects permit of half-answers; in math there may be a somewhat stark presentation of right and wrong. The moments immediately after a question has been asked carry increasing anxiety for the student. Among the group with whom I worked, despite the relaxed atmosphere that developed, an occasion when I did ask a question in a fairly demanding way produced the characteristic fear and defensiveness that we need to notice and if possible avoid in the classroom.

Some questions are clearly not hostile. A teacher will often use a carefully constructed series of questions, each in small steps, to help students to reach the answer themselves. The evidence of one subject, well worth quoting at length, is that this can be intensely irritating.

**Sarah:** I'm annoyed now because you're not going to tell me. You're going to go through all the bloody —

**Laurie:** What do you mean I'm not going to tell you?

**Sarah:** You're keeping a knowledge to yourself until it suits you. That's the feeling I get when you don't tell me what it is. You're presented with a problem. This bod knows the answer, whoever he bloody is, and he's not going to tell you till he's good and ready.

**Laurie:** So if I tell you the answer is $A + 3$?

**Sarah:** Then I can work. Then I can work and see. But you see, it's like any child, you see, we've got to go through all the bloody rigmarole and then they are going to tell you when it suits them.

**Laurie:** The intention is to get you to see it.

**Sarah:** I know. I know what the intention is and I'm telling you what the emotional feeling is. And I think with children...sod the explanation. Just tell me what it is. Don't play games with me.

It may be that this is an unusual or extreme reaction. It is certainly expressed in a highly articulate and forceful way which we are unlikely to hear in the classroom, but we do need to consider whether it might be felt, even if not expressed. The feeling of being driven unwillingly, like a sheep into a pen, is not a happy one, nor is the condescension implicit in the teacher's attitude.

Sarah comments again in a slightly different direction on the same approach: "It is interesting, this taking-through business, because the people who do it believe they are achieving something, because each step they question has been answered, but the subjects are not necessarily putting the steps together. At the end they still don't see the overall thing.

Another style of question used by many teachers is of the "Do you see that?" or "Do you understand?" type. Often these seem designed to encourage positive answers, which when given relieve both teacher and taught of the embarrassment of exploring whether anything actually is understood. Too often a response that the student does *not* understand only leads to the question "What don't you understand?" — and that can be very deep water indeed. Detail can be cleared up, but all too often the overall understanding, mentioned in the last quotation, cannot easily be tackled.

Another feature of this situation is a social one. One person in a group that has a certain amount of work to do (and teachers nearly all emphasize time pressures) cannot regularly hold up the group. It is only with difficulty that members of the experimental group have adjusted to the fact that the answer to "Do you understand?" must be genuine, and that if the answer is "No," everyone must stop and work at the business of achieving understanding for that person. It apparently results in a very slow rate of progress, but in the long run this may prove not to be so.

By no means everyone feels upset at being asked questions. For those who know the answers it may be an entirely pleasurable experience; but not all of us are going to know the answers all the time. The contention is merely that there is a higher emotional charge to asking questions than many teachers accept. If this is agreed, what courses of action can we offer by way of solution?

Much may flow simply from an increased awareness on the part of the teacher. Experienced teachers sense feeling quite as strongly as the purely cognitive response, and once their attention is directed sufficiently to observing reactions to questions, they will themselves adjust intuitively. It is possible though to make explicit some steps that can be recommended.

Questions in the main should be designed so that there is a high probability that they can be answered. It makes progress slow, and one must avoid, for reasons just explained, a whole series directed at one person. But properly structured sequences of questions, asked fairly quickly of a lot of different students, could have the wholly desirable effect of keeping everyone awake, while minimizing stress. There is, after all, much to be said for an interrogative approach, despite the difficulties.

The matter of delay after a question has been asked is very important. Silence is not easily tolerated by the person who has the task of breaking it with a sensible response. Most teachers realize this — or at least feel the need to break the silence themselves if it is too long. If it is left, the student, who already feels exposed, finds anxiety increasing to a degree that certainly inhibits an answer that is a genuine part of a discussion. The teacher may directly seek to relieve tension, in this case heavily imposed by time, by saying "Take your time" or "Don't rush at it." If the general atmosphere of the class is hardworking but unhurried (these are not in the least incompatible), this might be enough, but further intervention with extra information may be necessary. Sometimes, it may have to be left, but always with an assurance that it doesn't matter, that we'll try to look at it another way, or that it will be returned to later. At least for some people, it is necessary that their failure to answer is not interpreted in a disapproving manner. This may to some seem unnecessarily "soft" in approach; it is true that it is right only at certain times with certain people, but perhaps more than many teachers think. The evidence given by my subjects must not obscure the basic premise that *some degree of pressure is appropriate.* The avoidance of emotional blockages does *not* lie in a totally laissez-faire approach.

Questions are easier to handle if we feel that the answers we give will be treated with respect. As a general guideline, all answers should be regarded as of interest. This is reasonably obvious since there are clearly more teaching points to be made with wrong answers than with right ones. An experienced teacher is not likely to receive a series of answers without discussion until he or she gets the right one, and then stop; though this is a common fault early in a teaching career.

Much but not all of the tension derives from the exposing effect of questions asked in a class situation. Individual questioning of a more private nature is more easily handled. Classes conducted on an individualized basis are therefore much easier for the students in some ways; they are not subjected to "open" questioning, and indeed the burden of asking questions is to a large extent passed to them. There is some evidence that the situation may become *too* easy; the pace slackens, and even where the teacher has good control it is not easy to urge everyone on. As indicated, some pressure is needed.

The point about students asking questions is most important; it is more important that they should be able to frame proper questions than to answer them, and a well-thought-out question will usually contain the seeds of the answer. The ability to formulate a question properly is not widespread; it is an important language facility as well as being valuable in understanding new ideas. Anyone who has attended a magistrate's court will have seen the difficulty an average defendant has in framing a question. People find it relatively easy to speak in narrative form and recount how different it was in fact from the way the policeman says it was, but to ask the policeman a question is another matter.

In the classroom the student faces both this difficulty and the problem of knowing enough about the material to construct a question. Properly seen, mathematics is a subject in which exploration can take place, and the more the student asks questions, the better. This is presumably not confined to math.

A more recessive, moderator-like role for the teacher is also frequently espoused. This restriction certainly places more responsibility on students to express views and to pose questions to other students. This is a natural reaction from the very heavily teacher-directed approach, with information and questions flowing almost entirely from the teacher. It does, however, raise central issues about the role of the teacher.

One last style might be discussed. A certain well-known figure in mathematical education regularly refuses to answer questions and bounces them back. "I'm not here to answer questions," he claims. There is a lot to be said for this. In a one-on-one talk it may be inappropriate and annoy the questioner; but the general principle, that many questions could do with more exploration by the questioner, is sound. Classes well adjusted to the notion that they are expected both to raise questions and then pursue them can be a pleasure to watch. The teacher's role is more subtle but remains very important; the responsibility remains to provide material from which questions will arise.

We need, then, to think about asking questions. We need to recognize both their value and the tensions they may create in some people. There are ways to retain their value and to minimize their more negative effects.

# Goals and Feelings
_____●

We have assumed that the characteristic of intelligence in an organism is the ability to make models and to plan to reach goals. Whether we see our lives as largely goal directed (as some people certainly do) or not, there is a pleasurable emotional response to approaching a goal and a negative one to moving away from it. It is useful to use the idea of an *antigoal*. This is not purely and simply failure to reach a goal, and some examples will illustrate this. If I aim to drive to the station I have a very clearly defined goal, which I have every expectation of reaching. Since the expectation is high and the task routine, I shall expect only mild satisfaction in achieving it. If through some machinations of traffic control I find myself failing to reach it, my annoyance and frustration may be great, but getting lost or being blocked off from reaching my destination were not built into the original situation as antigoals. A goal alone was anticipated. Were I to be set down in a dense forest the antigoal of remaining hopelessly lost might more easily obtrude, though the goal might still exist. Approached by three large men in a dark alley at night the threat would be the most apparent feature — and that an antigoal. Were I to escape, the feeling would be relief at avoiding an antigoal rather than satisfaction at escape. It is not always clear-cut, but the general distinction is between the existence in the environment of a desired end or of something from which we wish to escape.

The matter of whether goals or antigoals are present is not an objective one. It may often depend on the view of the participant, and it is here that we can use for the purposes of illustration the common classroom occurrence of being asked a question. We could regard this as a goal-setting situation, where the right answer is called for, and that may be the perception of most teachers. Many students, however, may see a question as a threat; they will get the wrong answer and some unpleasant emotion will be experienced. The same situation is then seen in two different ways. Some, of course, will experience both hope of success and anxiety at failure.

Those people who are generally happy about being asked questions, presumably because of an expectation of success based on past experience, may read the situation as one where the goal is dominant (see figure 11–1a). Their emotional responses to the approach of success or failure will be on the one hand satisfaction or elation and on the other frustration or disappointment. For those who see a question as a threat (see figure 11–1b) there is an antigoal (giving the wrong answer) attended by anxiety as it is approached and relief if it is avoided, either by happening to give the right answer or by some act of God, like the bell ringing. Both the disappointment of the generally suc-

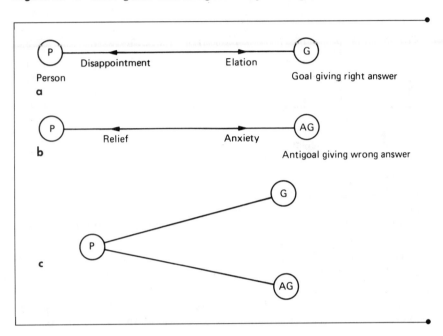

**Figure 11-1**   How goals and antigoals may be experienced

cessful person and the relief of the unsuccessful may be accompanied by surprise (an unfulfilled expectation). So we have two possible paths that may be experienced (see figure 11-1c), each yielding different emotional responses.

The problem in changing the attitudes of people who have developed a great distaste for maths is that the best we can achieve initially through success is *relief* at avoiding an antigoal. Both Lynn and Sarah, after each success, would feel relief that it was over and say, "That's enough for now—I've done that for you." Relief, although in some ways resembling pleasure, has one important difference—it is not an experience that we seek to repeat, since it obviously involves suffering anxiety first. It is only through regular experience of elation that one can want to continue. The initial, and very daunting, task is to shift people from the antigoal avoidance course to the goal-seeking course. There is a danger even if this is achieved, for someone newly on this route will experience the emotions in an enhanced form, and if disappointment is later experienced it is very bitter. This is well illustrated by the story of a very unsuccessful experiment with the group.

The problem I set needs to be stated. It is one produced by Wason.

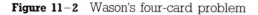

**Figure 11-2**   Wason's four-card problem

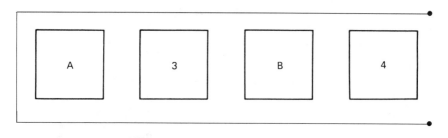

You are given four cards and told that each has a letter on one side and a number on the other (see figure 11-2). You are then given the statement: "If there is a vowel on one side there is an even number on the other." Your task is to determine whether the statement is true or false. How many, and which, cards do you need to turn over?

The problem is an interesting one and had several different purposes. My intention was to give them something involving logic rather than math and to see if they could reach internal certainty, independent of whether I agreed or not. The problem was set toward the end of one weekly session to be discussed the next week. In the event, the six members of the group arrived with three different (and certain) solutions between them. Eventually they resolved the matter by group discussion.

The distinct and important point is that Rosita who had, with reason, been gaining greatly in confidence through the sessions, had felt immensely pleased with herself, certain of her answer—and she was wrong. She reported to me the next morning that during the session and throughout the rest of the evening she had experienced feelings of bitter disappointment and deep despair, of an intensity totally out of keeping with the event. It was comparable to some of the statements of emotional response offered by Elaine. Of course, the mechanism is easy enough to see. She had felt she had moved to the upper route and the negative end of that route was extremely upsetting. Nonetheless the strength of feeling is not easy to understand, but it is necessary for us to know that it can occur. The effect may be to return the person even more firmly to the lower path or to introduce defense mechanisms of the "I don't care" variety.

So far then we can interpret certain emotional reactions in terms of our general model and use it to explain certain classroom problems. This is satisfactory in a fairly limited sense. To go beyond this we need to order and classify emotions in a manner particularly related to learning. Hume and Spinoza do not prove helpful here. There is an interesting study by Davitz (1969) in which people choose from a list of statements those appropriate to different emotions, but again the study is not related to learning difficulties. In attempting one classification of emotion that may be helpful, I am not suggesting that it therefore has more validity than others in general, but that it is directed at this specific area of learning.

# Analyzing Emotion

Consider *embarrassment*. Receiving the word generates the feeling, lightly, not at full strength, and at first without reference to experiences that had produced it, though some will soon come to mind. The feeling is highly specific — a shrinking, squirming that may manifest itself physically — and we have no doubt that what we feel is replicated in others.

Other emotions similarly seem to be quite specific. Disappointment and frustration are such feelings. I do not mean by this that only one sort of experience can produce them. There are many experiences which might produce either. But we know, clearly and without doubt, through experience, exactly what these words mean. In some sense they are as primary as the sensory experience we receive of actuality, though they reside within our inner reality.

Other emotions seem to be less specific. Fear, anxiety, elation can all be brought to the surface, with remembered physiological connections; but they seem less primary, more mixed or compounded. It may be that as in chemistry, there are elements and compounds, or perhaps it may be that the emotions can be arranged hierarchically according to complexity. Such an analysis may prove lengthy and difficult. It would be aimed not at the causes or effects, nor at the means of control and resolution of those that are in some way detrimental, but directly at the feelings themselves. It will be enough for now merely to accept that some emotions are more specific than others.

Other words perhaps generally thought of as expressing emotional states seem to have a different quality. Although the cognition may run over the events leading to disappointment (and thereby perhaps increase it) the feeling itself is in some sense "pure" emotion, and while it may seek attention from the cognition and deflect it from its proper function, it does not refer to a rational state. Yet if we take *bewilderment* or *panic*, they certainly appear to be in the emotional area, but they also express something about the cognition and indicate that it is in a state of disarray. So we shall assume that there are words that relate to the reason/emotion complex, tied together in their interactive relation.

We therefore have three categories of words to describe response: *specific emotions*, *general emotions*, and *states of mind* (for want of a better term).

**Memory and emotions.** What we have said about embarrassment illustrates a point not often made, but obvious when made explicit, that emotions can be and are recalled in the same way that events may be. At the first level, that of immediate recall, we can trigger a memory simply by a word. In the emotional area we have said that to offer the word *embarrassment* is to produce that feeling. If I were offered the word *classroom*, a visual image of the sort of classroom in which I had most often taught would spring to mind. I can see it and describe it; it is a model of actuality. It is also in the main a cognitive recall. There are emotions both pleasant and unpleasant that might accompany the picture, but it is basically perceived with the reasoning part of my mind. Here we are speaking of immediate response; the trigger mechanism seems similar but the area of the personality to which the recall is made is different. Many memories, even of an instant nature, may affect both areas, of course, though with different balance.

Let us take some memories less easy to recall, and start with an anecdote. Once at my office my young daughter (about ten) came to see me. I was just going to see a colleague whom she had met once some time before, and I asked if she remembered him. "No, but I remember I like him." This is one of the clearest statements I can imagine of the distinction I have just been making. In this instance recall touched only the emotions, and the cognitive aspects of what he looked like were not remembered.

It is tempting to suggest that the emotions are more important in the matter of memory than the store of facts and relationships of, for instance, academic learning, but this would imply some sort of measure (not easy to devise), and the matter may be largely individual. Certainly one of my subjects claims that she has extremely poor cognitive recall—though she can recognize memories when facts are put to her—but she has emotional memories that are quite clear. She also says that a close friend has the balance very much the other way and can remember detailed events easily.

Accepting both the distinction between reason and emotion, and their close interaction, this suggests that issues may be recoverable by working in either area. Events have in general a cognitive and an emotional aspect to them, though in particular cases one may be much more significant than the other. It goes even further than this, in that strong emotion experienced on a particular occasion may spill over from the event to which it properly belongs on to others, unrelated except in time. It is well known that strong feeling attached to a particular period in one's life may bring flooding back many more "rational" memories of details of that time.

A matter less easy to define is *willingness to recall*. It might be thought at first that it is easier to recall pleasurable than unpleasurable situations; this could be a matter of temperament. In fact there are often unpleasurable experiences and thoughts that return to mind unbidden and distract one from rational thought. Are we indeed *unwilling* to recall them? Certainly the strongest negative feelings, of a traumatic sort, result in memories being buried so that they may be virtually beyond recall. Other memories in that period of time may be buried with them. Among these may be pieces of learning such as math.

At first there may seem to be no good reason why this should occur in math rather than anywhere else. In part this is accepted; learning of a sort in any area may have been inhibited by unwelcome experiences that, sensibly or otherwise, have become associated with it. Nevertheless there are some special features in math. It is the major piece of school-based *developmental* learning that we all experience, and it is particularly serious if a subject so strongly structured is hindered at a particular time. It is clear that the interplay of reason, emotion, and the memory store is worthy of further investigation, and that dysfunctions in the process strongly inhibit learning.

**Ill effects and their remediation.**  Problems lying some way back in one's mathematical development are obviously difficult to resolve. Such progress as has been made with the subjects of this study has been as the result of fairly prolonged "therapy," tackling both the problem indicated here and the situations listed in chapter 7. Such work might be possible in small remedial groups in school, but the effort needed is considerable and the outcome uncertain. It would be more sensible to characterize particular things that we hope to avoid in future than to remedy the past. For this we may find a starting point in the analysis of emotion postulated at the beginning of this chapter.

We need to know what people are feeling when they are learning (or being taught!). This may seem an obvious statement, but it is perhaps less well understood by teachers of math than by those in other areas of the curriculum. Certainly, in some subjects, expression and the development of feeling are part of the material to be worked upon, and such explorations on the part of the students are encouraged. Math is regarded by many as an area where this is not the aim; it is characterized as feeding the cognitive area (which it does), and emotional responses are stifled, not dealt with. Yet as we have repeatedly seen, many adults have the very strongest (and negative) feelings about it. This contradiction must be dealt with. The teacher must recognize that some behavioral responses reflect not original sin but characteristics both of the material of mathematics and the way the teacher is teaching it. It is easy to detect serious distress; less so to spot certain discomforts in the learning of the subject, or to deduce them from the concomitant misbehaviour.

It will be easier to deal with emotions of the *specific* type, since the situations creating them are themselves more specific. More complex or generalized emotions such as anxiety may occur in such a variety of ways as to make analysis impossible. But a broad classification now begins to emerge based on the approach needed to resolve and abate the feeling.

The first class here contains those responses that may be tackled by a mainly cognitive approach. Feelings or *states of mind* such as irritation, frustration, and bewilderment, seem to be in this area. They are somewhat "inward" feelings not normally expressed by extrovert behavior. They are occasioned by failures to understand and by the individual's recognition (explicit or implicit) of that fact.

*Irritation* can arise from ideas that do not fit one's preconception or that may even seem to offend common sense. The fact that the product of two negative numbers is positive (or "a minus times a minus is a plus") many people find difficult to accept. It does not accord with our general understanding of the world, although it is in fact possible to relate it to real situations. Until this is done, however, it remains an irritant—known on another's authority to be true, but not accepted.

*Bewilderment* is a general state of disorientation quite common in math. It arises from a failure to comprehend the general area of study and to place in context the specific material being considered. The reaction "What is it all about?" is characteristic of bewilderment and related to the matter of "distancing" or understanding the general area in which one is working.

*Frustration* can arise with repeated failure in problem solving, especially when no strategy can be devised even to attack the problem.

Such emotions then arise from failure to understand that the resolution of them is cognitive. The teacher has clearly defined professional tasks: to resolve conflicts between mathematical ideas and common sense, to map out the area of study as well as deal with detail, and to teach strategies of problem solving. None of these tasks can be dismissed as easy, but they are well-known pedagogical problems. Much attention has been directed to them and, in all the mathematical topics taught, techniques have been devised. What has not been well tackled is the diagnosis of which difficulty an individual may be experiencing by examining his or her emotion.

The next broad classification is distinct. Feelings of anxiety, fear, embarrassment, and disappointment are not resolvable by purely cognitive means; they are more disturbing and do not depend just on failure to understand. It may seem an exaggeration to suggest that these feelings are regularly present in any strength in our classrooms, but many people can testify to powerful experiences of all these emotions at various times. They are not of course peculiar to math lessons, but there are particular features of math that may enhance them. There seem to be unusual opportunities for feeling diminished in math.

*Embarrassment* is readily occasioned by the exposure that a question in open class produces. Many people find themselves quite unable to utter anything, and silence is a deep source of embarrassment. The distinct feature of math is that very often no answer at all is possible.

*Disappointment* is often the result of the most well-meaning attempts. However bad one's performance in the subject has been to date, there is always hope, and a good teacher will work on this. Hope that understanding may come, and sometimes belief that it has been reached followed by an exposure that it has not in fact happened can lead to a despair out of all apparent proportion to the event.

*Anxiety* is a more general feeling, and may often relate to the presence of authority relationships. Implicit in offering an answer to someone is the belief that the person is in authority (however little the teacher may credit this!) and that one will be *judged*. This is a major (but not the single) cause of anxiety in the classroom.

This range of emotions must be dealt with by emotional and not purely cognitive means. That does not imply that one offers unspecific sympathy and pats on the head. The feelings, if they cannot be always avoided by the general ethos and atmosphere in which the classroom is conducted, must be dealt with directly by discussion. This does not mean any enmeshing of the teacher's emotions with those of the pupil. Detachment is the essence of professionalism. There are definite stages to be noted.

1. Recognizing that the problem is emotional and not resolvable by cognitive means.
2. Perceiving the emotion experienced.
3. Knowing the causes.

The resolution lies in getting the pupil to admit and discuss the feeling; and in the teacher explaining the mechanism leading to it. The student must feel understood and accepted (even if not right). It *is* a professional problem, but in the emotional area.

**Boredom: a particular problem.** Perhaps the most widespread response to math, occurring in large numbers of classrooms and throughout the population at large, is almost a nonresponse — boredom. It is difficult to categorize this as an emotion; like bewilderment and panic, it is perhaps a state of mind. Unlike the others it is unresponsive, but it is a central issue in teaching math. Some examination is needed of what is meant when someone claims to be bored. We must accept that it can be a perfectly genuine claim. If someone were to explain to me at length, and in a dogmatic and didactic fashion, something that I already knew, I would undoubtedly be bored (so I don't let it happen). The social constraints of a group visit to a place of entertainment that fails to entertain can lead to genuine boredom, again based on the lack of anything original to stimulate. Committees of all sorts are particularly effective in achieving boredom, again largely on the basis of expectations always being met.

The material within math is so varied that this situation never need occur. There is much reiteration, however, often with the same explanations. If the material is understood this is inherently boring; if it is not, the repetition of *method* becomes so familiar as to occasion genuine boredom, even if the idea is not understood.

It may be that certain areas of human knowledge and experience are simply not available to certain people. It is a commonplace that some people can derive no pleasure from music. It may be that for others (apparently with all their faculties) some quirk renders math inaccessible to them. If this be so, there is a general failure to relate over the whole area, and repeated attempts will only prove counterproductive.

Boredom can build up to large proportions. It can become a deep unwillingness, a great inertia, a feeling of "Why should I bother?" or "How does it matter to me?" Once it reaches such a level, further attempts to teach will result in sharp reactions. These suggest feelings, contained within the cotton-wool mass of boredom, but far more reactive than the person would accept. This may well imply that boredom is a defense mechanism built to guard against further unwelcome experiences of a sort previously undergone. I would speculate that this is a more usual situation than genuine boredom. Penetrating and remedying it is not likely to be easy, but given time it may be attempted.

**Summary.** There is a long way to go before we have a good understanding and analysis of the emotions that can be present in the classroom. (The experiment detailed in appendix B offers a small taste of a way forward.) In this large field, the categorization set out in table 11–1 is a very tentative beginning. It is not certain that we could accommodate all feelings into this classification; I have chosen those most commonly expressed by the subjects. Nor did the group generally agree with the placing of all those listed, but at least it is worth pursuing the basic question. Is the cure for your difficulty in math to be achieved simply through clearer explanations and new approaches to teaching the material, or does it reside in understanding your emotional response? I believe that for many the second answer is true, and that this has not in the past been understood as clearly as it might be.

## Do Emotions Show Through?

We have spoken of the need to recognize which emotions are present in a classroom situation, but are there then external manifestations that will tell us what students are feeling? Most teachers can remember situations (occurring very rarely) when someone they are teaching has become evidently very upset; but detecting lower levels of response, even if they do in fact indicate some distress, is not easy. The glazed look or the slight crinkling of the brows may be noticed, but not always precisely interpreted.

There have been fairly popular presentations of matters such as interpreting "body language"; this approach may indeed have something to offer, particularly in one-to-one encounters. Perhaps experts in the field of educational dance or movement can also tell us something

Table 11−1 Categorization of Classroom emotions

| Emotion | State of mind | Method of attack |
|---|---|---|
| Irritation<br>Frustration | | Through cognitive means and<br>increased understanding. |
| | Bewilderment | |
| Fear<br>Axiety<br>Embarrassment<br>Disappointment | | *Avoidance*: Partly through<br>organizational means — the release of<br>time pressure — concentration on<br>task and not interpersonal factors. |
| | Panic | *Resolution*: Through direct discussion<br>of feelings and not cognitive area. |
| | Boredom | Genuine — give up!<br>Defensive — try to remove the<br>protective barrier to get at the<br>underlying emotion, and deal with it<br>as suggested above. |

about what different presentations of the whole body mean about the way a person is feeling, though often it may be less specific than we would wish.

In a math lesson there is normally less freedom of movement and hence less chance of observing body posture. Most expressions of feeling must be seen through the face, therefore, and this is an avenue that we might well pursue. Here again, the drama teacher or actor may be able to tell us something. Since it has to be part of an actor's equipment to show very specific feelings (such as disappointment or embarrassment) by contrived facial movements drawn from remembered emotional experience, an actor might also be able to interpret such expressions on a face in a class.

Some of us, experienced in classroom observation but not in acting, have set ourselves this task, but have not found it easy. Math lessons tend to occur in a more formal way in secondary schools, and it seems that secondary school students, particularly in the fourth and fifth years, are adept at concealing what they feel. Perhaps this is what they have learned as part of the "hidden curriculum" of the math lesson.

Those with any experience in behavioral studies, particularly in group work, will be aware that it is possible to listen to what is being said in a class, but also possible to "tune in" to the emotional climate. This is a skill that many teachers have, though it is less strongly developed in those who adopt a heavily directive approach, and probably more widespread among teachers not in the scientific or mathematical fields.

Both at the group and individual level we need more explicit analysis of what we do. Some "natural" teachers may be very capable in the affective area, as others are in the cognitive, but they are often unwilling to analyze exactly what the skills are. It is not, however, helpful to others to say that a particular ability is something that one either has or has not. To omit any attempt to analyze such abilities would be to deny that one could learn in certain areas. What is clear is that it is a difficult area to tackle and one that needs a great deal more work.

## Emotional "Acceptability"

The stronger reactions, such as panic, seem to derive from interpersonal factors, but there are also emotional responses to the nature of the piece of math being presented. We can tie together a number of comments and attitudes here. The point has been made that irritation can result from knowledge that does not readily fit into one's present schemas. Roger put it more strongly, saying that such information could become carcinogenic to the whole body of knowledge. Among the commonly held beliefs about math is the view that it is "an affront to common sense in some of the things it asserts" (chapter 13). The prime example of this is the parroted phrase "a minus times a minus gives a plus," which moved Susan, after being logically convinced that it was so, to say, "But it's still a con!"

Another example, not previously mentioned, is from Elaine. When I discussed the angle sum of a triangle with her, she was happy when I moved the side of the triangle along "holding it at fixed angles to other sides," as in the diagram. But she still *emotionally* rejected the idea that the angle sum of the smaller triangle was the same as that of the larger. She *felt* (and that was why it was emotional) that the smaller triangle had a smaller angle sum. That is not to say that she could not perceive the logical contradiction this posed — she could and did — but it did not help her to *feel* that the sum remained fixed.

This then is almost in a different universe of discourse as far as emotional reaction is concerned, for it is not personal, it is related to the logic of the subject, and it involves us in assessing what is believed to be true at an intuitive level. Perhaps it is because our intuitions and expectations are attached to emotional forces that they have such strength.

Certainly it has been true at many stages in mathematical history that advances have been very hardly won against convictions that the new ideas were simply not true. The introduction of negative numbers in historical mathematics encountered far stronger opposition than any of my subjects offered, as did noncommutative algebra. Hamilton's realization of this latter possibility in developing quaternions involved a reversal of an emotional attitude of great strength.

Once new concepts have been grasped it is not easy to put oneself back into the position before that realization dawned, and yet this is necessary if as teachers we are to help others. A variety of cognitive approaches may help others achieve the step; if however the ideas are not emotionally acceptable in some way, the task is made much more difficult.

What has been said here relates to *reception learning*, or the acquisition of more knowledge and understanding of the subject. It is also true that in problem solving it is an important issue whether the problem can even be *accepted* and the first stage of solving a problem as described in chapter 7 achieved. This is another area in which there is much opportunity for further study.

# Chapter Twelve
## Reactions to Symbols

Much learning hinges upon the decoding of symbols, for it is mainly by means of written symbols that the knowledge the human race has accumulated is stored. Most of us learn satisfactorily to read our own language, though any of us can be confronted with passages of prose or poetry which we are able to translate from the written symbols to the spoken word, but cannot claim readily to comprehend. On the whole we remain comfortable when presented with a piece of our own written language whose symbols do not, with some reservations discussed below, occasion us disquiet. However, how are they regarded by someone who has not been able to learn to read? The range of unpleasant feelings is considerable. The mere sight of symbols of language will occasion fear, distaste, embarrassment, and shame. Anyone who has sought to teach an adult illiterate will confirm that this statement is not too strong. There is, in fact, a vicious circle whereby the emotional response to the symbols is such as to inhibit the individual's cognitive processes, which may in themselves be perfectly adequate to acquire the skill of reading. It is difficult to put oneself in the position of a nonreader (or even a prereader, though we have all passed through this stage). But once we introduce mathematical symbols, most of the population can be put precisely in this situation.

I shall describe three experiments on reactions to symbols, and I hope then to offer explanations of two of them. The first was conducted with various groups of people, most of whom knew some mathematics and had a generally positive attitude to the subject. The following statement was shown on a screen by an overhead projector:

$\phi(x)$ is continuous for $x = \xi$ if, given $\delta$, $\exists$

$\varepsilon(\delta)$ s. t. $|\phi(x) - \phi(\xi)| < \delta$ if $0 \leqslant |x - \xi| \leqslant \varepsilon(\delta)$

The assembled company was then asked to read it. "Reading" meant turning the written symbols into speech; it did not imply comprehension. No one was able even to "bark the words," let alone penetrate the meaning, so they were in the position, relative to this passage, of genuine nonreaders.

The group were asked individually to record their *emotional* response on seeing the statement. Some said "mystified" or "double-dutch," but there were a number of replies in the area of "fear," "anxiety," or "apprehension." This type of reaction, in fact, prevents people from even being willing to attempt understanding. We may assume that the symbolism of mathematics, despite its many advantages, can induce feelings inimical to learning the subject.

At this stage it is worth distinguishing between symbols and notation. By symbols I mean single characters, such as $\xi$, but by a notation I mean a grouping of such signs to convey a particular meaning. When we write (3,4) the symbols used are common ones, but the particular grouping of signs has a great deal of extra meaning (or to use a Skemp [1979] term, *interiority*) not detectable by anyone who merely knows the separate signs. The effect of this is to render the apparently commonplace rather mysterious. This is one of the features of the language of mathematics that makes it inaccessible to so many.

Returning to our first example of mathematical writing, it may be that the use of Greek letters accounts for some of the negative reactions. The second series of experiments with groups of people illustrates this, though there are other factors at work as well. When offered the suggestion "Plot the point (3,4)," most of the groups I was dealing with were happy enough, in that they understood the notation and the instruction was clear to them. Not all were sure which way one should measure the 3 and which the 4, but that was the only area of unease.

With the statement "Consider the point $(x,y)$," there was a sense of uncertainty and insecurity in some, deriving partly from the formality of the language and partly from the familiar numerals being replaced by slightly mysterious letters. Yet the statement was still on the whole acceptable.

Finally the group was presented with "Let $P(\xi,\eta)$ be such that..." Quite apart from the unfinished nature of the statement and the increased formality of style, the impact of $P(\xi,\eta)$ was such as to render extinct any hope that what followed might be understood. One person claimed that once such a statement was stated, "the shutters came down" as far as he was concerned. In part this derived from the notation of setting the letter $P$ next to the known notation, and in part from the Greek letters, which not everyone could even *say*.

Enough has perhaps been said to establish that the written language of mathematics has not only a density of meaning that renders understanding slow in coming but that the mere presentation induces an unease that will not allow one to make a start on penetrating the meaning. Those feelings laid down as a result of earlier failures in dealing with mathematical symbolism inhibit an appropriate cognitive attempt even at reading them.

There is another separate response that is of interest. In this third experiment, in which I again worked with various groups of people, another emotional response to symbols manifested itself. The evidence given so far suggests that unfamiliarity with Greek letters may be an important influence in producing negative reactions. Without refuting this, experiments in attitudes to single letters indicate that some are more acceptable than others and that certain Greek letters (such as $\alpha$ and $\rho$) are found to be pleasantly formed and quite appealing—and that this is not true of all the letters in our own alphabet. In presenting this issue to a group, I discussed the fact that some relatively unfamiliar letters, such as $\alpha$, did not seem to create unease. I then asked that the question of familiarity or frequency be cast from their minds and that each person should decide individually which lowercase letter of the English alphabet they found most *strange*. With every group of people, $q$ emerges as the easy winner. Even with groups of as many as thirty people not more than six letters were mentioned, with $x$, $z$, $k$, and $j$ appearing, but in every case with far fewer votes than $q$. It is not easy to guess what this may mean. Perhaps it is simply the shape. Certainly among the Greek letters $\xi$ is not as easy to accept as $\rho$. Why should we respond in this way, and what effect does it have on our being able to deal with mathematics? At this stage I have not even reached a hopeful speculation.

So we see that all purely cognitive approaches to the understanding of mathematical symbols and notation will be ineffective unless they recognize that an emotional dimension exists. *Acceptance* of a symbol or a notation is an emotional issue. It may come simply with usage and familiarity, but mere definition will never suffice. Even with signs to which we have become accustomed there may remain a flavor of distaste, which makes us less competent in their use.

So far the case is stated. If we now accept that there is a problem we have two things to do. The first is to give a rationale for why we should feel as these experiments indicate that we do, and the second is to suggest possible ways of preventing "symbol fear" from arising or (more difficult) remedying it when it has occurred.

Skemp (1979) has indicated that emotions may signal danger and an attack upon oneself. May we interpret the situation of reading a string of symbols in the light of this belief? Is an attack being made? Certainly all our early learning experience leads us to believe that demands are being made. When presented with symbols, including the language ones, the demand is that some response be made, such as reading them, understanding them, or working something out. The threat lies at the end of that process, because failure to satisfy the teacher's wishes can often have a negative emotional outcome! Even if in a present situation no demands are being made, our belief is that they are, based on previous experience. It may be that the symbols of mathematics make more difficult and heavier demands than other symbols. They are perhaps more functional, operational, active than the letters in which our prose is written. This is illustrated by the successive lines in which an equation is solved. So routine can become the various transpositions that we make that the symbols seem to have a life of their own in arriving at an answer. Even so, an illiterate probably does get quite strong negative charges from the printed work, and as we have said, most people are illiterate when it comes to "reading" mathematics.

The answer is not to avoid mathematical symbols in a child's earlier experience. Rather we should capitalize on situations in which the children feel a need for symbols. Several examples may illustrate this.

A group of children in one primary school were playing with some chime bars and at the end of one day had found a tune that happened to please them all. They wanted to play it the next day. No sophisticated derivation of musical notation arose, but the five chimes were labeled A, B, C, D, and E and they simply wrote down a string of letters. The beginnings of a notation, and perhaps the first step toward algebra? Certainly a code they all understood, and not discoverable from outside without further information.

A second case, again with primary children, arose in recording journeys. In going from, say, school to public library at every junction they used one of three symbols L, R, or A. A stood for *ahead*, L for *turn left*, and R for *turn right*. They worked happily with them and managed to establish how a string of symbols was transformed on the reverse journey. (Interestingly, if we introduce U for *about turn*, we have a group isomorphic to that formed by the powers of *i*.)

A last example comes from my own work with a group of experienced primary teachers. We were engaged upon an investigation of the regions created when straight lines cut each other, all in distinct points. We had arrived at a four-line configuration and at first I had labeled the spaces by a string of capital letters. This was readily accepted. Suddenly I wanted to convey the number of boundaries of a region, and whether it was open or closed, and without preparation I labeled it as shown in figure 12−1. One member said that she was totally lost. The *need* for a notation should have been raised and the group should have been asked for suggestions.

**Figure 12–1**  Unidentified and therefore confusing symbol notation

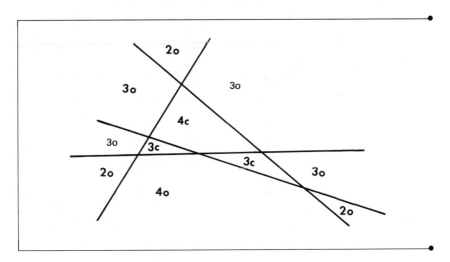

Regular sessions, then, at all stages in mathematical education, of experiencing the need for a symbol or a notation and the discussion of the notation suggested would greatly ease the situation. In most people's experience each addition to our complicated system has simply been produced like a rabbit out of a hat.

There is a related but distinct reaction to symbols that we may explain differently and perhaps remedy in other ways. A page of mathematics can induce not so much a clear and remembered threat as a feeling of insecurity, sometimes at a level that can be described as panic. Briefly, a failure to comprehend the symbols leaves the reader lost, with no sense of goals or direction, and with no sense of how to act appropriately. Panic ensues.

In general a symbol represents a concept, whereas a notation involves a whole schema lying behind it. We saw this in the plotting of a point described in various ways earlier. If the schema is not known to the student, even if the separate concepts are, he will be unable to operate. Approaches to mathematics teaching that are largely content based will attempt to develop it logically and to develop all parts of the *subject* in an ordered fashion—and this is admirable. However, more important than the schema lying within the subject (in Popper's world 3) are those in the mind of the student (world 2) (Popper 1973). We need to check with the students whether they find that the information conveyed fits what they have in their minds. An interesting experiment is to ask a number of people whether "minus times a minus is a plus" fits comfortably into their minds. When the student believes, rightly or wrongly, that the idea does fit, then and only then should you move on. It is the "emotional acceptability" of what we are told or read that is the measure of whether we can advance.

Most teachers check out whether their students understand, and by this they are addressing the *cognitive*. It is necessary to ask whether they accept—and that is *affective*. Once the strings of symbols are attached comfortably to those patterns we already have in our minds, we are secure.

Finally we should mention one counterindication to what we have said and point again to one question discussed earlier but not resolved. In the discussion on $(\xi, \eta)$ we did assume that the schema of two coordinate axes and the plotting of points were known and comfortable. Why did the use of unfamiliar symbols induce discomfort? Perhaps it is felt that they must convey something more, something mysterious—else why were such letters used? But the reason is not clear.

As for why $q$ is so "strange"—perhaps someone can help?

# Chapter Thirteen
## Demisting the Mystique

Both in the initial one-on-one interviews and throughout the group and individual work, people's views emerged concerning what math was about. How such views are formed would be a major study in itself. They are seldom explicitly transmitted (indeed *no* view of what math is about is usually transmitted), but they *are* received. In the classroom there seems to be a great deal of emphasis on progress in small areas of study, and no overall view as to what the whole discipline is about. In view of the lack of such information it is inevitable that those engaged in the study will try to form such a view. The following list of beliefs are in no special order. Some may seem to contradict others, but that is no bar to their being held at the same time, by the same person. Perhaps it is only within mathematics that we should expect such consistency!

## Attitudes toward Math

Math, then, is seen as:

1. Fixed, immutable, external, intractable, and uncreative.
2. Abstract and unrelated to reality.
3. A mystical science accessible to few.
4. A collection of rules and facts to be remembered.
5. An affront to common sense in some of the things it asserts.
6. A time test.
7. An area in which judgments not only on one's intellect but on one's personal worth will be made.
8. Concerned largely with computation.

When this list was presented at a meeting of the Institute of Mathematics and Its Applications, a member in the audience observed that he knew of some undergraduate math majors who would go along with a number of these statements! Yet we hope all these beliefs are wrong; many are positively harmful to learning the subject.

In this area there are a number of things that parents should avoid with their children, some of which derive from their own views about math and their feelings about it. It is sometimes difficult for intelligent parents who have done well in life to accept that they may not understand what is best for the their own children in a learning situation. It is foolish for teachers to believe that they are the only people who know and to gather the gowns of their own professionalism about them, but there *are* issues on which they may know and the parent may not. It would be wise for parents to test their own attitudes to math against the list — and to think about the result. If, for instance, you believe that computation is central and that speed is essential, please have a care! However well equipped you may be in many areas, if you really don't have a feel for math, try to avoid projecting your views upon your children. That is not to say that you should not involve yourself. The most helpful thing possible for children is that parents show interest in what they are learning and that parents ask questions — not probing, but seeking to get children to explain and articulate their own understanding.

It is not only parents who may hold these beliefs. Some teachers of the subject might agree with them. Check it out with your own beliefs.

Of this list, we have discussed number 5, shall deal with number 7 shortly, and will now comment only on number 4, the view of mathematics as nothing more than a collection of rules and facts to be remembered. If one single-question test were to be applied to a group of people to discover whether they knew anything about math it would be: "Is there a lot to remember in math?"

The feature that most marks a successful practitioner of the subject in an approach to an exam is the view that in math "there is not much to revise." Something has been said of this in chapter 9, where the poor practitioner sees the problem as rote-memorizing more and more material until he is overwhelmed. So it is a critical distinction, and one deeply tied in with whether we teach for understanding or for rigid programming of standard responses.

So let us now offer another list. The previous one consists of natural views deriving from many people's experience in the classroom, but contrary views exist, which are perfectly tenable and certainly very much more productive. They are that math is:

1. Experimental, exploratory, and creative.
2. Abstract at times, but often directly related to the most practical of problems.

3. Open to all, but (as with all areas of study) to be penetrated more deeply by some than others.
4. A network of consistent relationships, easily remembered when understood.
5. Always reconcilable with the internal logic of the mind.
6. A contemplative subject requiring concentrated and undivided attention at times but almost never needing to be done in haste.
7. An area in which judgments on one's ability should carry no more weight than in other studies.
8. About relationships in general.

Anyone who believes the first list is not readily going to accept the second, and the task of shifting belief is formidable. Only through good experience in the subject can we reach the second credo.

## What Is Relevant?

A great deal of play has been made in the last few years and in various parts of the curriculum with the idea of "relevance." This means the attachment of the material of the subject to real-life situations, and concentration on material that lends itself to such interpretation. The purpose of this linkage is the assumption that the students will recognize that what they are doing is significant and will both enjoy it more and work harder.

As with most criteria for improving what goes on in the classroom it has something to be said for it. Certainly in the group we made the rather odd start on the conic sections because Roger had a practical need to make helmets. Also, the final acceptance of directed numbers came through a house purchase, in which both Susan and Barbara were involved, and this was certainly related to the physical world (world 1).

Yet in this second case we were tackling something we *needed to do* in math using a starting point in life. We were not starting from the question "What math is needed in life?" and letting that determine what is taught. It would be extremely limiting if we were to do this. Indeed, there is plenty of material that may indeed be relevant in the world but is inherently boring. The "civic arithmetic" of rates and taxes and house purchase is not in fact the high point of the mathematical year for the slower groups in the fourth and fifth years!

Some material that has no apparent relevance in the world may attract and interest students. Reactions to puzzles and games are often polarized between strong likes and dislikes, but there are certainly examples of poor mathematical students working very hard at puzzles with a high mathematical content and enjoying them greatly.

We should be more aware of the value of what is happening inside the person, and, in math, whether we are helping him or her to think. It is sometimes not appreciated that this is an end in itself. In educating people we are trying to develop their general abilities in order that they may readily adapt to the various specific practical needs they may then meet. There is value in relating work at times to practical situations, but the real test is whether it fits patterns already in the mind. Some matters of an undoubtedly practical nature are inherently boring and others, totally detached from actuality, may catch the interest and fire the imagination. "It's what has connections for you," as was quoted before. Learning something that makes sense in our internal world is always satisfying. We often reject material that we cannot attach to anything inside. The test in the terms we used earlier is its acceptability into world 2, not its applicability in world 1.

## Math and Moral Worth

Characteristic of many of those who spoke to me was a feeling that their inability to do math was in some way shameful; they felt personally diminished by it. The failure therefore struck at *their worth as a person*. Once stated as baldly as this the evident unreason is very apparent, yet it is easy to understand how they have been driven to accept it.

Listen to the following statement:

> Nevertheless, the feeling of inadequacy, once it emerges from its burrow, is hard to kill or to drive back underground. It worms its way into your consciousness in the middle of the night, and obstinately refuses to listen to reason. An irrational inner voice says: "If I am no good at batting, painting, etc., then I am no good as a person." This argument is crazy, but creepy, in that if a person allows it to insinuate itself into his mind its presence there will make him both worse as a performer and weaker as a person. The defect in character does not lie in batting badly, but in believing that batting badly is proof of a character defect. There is certainly no need for failure in one's specialist role to affect one's efficiency as a captain, unless one allows it to. (Brearley 1979)

This brilliantly perceptive observation by Mike Brearley, the England cricket captain, points up quite sharply the unfairness with which failure in some particular skill attracts adverse *moral* judgments.

At the time he had lost a Test Match (the only defeat of his captaincy) and his batting left something to be desired at that level. Surely the only justification for personal attacks would be laziness or lack of thought about his cricket, or perhaps if he had been bribed by the other side. (Interestingly enough the distinctions between acts and intent is regularly made in law, where crimes of a moral nature, such as dishonesty, must involve intent.) In some senses it is understandable that people attack the England cricket captain, for they do not regard him as a person, but only as a captain and a batsman. These two features *are* his persona for many cricket partisans, and if he fails on either it *is* his character that is seen at fault, for it is a paper person that has been constructed. His position is very exposed and many feel entitled to make judgments on him. We have arrived back at elements that many feel about the situation in the math classroom.

The teacher exercises a very proper structural authority in controlling behavior in the classroom and is entitled to make moral judgments about actions that impede the task of learning, in which all are engaged. But this is too often carried over into whether students can actually *do* the math. It happens, of course, not only in math; but the status of this subject, the clarity of correctness or incorrectness in answers, and the terms *right* and *wrong* with their unfortunate moral connotations, all combine to make the situation in math more stressful than elsewhere. So failure to get the right answers is somehow seen as *morally* wrong, as in Brearley's failure with the bat.

Naturally, all we learn and know becomes part of us; in that sense our knowledge of math is part of our personas. If that knowledge is inadequate, then we may feel we are under attack as human beings. Certainly the school is an institution dedicated to the belief that knowledge is something all its students should have.

There is a slight digression we might pursue on the question of knowledge being a part of us. Many parents, employers, and the mass media express great anger at what they see as lack of computational skills in the present young (this is ill founded, but that is a line we shall not follow). What angers them most, however, is any suggestion that those routines, which they themselves established, are not as important as once they were. *A part of themselves is under attack.* Their anger is directed both at mathematical educators and at the pocket calculators that do the task with such contemptuous speed. It is not easy to distinguish the areas of personality in which a challenge represents a personal attack from those less central areas in which criticism does not imply any defect of character.

There is a widespread failure in educational institutions to distinguish between those areas in which moral values are involved and those in which we are concerned purely with learning (albeit broadly contained in the pastoral and academic structure). Students are constantly praised or criticized for their performance in learning, not for the efforts they make.

It goes even deeper than this. The institution regards it as *creditable* to be "intelligent" (using that term in the sense of intelligence tests). Within the curriculum the subject in which this "intelligence" is most necessary and manifest is thought to be mathematics. Those of us who were fortunate to be able at math were, from the primary stage, judged to be intelligent and were then praised for it! This was very ego building but totally unacceptable as a moral premise. It was also relatively few who were thus praised. All those who regularly got much less than all of the work right were found wanting — and inevitably this was most of the population.

We thus have a subject, the content of which is not concerned with moral values (even its propositions are not true or false but simply consistent or inconsistent), and yet around it and around our ability to do it is woven a false web of myth that imposes feelings of doubt and insecurity and raises questions of personal worth.

# Symbols

The difficulty the group had in distinguishing between $x = 2$ and $2x$ raises the question of exactly what symbols are. This issue extends far beyond mathematical symbols to the whole question of written and spoken language, but there are particular problems in math.

The idea or concept of addition arises perfectly rationally. If two of us join three other people the idea of addition is unambiguous. We write $2 + 3 = 5$, and by means of a string of symbols represent what has happened. The symbol + seems simple and concise. Yet problems soon arise. When we deal with fractions we need considerable modifications of the process, and hence a reinterpretation of the symbol. The difficulty increases with vectors, when we want to "add" two miles north to three miles east and find that it is certainly not five miles anywhere.

One of the main problems in dealing with simple permutations and combinations (say in the football pools) is when exactly the numbers need to be added and when they need to be multiplied. One could argue that if you were not always certain, you had not firmly grasped the concept of addition. Even worse is the notion of "add" as used in everyday speech. "Add the yolks of three eggs and then stir" may not have quite the same meaning as +! The symbol may have more in it than at first appears.

Modern teaching aims at an understanding of concepts at a level appropriate for the individual, and would seek to establish this understanding as well as the routines of operation.

Concepts are formed in world 2 by delta 2 (see figure 13−1). They may originate in the actual world or may be developed within the

**Figure 13–1**  Relationship between concepts and symbols

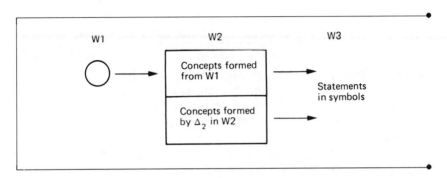

mind. Statements made and uttered into world 3 may be expressed in symbols representing these concepts. A cat exists in world 1. In my mind I have a general idea of *cat* and can recognize a large number of animals of different colors as being cats. I can also utter the word "cat" or write it down in symbols. These may be quite different in different languages. Fortunately in math the symbols used are international.

This distinction between concepts and symbols is very important. In an energetic discussion I had with Richard Skemp on this topic he asked and answered the question. "What are the operands of math?" (That is, what does it work with?) His answer was, "The hidden operand is the concept and the overt operand the symbols."

This thought has very important consequences for the classroom and has crystallized for me what is wrong in much of the teaching, particularly in secondary schools. I have often watched a teacher, with sound control, a lively manner, excellent relationships with the class, and a clear unhesitating presentation — and wondered what was wrong. I then saw that there was no discussion of concepts, and yet something was being described. It was the behavior of the symbols. The sort of thing I have heard is as follows:

> Here's our equation:
> $$3x - 6 = 14 - 2x$$
> Take the $-6$ to the other side and it becomes $+6$
> $$3x = 20 - 2x$$
> Now bring the $-2x$ over and it becomes $+2x$.
> $$3x + 2x = 20$$
> The $3x$ and the $2x$ give $5x$
> $$5x = 20$$

Now the 5 multiplies the left-hand side so it must divide the right-hand side when we take it over; so we get

$$x = 20 \div 5$$
$$x = 4$$

It gets the right answer, but it treats the symbols as if they have a life of their own, together with certain behavioral characteristics. The teacher is talking about what the symbols are doing, not what the operation is about and the concepts on which it is based. It treats the symbols *as if they were in world 1 rather than in world 3*. This is dangerous view of the subject and one that is widely conveyed explicitly or implicitly.

It is necessary, however, to make a distinction between the initial learning process, which is what we are at present concerned with, and the way the material is dealt with by someone competent in the subject. When I in fact solve an equation of the sort given above, the processes described are those that I in fact go through. I do change the sign when I change the side, and I operate largely automatically. The justification is that I do know why it works like that, and it is now for me a dead part of the subject, which I am willing to treat by routine. Yet I would not be psychologically able to do it if I did not know that it *was* justifiable. It might suffice that I knew just that and could not even recall the underlying reasons; the knowledge would fit and not be uncomfortable. It may be that some people do not feel this concern about rules without reason, but I doubt it. If any do, then they have been badly taught.

Symbols in math do have an odd power of their own at the higher levels. Treating them as having certain behavioral characteristics can lead on to new and important ideas. There is a telling phrase of Gödel's where he deals with strings of symbols "drained of meaning" (Shanker 1988). Here they are deliberately detached from the underlying concept. Symbols can also be allowed to carry forward ideas to reach unsuspected conclusions. These, however, must be reinterpreted in conceptual terms. They must not remain permanently detached.

The role of symbols generally is therefore important in our thought processes. There are those working in the language field who believe concepts cannot form without symbols — the symbols of language. Unless we stretch the idea of language to a point where it is identified with thought and the statement becomes tautological, this cannot be accepted. What can be accepted is that the symbols stabilize concepts and allow them to be thought about more concisely. They have a most important function in building up our schemas, and the work of delta 2 in so doing is greatly facilitated by their use. The ability to use symbols is another characteristic of human beings; the difference in our capacity to that of other animals is so marked as to be one of quality rather than quantity.

## Links with Freudian Theory

Our present theory is concerned with emotional response to learning; it suffices if it can help us interpret and improve classroom work. Certain Freudian interpretations were suggested in chapter 7 but it was made clear that that was not the underlying theory on which this work is based. It may be that the present model will not match with Freud's, but it would be pleasing if at least it were not incompatible. So we must seek some pointers and, briefly, raise some questions.

The combined activities of delta 1, delta 2, and the emotions can work toward general personal development. The ability to cope with an extended domain is a growth in the ego, and to be desired. As Skemp (1979) expresses it: "There's that which corresponds to the enlargement of the ego, in its best form, where freely and cheerfully one receives communication from others because they will enlarge one's comprehension."

On the other hand, the wrong sort of authority projected by the teacher has a quite different result:

> If one feels a teacher to be in a position of *power* then one alters bits of one's inner reality so that one can behave in ways acceptable or even pleasing to the structural authority of the teacher. This is not an enlargement of the ego, but of the super-ego which by presenting an accurate model of the authority enables you to behave in ways pleasing to it or demanded by it. It is pro-survival but is not enlarging of one's own inner reality. It is done at the expense of it.

Our thinking does not then conflict with ideas of the ego and superego. Nor, since we have indicated that delta 1 reacts to instinctual drives from the emotions, does it conflict with the id. We have paid little attention to this only in that we are at present concerned with cognitive activities, which are not exactly those of the id.

But there is a problem. How does delta 3 fit into the picture, accepting only the basic Freudian concepts? It is this problem that makes the definition of delta 3 more tentative than our earlier deltas, yet we need to use the idea if we are to suggest any form of self-help in shifting our attitudes to those matters that create anxiety for us. We have assumed that the operand of delta 3 is the delta 1, delta 2, emotions system, and that it therefore observes upon behavior and thinking. It may assert priorities. At this stage it therefore has a remarkable similarity to the superego, though the latter's assertion of priorities is in forbidding things to be done or thought about. We have seen delta 3 as cool, detached, and the seat of wisdom and judgment. The superego is certainly judgmental, but is none of the other things. Yet it *is* another voice in the mind, and both delta 3 and the superego are authority figures in the mind. Is it feasible to speculate that the image of authority built in the mind at an early age may in fact develop so as to become supportive rather than punitive? As we develop in confidence and take authority within ourselves do we in fact develop our superego into something rather else?

Certainly, both with the group and with the individual subjects the regular acceptance of moving into discussion of how their thoughts and emotions were working proved of great benefit. In a sense, this was encouraging the use of delta 3. It may well be that this is what is happening during psychoanalysis.

## Nonpanic

There is another phenomenon that it would be satisfying to explain, though it does not seem to occur in the educational process. That is the experience we have all had of a sudden calmness and enhanced ability to cope when in certain difficult circumstances such as going down a steep hill without brakes. The model suggests that difficulties arise when delta 1 and delta 2 both seek to work on the same problem at the same time, and that a flicker between them produces the paralytic form of panic, with the two locked together, uncertain which should operate. The feeling of calm and of everything slowing down is obviously connected with physiological changes. In terms of our model, we can only suggest that delta 2 somehow gains direct access to the sensorimotor system and plans and acts at the same time. Certainly the conflict is somehow resolved. The slowing down may be accounted for by the difference in "internal" time and that of world 1. Our world 2 thoughts certainly move faster than world 1. If delta 2 is permitted to operate in world 1, then it would find it slow. The reaction does not seem to be under our control, however, and depends partly on chemical changes not as yet dictated at will. It is therefore outside the realm of this particular study. But it would help if it did fit.

## Sex Differentiation in Mathematical Ability

Theories abound as to why more advanced classes in math seem to have many more male students than female. It has become a contentious issue as far as some feminists are concerned (Tobias 1978), and we should perhaps tackle this point first. The standpoint adopted later in this chapter indicates that no special virtue should be attached to ability in math, so in the unlikely event of its being established that men were better at math for some physiological reason, it would be no cause for rejoicing among male chauvinists. Before picking up some of the pointers that this study has afforded, let us examine some common ideas.

The cultures in the centuries during which math has developed have been male dominated and the creative work has been done largely by men. If therefore there were basic genetic differences in the brains of men and women (differences, not superiorities or inferiorities), then it might well be that such material created by mankind (world 3) would fit men's minds more readily than women's, because it had been uttered by men. The emancipation of women in academic learning has not advanced sufficiently to state categorically that their powers are no different from men's in this respect, but the evidence is growing that this is so. Math, however, is the study on which there is probably least evidence. So at first sight it seems a possible standpoint.

The next point is cultural, not genetic. It is suggested that there can be no essential difference in the brains of men and women, and that different abilities develop and different choices are made because of roles thrust upon them. There is no lack of evidence that different roles *are* thrust upon them, and from a very early age. Boys' toys and girls' toys are different in most families, there are different expectations in behavioral terms, and it is assumed that different things will interest them. Certainly this sort of environmental influence will create differences. This might be most marked in subjects such as physical science and engineering, for there is much more encouragement for boys to learn how mechanical and electrical things work than there is for girls.

If we accord a major role to such influences, then we must accept that they operate from early on. If we believe them to affect girls' performance in math, we should expect to find evidence of this at an early stage — and we do not. At the age of eleven, results are very comparable among boys and girls. It is during secondary school that the position shifts.

Various reasons are offered for this. It is sometimes said that single-sex schools heavily emphasize orientation toward certain subjects, and this may be so. It is also said that more math teachers are men, and that girls have fewer teachers of their own sex to offer them a favorable image of a woman interested in math. Yet I know of a two-tier mixed comprehensive where women are in charge of math in both sections, where the upper school has only one male math teacher out of five (and he fairly junior), and where the boys and girls have been in coeducational classes since they were five—and yet in sixth form math courses there is regularly a heavy preponderance of boys over girls. It may be that the cultural pressures eventually affect them, even if it has not happened at eleven.

Tobias (1978) claims that in the United States, with its highly elective system within the school, girls are consistently advised to pursue studies that mean they have by high school graduation taken far fewer math courses and are therefore unable to compete with men. This may well be so there, but experience in Britain does not support the view. Math is seldom optional up to the school-leaving age, and girls have the same background as boys when they choose their sixth-year courses. It is just possible that the choices they make in the fourth year give them a balance that leads them away from math in the sixth, but they do not do less math before then.

From the study of these relatively few adults we have discussed in this book, it would be unwise to offer any interpretations intended other than as starting points to another investigation. To come to any conclusions, even tentative ones, there would need to be some solid statistical evidence.

One possible explanation involves attitudes to authority, and we have constantly mentioned the role that authority figures may have in inducing negative feelings. If therefore we could claim that the sexes may, particularly when young, react differently to authority, either from some inbuilt difference or more likely from cultural expectations that they would do so, it would offer some basis for a guess. Certainly boys are expected, and therefore perhaps encouraged, to be more venturesome, and to have the limits of what is permitted set wider than is the case for girls. Girls are generally more protected and expected to be more obedient. Boys are not only allowed to stray further but even if firmly handled are expected to challenge that authority. So it would not be unreasonable to expect the sexes to react differently to manifestations of authority in the teaching of math.

Two further possibilities arise from this. The first is that such strongly negative feelings some of my subjects acquired may be more widespread among women, because they arise from a fear of authority. We do not even know if the panic we investigated is more widespread among women or only more honestly admitted by them. Again, we need statistics, but there is a question here to examine, and a reason for doing so arises from a central theme of this book. The other possibility is that, by its nature, mathematics appears early on as a set of neat and well-controlled situations, with rules that may be memorized and applied. Someone brought up to obey rather than to challenge rules may find that acceptable. Yet one cannot progress far in math before one has to "accommodate" rather than "assimilate" (in Piaget's terms).

Perhaps we should use a term more in current vogue — "restructure." Not only do we learn new things, but we have to *alter* some of the things previously learned. Later in mathematics new developments may occur only through challenging rules that have great authority (such as commutativity). Such a challenge to authority, represented in this case by mathematical rules, may be more acceptable to boys, because of the particular attitudes they are encouraged to have, than to most girls. This particular speculation may be even more difficult to explore than the last.

In any case the issue of sex differentiation in mathematical ability is certainly an interesting one, and there seems to be no satisfying explanation as yet.

# Section Four

## Additional
## Group Sessions

# Chapter Fourteen
# Textured Learning

Textured learning is a teaching style that originated in the group sessions described earlier. Since then I have refined and developed it, using it with a variety of groups of different ages and abilities in mathematics.

## The ILEA Team

The most substantial work was done within the Inner London Education Authority mathematics team, which, as staff inspector, I headed. The whole team consisted, at full strength, of four other inspectors, four wardens of mathematics centers, their deputies, five primary advisory teachers, thirty primary consultants, and a number of people working on special projects. They provided a strong force for affecting the schools, mostly by direct intervention. The primary consultant role may need some explanation. These people, generally in their thirties, with ten to fifteen years successful experience in the classroom, were allocated to schools on a one-day-a-week basis. Thus an individual would have four schools and would visit each once a week on a fixed day. An essential and very important part of the program, however, was their own day for in-service education, which took place every Friday.

The team split most weeks, a quarter of them being based at each of the four centers. The first hour and a quarter for every group consisted of learning some mathematics. Many of the team members were not particularly well qualified in mathematics, though expert teachers in other ways, so deepening their understanding of the mathematics they would be teaching was a high priority. From September 1978 through to July 1984 (despite my retirement from my post in

December 1981), I taught one section of the team for this first session on Fridays.

# The Nature of Textured Learning

In most classrooms, teachers see their role as explaining, as clearly as possible, the mathematics that is to be understood. This is so widely accepted that the statement of it may seem to many to be a platitude. Yet the perception is in fact a very limited one.

Textured learning is an attempt to extend the notion of teaching and learning well beyond this particular perception. It is based upon discussion. The conduct of this discussion will be dealt with shortly; it is the content that leads to the description of the technique as "textured learning." We define six areas that are permitted in the discussions. In one sense this limits, though the bounds are wide, but in fact, it points to the need to enter areas that are not common in mathematics classrooms. The six aspects are these:

1. Mathematics.
2. How we think about it.
3. How we feel about it.
4. Interpersonal reactions.
5. Observations on the way the group is functioning.
6. Pedagogical issues applicable elsewhere.

The interweaving of these six elements provides the "texture." Each element needs further explanation and illustration.

**The mathematics.** The "leader" of the group (a concept to be considered later) normally defines the general area of mathematics to be looked at. Ideally, from there, the leader should direct as little as possible where the group moves. In one group, I defined the area as geometry and introduced the elements as points, lines, and planes. The work rapidly went in directions I could not have forecast, and questions arose concerning configurations of lines that I could not answer. In another, a discussion of measure led us into difficulties of a philosophical nature that remained unresolved.

An implication of this freedom is that the leader must not prepare in advance, other than in the most sketchy of fashions, and must not have aims and expectations of where the work will lead.

**How we think about math.** The second strand of the texture is effectively a study of cognitive psychology, conducted while the mathematics is being worked upon. This involves the participants in the task of reflection at the same time as actively thinking—a skill that has to be developed with practice.

For instance, in mental work on a three-by-three-by-three cube, the members of the group described what their internal visual display was like (their "skull cinema" as J. W. Dunne once put it). There were surprising variations. Mostly they had large spaces inside their minds (bigger than their heads!) though the size of objects in it, such as the cube, was sometimes undefined. The edges of their minds were fuzzy (as were some of the minds themselves), generally in black or gray, and the object they were asked to look at in their mind might be placed on a sort of stage, or simply float. The object itself might be made of wood or plastic, it might be solid or skeletal, it might be colored or not.

On another occasion they described how they got started on the "milk-crate" problem. This has been used widely with young children and asks you to put eighteen milk bottles in a crate with twenty-four spaces (four spaces wide by six spaces long) so that every row and column has an even number of bottles in it. They had moved from random trial and error, through a search for other problems that reminded them of it, to the technique of considering the complementary question. By this I mean they looked at the spaces and not the bottles. Such general methods, often new to them, permanently enhanced their weaponry for tackling not only the present problem, but future ones.

**How we feel about math.** Integrating an affective dimension into the teaching of mathematics is not easy, yet it is the main need to which my studies point. The heavy anxiety experienced by many of the subjects I have interviewed had been built up through emotional pressures over the years whose effects were not seen at the time. Textured learning permits discussion of these pressures as they arise. We cannot expect that it will resolve the accumulated concerns of many years, but it might at least permit effective progress in the topics of the moment.

The third strand is the first that tackles this aspect. Members of the group are expected to comment on their emotional reactions and to analyze why they occur. They discuss whether and why they are interested or bored with the material we are working on. They have explored a general fear of figures (or more often, of other symbols) and explained strong reactions to situations in terms of emotional echoes of earlier experiences. Positive feelings have also been described with great clarity, such as the feeling of "rightness" and deep satisfaction when something has been grasped in reception learning, or the elation experienced as the way through a difficult problem is glimpsed. In our way forward we clarify these issues as we advance.

**Interpersonal reactions.**   Interpersonal reactions, sometimes of a violent nature, are characteristic of behavior in small groups; this is peculiarly so when they are leaderless and have the sole task of examining these reactions. I have reservations about these methods in group dynamics, at one time widely used in sensitization and management training. Some use of them is appropriate when they form part of a more complex process such as textured learning. I was always prepared that animosities would develop (they did) and that we would be able to explore what was happening (which did not occur as much as I would have liked). There were, however, at least two occasions when hostility to a "know-it-all" was evinced quite strongly and discussed in some depth.

**How the group is functioning.**   Anger between two people and the development of a more general turbulence in the group are distinct but related. This turbulence has manifested itself strongly on occasion and is part of the fifth strand. One such occasion arose in an early group, where a strongly competitive atmosphere developed. Over some weeks, this made some people more and more angry, until the tension was resolved with explosive force by one member, who was then strongly supported by another. I think this was a powerful learning experience for all of us. My problem as the situation built up was to avoid intervention and to restrain myself from helping those who were clearly finding the pressure unacceptable. My expectation, happily realized, was that they would eventually handle it to much better effect themselves, rather than have an authority figure resolve it.

As is natural, a main focus of attack is the leader of the group. There was one very powerful attack on my being manipulative; other attacks expressed frustration at my not teaching them "properly." These led into important explorations of general attitudes to authority figures, and by decentering, to the feelings they attract in their own work roles, in which they are often the authority figures. Not all the observations about the behavior of the group were in the affective area. There were many times when we commented as to whether the style was becoming didactic, whether we were spending a long time on one strand, or whether we were working as a group, in pairs, or singly.

Some observations supported the analysis of Bion (1961), which saw the group mood as being "dependent," "pairing," or in a state of "fight" or "flight." Generally, however, the textured learning groups, not being of the same kind as those studied by Bion, did not have such clearly defined moods.

**Other pedagogical issues.**  Because the ILEA groups were teachers, regular observers of classroom practice, and experienced in-service trainers, the sixth element of the texture was of special interest. The group was an analogue of the classroom, though there were many obvious differences. Happenings in the group, such as the reaction to someone who appeared "too" clever, and the constant concern not to hold others up, are often mirrored in classrooms. Their occurrence and the feelings experienced were directly relevant.

It is easy to argue in cool terms against, for instance, competition in the classroom. It is much more profitable to do so after some traumatic personal experience of it; the group sessions provided these uncomfortable experiences, but then offered the chance to reflect upon them.

There were no rules about how much or little time we stayed on each strand. There were times when some members were obviously bored by staying too long in one area, though this was a personal matter; some preferred mathematics, others liked to pursue pyschological matters. I tried not to manage the movement from strand to strand, and to allow the group to make its own decisions, which it generally did.

These then, were the six strands of the texture, but the style and mode of working were also important.

# Making Small Groups Work

The best size for such groups is between eight and ten. Above that number, some people find it increasingly difficult to contribute. One year, circumstances led to an overly large group, with the result that one person did not speak during the whole year and became very concerned at this inability. I felt that such matters should be picked up on by the other members and worked through, but this one was not. The existence of a leader meant that the members of the group did not always learn to take full responsibility for happenings or for their own learning.

Below about seven or eight, the feeling of being a group does not develop, and people either pair or work by themselves.

The members sat at tables in a circle, with exactly the number of chairs to match the full membership. If someone was away, a chair was left empty. There was no rule as to who sat where, though some members exercised a preference for certain positions.

Every session save the first started with us all reading the prepared notes of the last session. These were normally written by myself, though at one time members began taking turns at writing them. I stopped this when we found that two members were becoming quite neurotic at the approach of their turn. The level of stress was surprising and interesting.

The notes were an important feature of the whole style. They represented a policy of always reflecting on what we had done, while not prescribing what we were going to do. In them I wrote my perceptions of what happened last time. There was always a seating plan, which helped us remember, notes on the mathematics discussed, and my observations of behavior. I did not claim that these were accurate — they were merely what I thought. No corrections were made; they were not minutes. If objections were made (and this was frequent), these appeared the next week in the account of the session. At one time I was strongly challenged on the policy of observing adversely on people; it was felt I could say it but not write it down.

The notes were always the starting point for the week's session and established the continuity that I felt important. They were confidential, to be read only by group members; I typed them myself. If someone was away the notes were put aside for them.

**Confidentiality.**   Confidentiality was a complex issue. It was linked to the notion of trust. In work that on occasion touches upon deep emotions, it is clear that statements must not only be treated with respect, but cannot be referred to outside. This did not, of course, apply to the mathematics involved; the ILEA groups were a testing and development ground for material that would then be used in the classroom. I also felt that if they were unhappy about what was happening, the proper place to say so was in the group; I did not like comments fed back from outside sources as to what members felt. Yet the method provokes interest and comment, and naturally people discussed it at home.

How trusting people were is hard to assess. Certainly admissions of incompetence were made more often than is customary. Some powerful emotions were expressed and were clearly genuine; others were certainly concealed. There were some matters that I hoped would be brought out that were not. Not surprisingly, people were not frank in their views of each other's behavior. Their need to work together during the rest of the week made this difficult, but greater openness might have been valuable at times.

**Boundaries.** Textured learning groups need clear boundaries. The weekly session is an event encapsulated and set off from the rest of the week. That is not to say it is more important, simply that it is separate. The issues of the last paragraph in part explain this. The group, to function at its best, needs to be conscious of its own existence; this is enhanced by practices emphasizing its separateness and completeness.

The two most emphatic boundaries were of time and of "closure." It is important to start and finish very promptly. During that time the group takes priority over other calls upon one's time. One does not casually arrive late because one has been trying to catch up on phone calls. It is also important that no one enters the session for any purpose. This is not just because the boundaries of the group need to be respected, but at times the thinking can be intense and interruptions should not be tolerated. Though this rule caused groups to be invested with a sense of mystery by those outside, the reasons are simple and of clear educational purpose.

The sharp finish sometimes meant that we broke off in the middle of an intriguing problem. This offends some educational thinking, but I welcome it. An unresolved problem lingers in the mind and helps the continuity that the sharp boundaries might militate against.

Regularity was seen by all who have participated in these groups as very necessary. A gap of once a week and a session of one and a quarter hours seems to work well. The style is demanding, and a higher frequency might be too much for some to handle.

Long-term membership is necessary to settle in. New members had to be absorbed into groups as they were appointed to the team, and said they did not feel adjusted to the style for upwards of a term. A sensible time for a satisfactory exploration of a piece of work was a year.

We seldom used concrete materials, though there was no bar to doing so, and people moved off to find materials if they so wished. This again is in conflict with modern attitudes, but there is a clear rationale. Concrete work can help to make the mathematics simpler, but that was not my aim. My aim was to encourage thinking and to change attitude. Developing the mind and seeking clear ways to demonstrate things may not go hand-in-hand.

The main mode in textured learning is discussion, and people speak when moved to do so. In the groups near the optimum size this resulted in a reasonable balance of input. In larger groups, the talk often became dominated by a few, and I wished this had been more strongly commented on by others. On some occasions sexist issues were pursued, in particular the extent of male contributions or the deference it was (falsely) claimed that I accorded them!

There should be no time pressure. The intention is that those who do not understand should be willing to hold up proceedings until they do. All the work that led to this book showed that time pressure was one of the most powerful influences that led to people's disaffection with mathematics. Some group members fully accepted this principle, yet for many there remained a great unwillingness to "hold others up." Many people believe everyone else understands better than they do. On occasions when a member did stop us and ask for further discussion, the relief on the part of others was evident. On one occasion a member said that she had not fully grasped something, but was confident she would when she thought about it later and would prefer to move on. This was accepted.

In the ILEA groups, I asked that when someone did not understand and said so, those who did understand should move from the student role to the teaching one, which should be natural for them.

In these groups it was also emphasized that we had no specific goal, that there was nowhere we had to reach. We merely sought to deepen our understanding of an area of mathematics. Hence we did not need to move on all the time. Yet some perceived a social pressure to do so. Questions were raised as to whether this apparently relaxed pace could be transferred to the classroom, for it is the general view of teachers that they have to rush to get through any syllabus. I later discuss working under examination pressure in a local school.

**Leadership.**   The question of leadership in such a group is interesting. It is important that the rules described are understood and followed. So someone needs to understand them and their purpose at the start and persuade everyone to adopt them. Once established, they are not seen as confining—rather the reverse. They soon cease to be thought about. This chairperson role can recede as the group progresses.

It is necessary that someone is well acquainted with the mathematics and is confident in moving into unfamiliar work. In one year, I established a group with one person who had this role, but was not otherwise seen as a leader; this was very successful, though I could not tell how far the style altered, since I could not watch it. It also helps that some present have a grasp of group dynamics, but this need not reside in any particular person. Ideally the group should take full responsibility for its own learning. My presence may have been helpful in some ways but it acted against this aim.

Learning to work in such a way takes time and a high level of commitment. This needs agreement or the discipline of a job. It may be preferable to have no examination pressure, but in fact that may improve commitment to some extent, provided time pressures do not obtrude into the group.

# Modifying the Method

Modifications of the full textured learning method were used with some other groups, and this threw up various matters of interest. It chanced that I was asked to help out at my wife's school when a teacher left suddenly. My wife was then the head of the mathematics department at a large mixed comprehensive school. She was also pursuing a master's degree for which she was writing a thesis on discussion methods in teaching. So the concatenation of circumstances was quite remarkable.

I took over a group of nine sixteen-year-olds who were working toward an examination, half of which was mechanics. There were two girls and nine boys. Unlike the ILEA group, this involved school children with an examination objective and would therefore properly test my assertions that one does not need to hurry to cover a syllabus. They were an able group who had all passed O level, but some were not strong candidates for the next examination, A level. This examination is taken after two more years, but an examination of easier standard, covering most of the concepts, was proposed for them after one year.

The school agreed to my terms of having two sessions of seventy minutes, each run on the closure principle. I did in fact relax this by having my wife present on occasion. I used her room, and she sometimes stayed, apparently doing work of her own (as the students supposed). On one occasion one of her colleagues attended under a vow of silence, which, owing to her personality, she found quite irksome!

I did not mention the term *textured learning*. I merely said that I proposed to work in a way they might not find familiar, and they must trust me. I preserved the idea that I purveyed very little information, to such a degree that late in the sessions, one boy turned to ask me a question and then looked back at his colleagues and said, "Silly of me, *he's* not going to tell me."

We waited until we had worked things out; there was no sense of hurry. The colleague who attended a session found herself bursting to tell them what they were trying to find out, but ended up, when they had worked it out for themselves, greatly impressed with my restraint.

Closure was maintained; people respected the note on the door saying no one should enter. On one occasion the deputy head looked in and then withdrew with a "Sorry" when I glared. A member of the group remarked, "That's the first time I've heard her say that." Time boundaries were sometimes a problem; they were respectful of them, but if delayed by their last teacher, could do little about it.

There were elements missing. I did not feel it right to allow emotional tensions to arise in the way I hoped they would in other groups. Yet there was a good deal of spirited interaction between them. Though the sixth element, pedagogical relevance, was not dealt with as it was among the professionals, there were times when I explained my thinking about teaching and about what I was doing. It was the mathematics I left to them. On one occasion, for example, I started by asking what happened when a stone fell from a window. We talked and talked; I asked occasional questions but would not answer theirs. They argued with each other, but eventually they arrived at the equations for constant acceleration. In another session, one of the girls was convinced of an answer to an issue and all the others thought she was wrong and had another result. She argued, she explained on the board, she appealed to me to help. I refused. Then came the crack in the wall. One of the boys saw that she was right, and gradually they all gave in. It was a joy to watch! Another time I drew a wheel rolling, without slipping, along a road, with its center traveling at 30 miles per hour. I asked how fast the top and the bottom were traveling. After some time one boy said that the bottom point was stationary. Then he laughed the idea away. None followed it, but a long time later they all came to see it was so. As a final example, we once had a long discussion as to the effect of a constant force on two different-size people (me and a small lad). They linked this with the fact that we both fell at the same rate on Earth. This they saw as a paradox, but its resolution led to a great clarification of the distinction between weight and mass.

I enjoyed the group, and I think they enjoyed our sessions. My wife was teaching them pure mathematics and said, on one occasion, "Think." "I thought we only had to do that in Applied" came the answer!

In the time I had, about two-thirds of a year, we covered all the essential concepts for the whole two-year course. They performed well in the examination they took after one year, though little could be drawn from this since it covered both pure math and applied math. However, it made me totally confident that even under examination pressure, there was absolutely no question that my refusal to be hurried could be maintained to no detriment of the students, and also that placing the responsibility of learning on the students was completely capable of success.

Also with an eye partly on my wife's dissertation, I took another group of twelve first-year pupils (eleven-year-olds). We talked exclusively about the basic concepts in geometry. We spent a great deal of time examining exactly what they meant by *line*. This was partly stimulated by some work done by another friend who examined the terms used in a number of standard textbooks to see if they were well defined. She found, without the authors presumably being aware, that *line* was used in seven distinct ways.

I taught these students for only four sessions of about an hour and a quarter, and they introduced me to many new notions. Not until these sessions had I realized quite how important the preconceptions that people bring to any study could be. Children of this age can teach us a great deal if we allow them to.

I will briefly describe two other short-term experiments, before looking at a direct attack on anxiety in the next chapter.

Morley College is an institution connected with the Old Vic theatre. It runs a large variety of courses. Through a contact there, I suggested that they advertize a course for seven or eight people who knew very little math but would like to look at some. I ran this course for about ten evening sessions of two hours each. We worked each session as a group, engaged in group discussion, but, their commitments being what they were, regular attendance was not achieved, which took away from the full group experience. Assessing such a purely recreational activity is not possible, but all expressed pleasure at what we did, and we had a grand end-of-term party at the house of one of them.

Finally, I conducted one session of one hour with a class of eight- and nine-year-olds in a primary school. I spun a wheel-shaped disk of some thickness about its axis and posed the question of how they would tell someone outside the room how it was placed and what it was doing. Among the results they got, without my telling them, was that it occupied the same space all the time it was spinning, that every point on it was doing "something the same," and that a point halfway in was moving half as fast as a point on the edge. I reckon that is pretty smart!

Textured learning is the first attempt to integrate so many aspects of what goes on in the classroom. There have of course been many studies that discuss elements other than content and learning theory. But it is the recognition that so many elements can be regarded as an overt rather than a hidden part of the curriculum that is new.

# Chapter Fifteen

## Interlude in Cambridge

Madingley Hall is an Elizabethan mansion some three miles from Cambridge. It houses the Cambridge University Department of Extra-Mural Studies, which provides a wide range of cultural offerings in some style, with good food and graced by charming surroundings. I first came to know it while attending a course for magistrates. Next I went on to two courses on philosophy and began to feel at home in the place. Noticing that there was little in the area of mathematics or science, I suggested to those in charge, that I run a course entitled "Overcoming the Fear of Mathematics." They agreed.

In doing this I was returning after some years to my original problem. I hoped to attract people even more afraid and with even less to their credit than those with whom I originally dealt. Since I was using group methods, I did not want more than about nine people. In contracting to provide an experience, it is important that the terms are spelled out as precisely as possible. Parodoxically, this is particularly so when the sessions may appear to be unstructured. We therefore advertised in the following terms:

> Some people's feelings about mathematics seem quite irrationally strong, and this is not surprising since feelings are not rational. In my researches adults have told me that experiences in the mathematics classroom have left them permanently diminished. They report emotional responses that, presented coldly, appear absurd, but when heard repeatedly from a number of subjects are totally compelling.
>
> The study of, and experiences in, small groups have led me to adopt modified techniques in this area to explore and to resolve, at least to some extent, these feelings.
>
> The sessions on this weekend will therefore be closed and sometimes intense group discussions, where we will explore these reactions, seek to analyze them, return to specific occasions in each person's past where feelings were most strong, and suggest remedies.

There will be no attempt simply to teach chunks of mathematics more expertly than before, but if a person wishes to return to a particular black dragon to try to understand both cognitive and affective aspects of the difficulty, we may well do so.

There will be no predetermined structure of the sessions, which may develop as you decide, but a small amount of material may be presented, to relieve the demanding nature that discussions can sometimes take.

The advertisement attracted eight people. In a sense I was disappointed that no more than this wished to come, but against that it was the exact number that I had wanted for a group. At the last moment one dropped out and we were eight including myself, three men, and five women. The fact that the sexes were reasonably balanced was very pleasing.

The course was held October 20−22, 1989. What follows are some notes recording things I remember and impressions I had. They are not, and do not pretend to be, minutes. A number of remembered things may well appear in the wrong order, and the impressions I give are simply my perceptions.

## The Participants

The seven people in the group were all highly articulate and *intelligent*, insofar as we can attach an everyday meaning to that word. They all (except perhaps John) arrived feeling that they would know much less math than anyone else and were concerned that I might be dismayed at the depth of their ignorance. Depth of ignorance was what I was looking for! A brief description of each follows.

**John:** *A man rather older than the rest of us; older even than me! Quietly spoken to such a degree that Julie commented that he was difficult to hear. I agreed; he was surprised. He had obviously pursued math to a higher level than the others, but said he could not do simple calculations.*

**Chris:** *A carpenter who came off as warm and confident. He was very sure within his realm of knowledge but was conscious that he had drawn boundaries beyond which he did not go; now, as he approached fifty, he wanted to extend himself.*

**Pam:** *A teacher, strong and forceful, angry that certain areas of possible interest had been cut off by a deep fear of anything mathematical. Historian.*

**Cynthia:** *Calm, contained, and assured. It was not easy to see how concerned she was at her deficiency in math. But the evident delight* *that showed when a step forward was taken assured me that there were things she wished to resolve.*

**Julie:** *A bright and lively teacher of five-to-seven-year-olds a bit guilty lest she lead her charges astray in math. Became very confident in describing and resolving her problems in understanding, after initially crumbling if asked a question.*

**Sally:** *Exhibited very strong reactions to any math, and wanted us to go on and leave her when she stuck. Never! She couldn't get back to any of the origins of the fear. Most of school blanked out.*

**Jill:** *Taught poor readers, so had a link with this. At first I could tell little from the minimal reaction she showed to issues, but when asked, she responded and showed real pleasure when she had seen something new.*

The social climate of the group was very friendly and trusting. Setting any exploration in the form of a small group can lead to tensions and clashes, for which I was prepared, but none came. On the whole this was helpful. If the exploration gets slow and sticky, an explosion may be a necessary catharsis, but at no time did I feel that we were running out of steam. In fact, on a number of occasions I suggested something they might want to do or see and was delayed considerably by their wishing to follow other lines; this was very pleasing to me.

I wrote the notes on a particular session at some point rather soon afterward. Drawing the plan of names helped me remember, as I could see in my mind people saying things. I then wrote my notes up in a (slightly) more coherent form days later. I started this rewriting on Monday afternoon, when the events of the weekend were turning over, pleasurably, in my mind.


# Friday Evening

We introduced ourselves. (Our seating configuration around the table is shown in figure 15–1.) John spoke first, saying he had taken math some long way (this introduced shudders in others) but that he could not add up figures. He described how he tried to add up the nine numbers on each column of a golf scorecard, looking for pairs of numbers that made ten, then losing track and finding himself adding two sevens. He had to avoid others seeing what he was doing. I asked for the feeling he had, and he hesitated. Pam and Julie both said, "Shame." Pam gave a vivid picture of the shame and panic she could feel, with it rising up, apparently from her feet.

**Figure 15-1**  Friday evening seating configuration

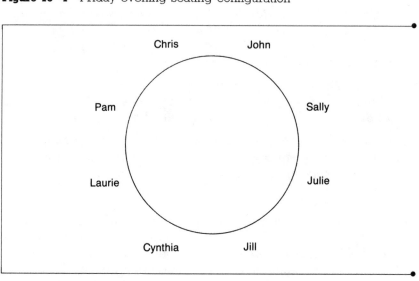

Chris worked in the construction industry, and he described how he avoided calculations. When he had to place trusses at equal spaces over a distance, he guessed a distance and put them all at this equal distance; he then saw how large the last gap was. On the basis of this he revised the equal spaces downwards or upwards, and gradually arrived at a satisfactory distance by successive approximations. He did not feel he could do the division sum, dividing the whole distance by the number of gaps needed.

Cynthia described her school days and her inability to relate math to the world, as well as her need for absolutely concrete things. She was quite unwilling in class ever to ask when she did not understand. She believed the teachers knew everything but could not explain things, and she did not appreciate that others could not understand. I told her that they did not understand in the proper depth, and that their failure to be able to respond to questions derived from their consciousness of their weak grasp and their unwillingness to expose it. The teachers too were in fear. These two issues — whether math did or even should relate to the world or be "useful" in a worldly sense, and the sapiential authority of the teacher — were returned to often.

Sally worked in a tax office and could not do figures (I always suspected they chose innumerates for these jobs!). She described graphically her problems with her time sheets.

Jill spoke of her father's attitude to her not understanding. She said there was some resolution of her feelings toward her parents, but they remain significant. This was the first of several concerns about parents, who are clearly additional (and more important) authority figures, though teachers are a bit more likely to be at the back of fears about math. I told them that since math is a highly structured subject it provides a "ladder to the past" (see chapter 7). Therefore, when I ask about learning certain multiplication tables I am talking to a child of the age when that was learned; I can see people adopting a "pupil posture" appropriate to a child in junior school.

We talked of attitudes to authority. How rule bound are they? John and Cynthia seemed most prorule. Jill maintained she was anarchic and went against accepted practice with her class. I said that if the primary aim, the learning of the students, is achieved, that overrides all issues of the rules by which the institute is conducted.

Sally described how there were always set rules for how everything was done in her office, and if another way was suggested, it could not be considered. Pam talked about the rules in math, which she thinks of as logical but does not see the reason. She gave long division as an example. Shall I teach them long division? What a challenge!

I do not remember how it came up, but I asked Julie how long it would take to travel 90 miles going 30 miles per hour. She cowered away and crumbled up. Laurie is the greatest fear inducer in the business! But a bit later she came back to say that if she was traveling in her car and saw that somewhere was 30 miles away, she would reason that it would take an hour if she were going 30 miles per hour; if she were in fact going 70 (not more, of course, in the presence of a magistrate), it would take her a lot less time, maybe about half an hour. I said that this sort of understanding was conceptual, and a better start than learning a rule about which number you divided by which. The others answered the question correctly, and I asked whether they had twinges of anxiety as they started, followed by instant relief. But they had not been asked directly and pointedly by me as Julie had.

Pam remembered learning tables by rote, and she still had to go through each from the bottom up to get the answer she wanted. John thought learning tables by rote was a good thing.

Next session I want to look at shame and authority, and further explore with Julie her understanding of speed, etc.

# Saturday Morning

Only the third session and already we had changed our seats around

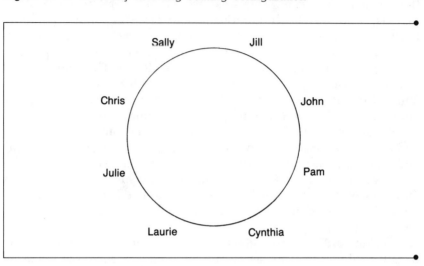

**Figure 15–2**  Saturday morning seating configuration

(see figure 15–2). In small-group work I might have examined the significance of seat shifting, but I didn't here.

We got into fractions and decimals. At some stage we had actually to do a little bit of math to see how much it hurts. Cynthia said that she had had it made very clear by her father why ⅛ was bigger than ¹⁄₁₆. He demonstrated this up cutting by a potato, and the concrete nature of this was firmly convincing. Chris also was very sure because of using a ruler with those measurements on it (if they had been other fractions than those on a ruler would he have known?).

I asked Cynthia whether she felt sure enough to defend her knowledge against anyone who attacked it. She was confident of it. I described what I call the "authority of the subject." This means that some facts that are simply true within the subject of mathematics can be seen by people and made their own, and do not depend on the say-so of a teacher. There is an emotional acceptance that something is so.

I asked whether anyone else could tell about a breakthrough to understanding. John mentioned logs and seeing them in relation to a graph. Pam could not take graphs, this high-powered stuff was a bit much for her. Jill related how a substitute teacher had made geometry clear, and how a practical approach to Pythagoras allowed her to understand it. Sally had quite recently learned her alphabet (she was a great reader), and the fact that she could do this and the benefits arising from it were very pleasing to her. She had never learned her tables. Her husband goes on at her about its being easy, and she must do it...but he doesn't read anything! It is absolutely no use telling someone they must be able to do something.

We got onto reading a bit. Not being able to read is the worst intellectual disability. Chris had recently taken up a lot of reading; he asked how to cope with interruptions. I answered that in reading or doing a math problem, I felt that breaking off would be all right, but that interrupting a session such as ours would be very difficult. They all agreed that no one should be allowed to come in. But we needed rests in thinking. A weekend like this was hard work for them (and me) and I found one and a half hours a bit long.

I had mentioned that I was going to show them a bit of Elaine on video, but they had taken control of the pace and were deciding what they would discuss and were prepared to stop me — great. But we did show the bit in which she described her feelings about math. They mostly related strongly to it. She again mentioned shame and I tried to get a further description of what shame feels like. Pam said it was not achieving the norms of one's society or one's own expectations. John asked if guilt and shame were different. We decided they were not. Why is panic often described as "rising"? I went back to an earlier physical demonstration by Pam. She now said it really did not start at the feet but in the guts. But although we said something of causes we did not get very far with deeper descriptions.

I got them to take in the word "embarrassment" and describe its "taste." We got something of the squirming, hiding-away flavor. We also talked about the attitudes Elaine described her teachers showing — the "jollying along" and the condescension. Do most teachers do these very negative things? Do those of us who teach now do so?

I asked them to take the number 7 in their heads. Then they described it. All envisioned the symbol for 7 and did not try to represent the number. If you try with kids you may get groups of seven objects. Also with literate people, I sometimes get the written word "seven." Another useful picture is the position on a ruler, showing where it lies between 0 and 10. I tried to get a picture of the inside of their minds. The only 7 that was at all different was Sally's, whose numeral was a bright red. I said that the numeral 7 is the way we write what we see with a collection of seven things, but that the actual number 7 is abstract. Comparing it with *cat*, we have a symbol representing the real animal, but there is not really an abstract idea involved. So they agreed that the difference between number and numeral is clear, that they had never seen it before, and that it was important.

Back to decimals. Pam used the image "the curtain comes down" when confronted with them. She could not see which is bigger, 0.534

or 0.25. Various people tried to help, even comparing the decimals with ½ and ¼. So I gave a purely instrumental explanation: this enables you to do something without understanding why. I compared it with alphabetical ordering. Look at the first number of each decimal. If one is bigger then that number is bigger. If the numbers are equal, then we compare the second numbers. It is exactly parallel to putting things in alphabetical order. Pam grasped this rapidly. I said that if something relates to a schema already present in the mind, then it is accepted easily.

What does math do for me? It enhances my mind. I do not mind whether it is "useful" or not, or whether it relates to reality. There is excitement in process. But some math can be more useful than you may think. Quadratic equations may seem a bit abstract, but they give the flight of an object thrown under gravity. Julie thought it might go straight if you threw it hard enough—it doesn't! Pam wanted to roll it along the floor. No, I meant thrown in the air. And what could be more useful than learning how to drop cannonballs on people you do not like?

# Saturday Afternoon and Evening

The seating configuration after dinner is shown in figure 15–3. Having got thoroughly into the group mode, it seemed a long time from the morning session to the late afternoon one, yet they are demanding, and to have five sessions in one day would have been a lot.

I did place value, showing how each column implied ten times that to the right and a tenth of that to the left. We compared sizes of whole numbers with no trouble. Then we moved to decimals, and Pam very rapidly saw that the process was the same. The point about decimals is that it continues the pattern of numeration for whole numbers below one. Fractions adopt a completely different system, which does not really make sense. Pam wanted to go on and add, to see that it was the same. We added 9 and 7 in the ¹⁄₁₀₀ths column and get 0.16. We saw that the 1 is ¹⁄₁₀ or ¹⁰⁄₁₀₀. Sally got lost here and wanted us to go on (avoidance tactic?). But no, we got her to see which is bigger, and the principle of carrying. General euphoria at conquering something for the first time. Julie gave an answer that I misheard and thought was wrong. She retreated and then revived as everyone put me right.

I looked at large numbers. Described how I saw a millionth of a large tennis playing area. Took ¹⁄₁₀₀₀ of the distance across by using the fact that there were 200 planks, each 6 inches wide. A fifth of a plank was just over an inch, so that was ¹⁄₁₀₀₀th of the way across.

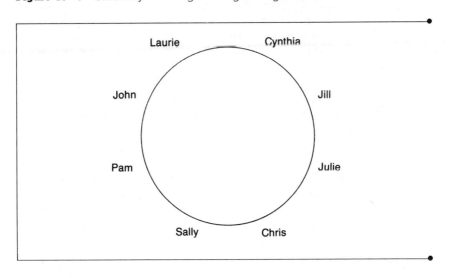

**Figure 15–3**  Saturday evening seating configuration

Since the whole area was roughly twice as long as it was wide, a millionth of the area was a piece two inches by one inch. We asked how large a case we would need for a million pound notes; they complained they no longer exist. Well...

We looked at a book with 300 words per page and 200 pages. Julie got the answer of 60,000 total words. It is worth playing with big numbers like this to get used to them, but almost no one had much conception of them.

We talked more of emotional words and their relative strengths. I did the eight questions (see appendix B) and then handed out the results from that large group at the Institute of Education. When they were doing the questions there was concern about whether they would have to hand them in. Jill was concerned that she would have to explain why she used the word. They compared what they had said with the lists from the large group, and they had found some different words. There was still lingering concern at times over whether they were getting the right(!?) answers. The answers are what they think, not what I want them to think. Pam mentioned "regret" for the first one, for that is what she felt when she left school, empathizing with the teachers. Julie gave "dismay" for one, which she did not see as very heavy. "Elation" appeared as short term compared with "satisfaction," although it is stronger.

We discussed "relief." Cynthia forced herself to do her bank statements every month; she could do them and was getting better, but it was always a relief. On the overhead projector I showed the diagrams in figure 11−1a, b, and c, with their depictions of elation when one is successful and disappointment when one is not. When it is an antigoal, something we do not want to do, we feel fear at failure and only relief at success. Elation encourages us to learn some more, but relief, though pleasurable, does not do so. I also told them of Rosita (chapter 11) and the effect of disappointment on her.

John brought up the matter of having time to do things. Although we were working hard and continously, there was no sense of rush, because I did not have somewhere I had to reach. Time pressure is the most destructive thing in learning, and the whole point of mathematics is that it should be ruminative, contemplative. Sally said that when left to herself at work, she could get something done in her own time, be confident that she would succeed, and quite enjoy doing it. Right!

Chris talked of the pressure in his school days, starting with the whistle, the lining up, the going in to school, and the harsh discipline of the classroom. I told them of the classification of authority. They had seen their teachers very strongly as both structural and sapiential authorities. Chris was coming to terms with teachers not knowing everything. From what he said I bet his teachers knew very little. A class, or society, needs rules and control, but learning needs freedom. So the two roles must be exercised by the teacher with different strengths.

We went back to the condescension of teachers and others, and the failure to understand that one might not understand. Jill spoke of her relation with her father, who did not see her difficulty. John described feelings from early childhood, of being condescended to, and of dreams of very early life.

# Sunday Morning

I did the notes on to tape when driving back on Sunday afternoon, and did not have the seating plan. I wrote them up on Tuesday morning. This lot may well contain material that in fact came earlier. As I said, the order of the notes will often be wrong.

We talked a bit about working on video. I explained that the Elaine tape had been made by me in an ILEA studio, that I knew the area I was going to cover, for I had to have the graphics prepared, but I had no idea what Elaine would say. She was very used to my way of working, however. During the program I had to follow what she was saying and keep an eye on the monitor to see the camera was right.

This is evident sometimes in the tape, where I am waiting for the camera to show what I want. But it could not be prepared, because of the need for total spontaneity.

They watched the tape, mostly very absorbed and sometimes amazed. Jill was amazed that she understood. The point made by Elaine about unresolved conflicts was taken very strongly. They were conscious of these in themselves, and cross with their teachers for leaving them.

In the tape Elaine controls me. That is the right way round. The learner should control the teacher as to rate of input. In one of my schools there had been a partially hearing unit. Here the teachers accepted the childrens' control to be sure they had heard. Every teacher should accept the control of the pupil not understanding.

The question of whether something was "perceptually evident" came up. With vertically opposite angles all accepted this. But I claimed not to see, in a naive sense, why the angle sum of a triangle is 180 degrees. Chris knew it from practice, but that was not knowing in the sense I meant. So I looked at a line crossing the shelves of a bookcase and asked if it was obvious that certain angles were equal. Julie thought they looked it and probably were. Not good enough. So Chris took over and did a wonderful job. Working with pencils, very slowly and calmly, he got Julie to see that there were eight angles, four of one size and four of another. This was a very positive experience for her but also for him. He had adopted a teacher role with a teacher, and from not seeing why someone could not see he had progressed to find the difficulty. I felt we were all achieving great things. Chris asked whether adopting the pupil role in this piece of work had evoked any unpleasant memories in Julie. But no. . . .

Julie also wanted to know why I had extended the sides of the triangle, so I went through it again on the board. We worked on how a straight line could also be an angle at 180° with Pam. We also found that she had looked at the wrong side when I had cut the corners off the triangle. With Cynthia we had a semantic discussion about the use of 90° into which we divide a right angle. It is now fixed, but the number of degrees we originally decided to use was at choice and arbitrary.

They wanted to do long division. They accepted that it was a totally useless skill now, but learning how might kill off past dragons. I looked at 1,537 divided by 29, which they thought a bit hard. First I took off 29 at a time, keeping track by tally marks how many 29s we had taken. Sally again said to go on, but she was blank and could not do subtraction, let alone long division. So I asked her the gap between 37 (in the 1,537) and 29. She guessed it might be 6. So I gave her the image of a number line, and she promptly saw it is 8.

Cynthia had been unaware, as had others, that division could be repeated subtraction. A revelation. They agreed this process would get them there, but only very tediously. So I suggested taking off lumps of 290 at a time and keeping a tally of the tens. This would in fact get us there pretty quickly. But the usual method for doing long division (which is not sacrosanct) involves taking off the largest chunk you can each time. Here we took off five lots of 290 (which is fifty lots of 29), leaving ourselves with 87. This is $3 \times 29$, so our answer was 53. Cynthia asked what happens with remainders. If the large number were 1,539, we would simply get 53 and remainder 2.

Amazingly, everyone seemed to see it and Sally was particularly pleased. She said she definitely understood, but might not be able to do it, because of the subtraction problem. I suggested she work at it, entirely by herself and quite without hurry, until she was successful.

General advice: take a piece of math you can not do and work at it, unhurriedly, by yourself. Expect it to take a long time. Always make the understanding your own. Do not rely on the say-so of a teacher. Elaine said that generations of math teachers had said that there are 180° in a triangle but she does not initially credit it. As the Buddha says, "Accept nothing on hearsay. Do not believe in traditions because they are old, or in anything on the mere authority of a teacher, myself or any other."

We had several goes during the weekend on whether mathematical ability was innate. We decided yes, to some extent. There will always be some people better at it than others. But with all of the participants, a major part of the trouble was what had been done to them by parents or teachers.

We went back to the "usefulness" issue. I wrote the square numbers on the board. Jill said, "So what?" Pam said she remembered her husband having to use square roots in his work. I looked at the gaps, which are the odd numbers. Was that interesting? Not sure. We looked at arranging counters in rectangular shapes. If you cannot, the number is prime. Cynthia defined them as having no other number (leaving aside 1) that goes exactly into them. Pam thought this definition much easier. It depends on the balance between spatial and numeric in an individual's mind. To see both gives deeper understanding. Is the question whether primes go on for ever interesting? Chris did not think so, others did in varying degree. I did the proof and was not sure of its accessibility.

As we ended Cynthia said that when she came she could not see how we could spend all this time on the topic of fear of math. Now she did not see when it would stop.

# Participants' Responses

It is a principle of my way of working not to continue discussions outside the group sessions. The rationale is that it is a group experience and that all of the group should be present at all of the event. It would also be rather too much of a good thing to exceed seven ninety-minute sessions. The notion of an encapsulated experience is important.

However, there was one thing of interest outside the sessions. One of the other courses during the weekend was on poetry. The members were all keen to know what we were doing. The nature of group work and its stated secrecy always attract curiosity from those outside it. Several members of this other course said how much they needed just such a treatment themselves, so maybe they will be there next time.

Through my work I have become more and more concerned with the importance of reflection rather than planning. Despite being clear about the general terms of what I wanted to do, I specifically avoided building in what I wanted to achieve at each stage. I followed what the group wanted to discuss, though I did firmly hold it within the stated terms. At the beginning of each session I asked that we reflect on the last session. But perhaps most important of all was the long-term reflection. As I said in the notes to the group, I was most interested in a report after two or three months. After some pursuit, all replied at some length on their memories and their assessment of the weekend. The letters I received were warm and chatty, but here I reproduce extracts related most directly to the work we did. They are a selection, but I have not simply recorded the positive things said — it is just that nearly all of it was positive!

## John

*"The weekend was my first experience of group working. Sitting with a group of agreeable people and just talking things out seemed a great luxury to me. I felt much like an old duck going into water for the first time."*

*"One weekend is not enough. One needs at least another to look at the questions which come to mind after."*

## Chris

*"What a hornet's nest was stirred up in me when we were dealing with the problem about triangles."*

"...then coming to realize and understand how Julie felt not being able to do it gave me a very warm feeling inside, reversing roles [teacher-pupil]..."

"How tearful and sorry for myself I felt when I realized that the short time I had spent with Julie over the triangle problem was time that I would have liked for myself as a lad—just a few moments of someone's time to give me some help."

"I have become aware that when I go into a shop now I will sort out the right money if I have it. I would always have given a large coin or a note and received change. I have lost a fear of being wrong over numbers."

### Cynthia

"I do, in fact, bless you every day for holding the course and pat myself on the back for having the initiative to attend."

"These days I approach my everyday math with a lightness of spirit and confidence that I am probably as good as the next person."

### Pam

"I found the course stimulating and helpful. It helped me to change my attitude both to myself and to mathematics. I think I have managed to shed the minor but irritating feelings of inferiority I had. Looking at my abilities in a more detached manner, I have decided that I'm really not as bad as I thought I was."

### Sally

"What did I get from it? Enjoyment, relief, confidence. Your method of making sure everyone understands a concept—before moving on—is so vitally important. It was so reassuring and the complete opposite of my school experience."

"[I was able] to admit to various groups of friends just what my weekend course had been about—and I didn't feel shame or embarrassment."

"A strange confidence came from just being able to talk about it... and the knowledge that even I can improve."

### Julie

"I tried several tables in this way. I used my fingers! I felt very confident, and I was surprised how easy it was. I surprised Jill (and *myself) by saying I wanted to continue with my math. I even tackled the dreaded decimal point. Even though this was difficult I still kept going."*

*"Eddie, my husband, began to help me. After seeing it in print he stopped telling me that math is easy."*

*"The more math I have done the greater my confidence has increased. I don't give up even when it is difficult. Even getting it wrong sometimes, which used to make me stop, hasn't made any difference."*

### Jill

*"The weekend after the course I sat down for several hours and attacked the kind of sums that gave me problems at school. I have never felt so calm in my approach to 'sums.' In the past I would have struggled with my own feelings of inadequacy. Tonight I sailed through the chapters at speed, feeling genuinely confident."*

*"When I reached the 'problems' section I remembered my old feelings of fear, but did not actually experience them. . . . Gosh, after all these years of thinking I couldn't do this, to find it so easy."*

## Reflections on the Process

The conclusion is clear. People who have suffered most of their lives from a feeling of diminishment, ranging from a mild irritation to a full-blown life impediment, can be relieved of it in an intensive series of sessions such as these. The length of this therapy was not designed by myself; I simply fitted the pattern of courses run at Madingley. Yet it seemed an appropriate "dosage." I would not have liked it to be much longer, for it makes great demands on the "leader" of the group, and indeed on the members.

It is not easy to codify what was done in the sessions. I cannot supply a blueprint that allows others to do the same, but there are things that can be said. The explicit removal of the twin pressures of authority and time was essential. They then had to be brought to an angry acceptance that their condition had been caused by an authority that judged and was cross at error, together with constant demands that time conditions be met.

There is an odd paradox here. Their acceptance of these facts — that mathematics was a contemplative subject to be done at a pleasurable and leisured pace, that no one would be cross when they made mistakes — depended on my presence. They accepted that I was a greater authority than their teachers. So in part I was using authority to overcome the ill effects of previous authority figures.

One powerful therapy for participants was hearing others saying the same things that they had themselves had experienced and believed to be particular to them. Several expressed great relief on hearing a "horror" story from another's past, and matching it with their own.

The other skills involved in running such groups are those of the counselor or therapist — the need to listen very carefully, to empathize, and to feel your way into their feelings. But it needs much experience and the accumulation of anecdotal material that can be used to parallel what one is being told at the moment.

# Last Words?

Of course, they cannot be last. With much of the material toward the end of this book, mere indications are offered of where further research my take us, and there is much to be done.

Some things should and must be said, however. Many people have been made to feel guilty, embarrassed and ashamed by their experiences in their mathematics lessons. This is little short of criminal on the part of those who taught them. If you are such a person, be assured that they, not you, were at fault.

I hope that the great majority of caring, concerned teachers will, after reading this book, further enhance their awareness. In particular, may they always be on the lookout for signs of negative emotional response. I do not ask that they seek a point-by-point formula to ensure this. Awareness is all!

# Appendix A
## Problems, Puzzles, and Diversions

Various materials were referred to in the accounts of working sessions, and they are collected together here.

## A Graded Problem in the Cube

This particular series of questions was widely used to explore people's spatial perceptions. The $3 \times 3 \times 3$ cube offers the simplest model of three-dimensional space, allowing all directions to be explored in a very limited but effective manner. At many levels the answers, once seen, are such that one can be confident of their correctness. Most series of questions stopped at no. 8, but some people or groups attempted as far as no. 12. The last result, no. 14, would be beyond the capacity of many people not practiced in problem solving.

1. Visualize a cube and hold it firmly in your mind.
2. How many faces are there? (Easy for the dice player.)
3. How many corners are there?
4. How many edges are there? (The first level at which people are likely to stumble.) If people showed hesitancy about the words *faces*, *corners*, *edges*, I clarified what was meant.
5. Imagine the cube made up of 1 inch cubes and 3 inches in each direction.
6. How many small cubes are there? (Some see this immediately but others have very great difficulty. One person tried to visualize just the bottom layer and arrived at the conclusion that there were three on each of four sides, making twelve, and a good many more 'in the middle'.)
7. Paint the outside of the cube black.

8. How many of the small cubes have no paint on them?
9. Three faces painted?
10. One face painted? (Generally people found this interesting and were quite successful. Also, they were not sure it was math and showed less anxiety than with other problems.)
11. Imagine the 3-inch cube whole and undivided. How many saw cuts are needed to reduce it to 1-inch cubes?
12. Can this number be reduced by rearranging and restacking the pieces after each cut?
13. Allowing for this rearranging after each cut, how many cuts are needed for a 4-inch cube?
14. What is the general result for an $n$-inch cube?

# Wood-Block Puzzles

These puzzles were devised by a wood sculptor, Brian Willsher. His sculptures are developments of a single block of wood with sections cut and slid, offering beautiful shapes in a range of interesting woods, many being African hardwoods with strong coloring and firm textures.

The puzzles have a similar theme, being developed from a single block of wood. These particular puzzles (not sculptures) are both intriguing to work at and pleasing to the touch with their various shaped pieces. The design is simple in the extreme, enhanced by the beauty of the wood and the nature of the curves.

A rectangular block of wood is cut lengthwise in curved lines using a bandsaw (see figure A-1a). The difficulty increases greatly with the number of cuts and once the number of separate pieces exceeds one hundred the task of reassembling them becomes formidable.

Puzzles can be made with only four pieces, for very young children, but about twenty or thirty pieces provides a sensible level of challenge for most people. As with a jigsaw (and this is a three-dimensional jigsaw) trial and error alone will make the task extremely tedious. Shape recognition, matching, and pattern spotting, all activities of value in math, need to be employed.

A puzzle with fewer pieces (nine), but providing slightly more difficulty in actually fitting them together, is a cube in which the pieces resemble more closely those of a jigsaw when viewed from the side (see figure A-1b). Separated out, the pieces are weird and strongly curved, and starting on reassembly for the first time proves harder than one might expect.

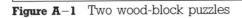

**Figure A−1**  Two wood-block puzzles

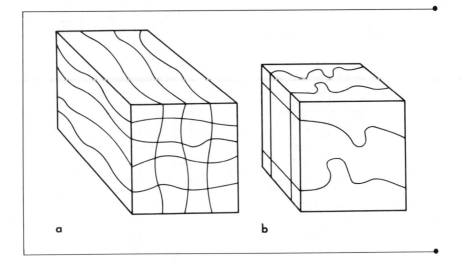

a          b

## "Passalong" Problems

I encountered sliding block problems for the first time when I was about ten. At the local toy shop I bought two, one of which I managed to solve, though the other eluded me until I was about eighteen.

My friend Warwick Sawyer, who has interested so many people in math (his best known book is *Mathematician's Delight*) told me that a series of such puzzles had been devised in the 1930s by a psychologist interested in spatial perception in children. They had been given the name "Passalong." Several are shown in figure A−2a.

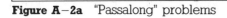

**Figure A−2a**  "Passalong" problems

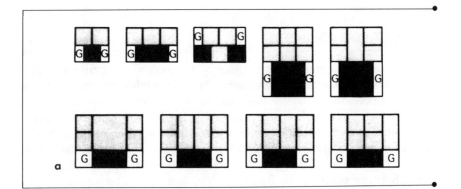

a

**Figure A–2b** "Passalong" problems

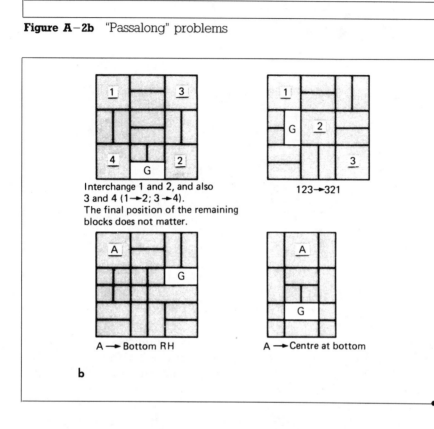

Interchange 1 and 2, and also
3 and 4 (1→2; 3→4).
The final position of the remaining
blocks does not matter.

123→321

A → Bottom RH

A → Centre at bottom

b

More complicated and sophisticated ones have been developed; L. Edward Hordern told me of several. It was these, quite hard problems involving a considerable number of moves, that I gave to Elaine. Four of these are indicated here (see figure A–2b) for those who have a taste for this sort of thing.

## De Bono Problems

Edward de Bono has been extremely productive of problems that appear to offer no real starting place. They involve a creative leap, an unusual perception that he has elaborated as "lateral thinking." The problems reproduced here are used with Dr de Bono's express agreement, and may be reproduced only on this same condition. In the diagrams each shape, can be divided into two equal halves by a line that may have angles. The two halves will be equal in size, shape and area. (See the example in figure A–3a.) Seven similar problems are

**Figure A–3a**  De Bona problem example/solution

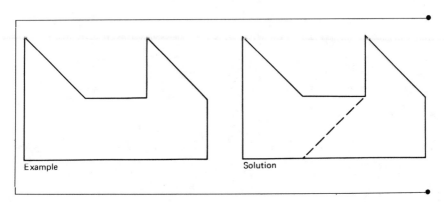

Example                                    Solution

provided in figure A–3b. These puzzles were used with some of my subjects because they involved spatial perception (at least two people · were strongly interested in art), because they did not depend on any real mathematical technique, and because once the correct answer had been found it was possible to check that they were correct without referring to anyone else. Lynn's comment, given earlier, was, "What proof have you that you are right? Oh...you have your own proof."

**Figure A–3b**  Seven de Bona problems

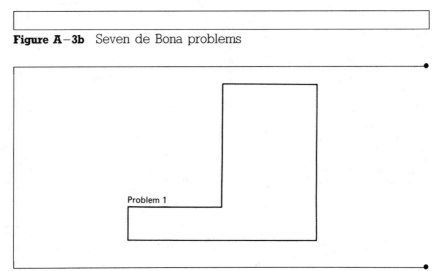

Problem 1

continued

**Figure A-3b** (continued)   Seven de Bona problems

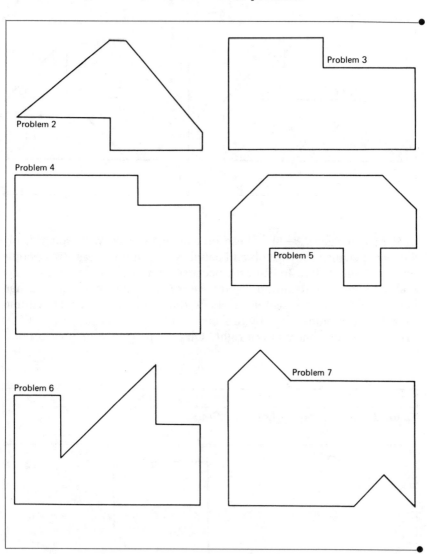

# Appendix B
## Emotional Responses in the Classroom

In chapter 11, we started on the very difficult notion of an analysis of emotional words and, presumably, states. The original objective of this book was to examine one specific reaction, panic, to find its causes and the ways to avoid it. The more general task of examining the emotional climate created in a person by certain classroom situations gives us scope for much future research.

I have now, with a number of different groups, sought to discover what a particular range of events in the classroom may generate. In giving an account of one particular experiment, I am merely sketching an idea for an approach. As I have indicated earlier, it is not my intent to seek statistical validity, for I do not consider that the areas we are discussing are ready for that level of analysis.

The material in this one experiment was gathered at a lecture I gave at the London University Institute of Education. All the various groups pursuing the year's teacher training that followed their first degree came to my talk. They were all due to teach in secondary schools (eleven-to-eighteen-year-olds). The group was atypical of the population at large since all were pursuing this Postgraduate Certificate of Education, had quite strong mathematical backgrounds, and presumably had suffered less unpleasantness than most in their own school experience.

They were asked to recall eight hypothetical situations from their school days and to respond immediately, without cognitive searching, with the single emotional word that came to them. The first two situations were general, and the remaining six tried to reflect characteristic situations.

The eight situations, with a breakdown of the responses, are presented in tables B−1 through B−8.

Table B−1

Recall the worst experience you had at school, taste the emotion, and name it.

| Female | | | | Male | | | |
|---|---|---|---|---|---|---|---|
| Panic | 5 | Belittled | 1 | Hate | 3 | Sad | 1 |
| Hate | 3 | Humiliated | 1 | Frustration | 2 | Anger | 1 |
| Shame | 2 | Worried | 1 | Fear | 1 | Helplessness | 1 |
| Fear | 2 | Inadequate | 1 | Fear/contempt | 1 | Pathetic | 1 |
| Sick | 2 | Very | | Hateful | 1 | Shame | 1 |
| Anger | 2 | uncomfortable | 1 | Injustice | 1 | | |
| Confusion | 2 | Unhappy | 1 | Boredom | 1 | | |
| Terrified | 1 | Failure | 1 | Chaos | 1 | | |
| Depression | | Embarrassed | 1 | Embarrassment | 1 | | |
| (tears) | 1 | | | Panic | 1 | | |

Table B−2

Recall a good experience.

| Female | | | | Male | | | |
|---|---|---|---|---|---|---|---|
| Elation | 4 | Enjoyment | 1 | Pride | 3 | Happy | 1 |
| Pride | 2 | Satisfaction | 1 | Excited | 3 | Valued | 1 |
| Excited | 2 | Lifted | 1 | Enlightenment | 2 | Exhilaeration | 1 |
| Exhilarated | 2 | Delighted | 1 | Elation | 2 | Pleasure | 1 |
| Self-satisfied | 2 | Exhuberance | 1 | Self-righteous | | | |
| Happiness | 2 | Chuffed (proud) | 1 | pride | 1 | | |
| Pleasure | 2 | Calm | 1 | Eureka | 1 | | |
| Bursting | | Power over | | Joy | 1 | | |
| with | | pattern | 1 | Cheerful | 1 | | |
| pleasure | 1 | Scientist | 1 | Clever/proud | 1 | | |

Table B—3

You are having a mental arithmetic test, teacher standing with a watch. He asks the fourth question and you have not done the third.

| Female | | | | Male | | | |
|---|---|---|---|---|---|---|---|
| Panic | 13 | Highly charged | 1 | Panic | 8 | Hurry | 1 |
| Terror | 3 | Angry | 1 | Anxiety | 3 | Absurd | 1 |
| Anxiety | 2 | Tense | 1 | Worried | 2 | | |
| "Oh, Shit!" | 2 | Challenge | 1 | Despair | 1 | | |
| Frustration | 2 | Bewilderment | 1 | Anger | 1 | | |
| Anguish | 1 | Lost | 1 | "Stay cool" | 1 | | |
| Grasping | 1 | | | Scared | 1 | | |

Table B—4

You have been working for some while on a math problem that is close to the limit of your competence. Then you see the way it is going to come out.

| Female | | | | Male | | | |
|---|---|---|---|---|---|---|---|
| Relief | 5 | Amazement | 1 | Relief | 3 | Good | 1 |
| Pleasure | 4 | Thrill | 1 | Euphoria | 3 | Manic | 1 |
| Joy | 3 | Excitement | 1 | Delight | 3 | | |
| Elation | 2 | Enlightenment | 1 | Elation | 2 | | |
| Great | 2 | Satisfaction | 1 | Warmth | 1 | | |
| Incredulity | 1 | "Thank you" | 1 | Pleasure | 1 | | |
| Wonderful | 1 | Happy | 1 | Wonder | 1 | | |
| Jubilation | 1 | Overwhelmed | 1 | Thrill | 1 | | |
| Bliss | 1 | | | Satisfaction | 1 | | |

Table B—5

You have been trying to understand a piece of mathematics and
have at last grasped the idea of it. (This is reception learning as
opposed to the problem solving of the last question.)

| Female | | | | Male | |
|---|---|---|---|---|---|
| Relief | 10 | Elation | 1 | Satisfaction | 8 |
| Pleasure | 3 | Pride | 1 | Relief | 5 |
| Satisfaction | 2 | Contentment | 1 | Happy | 2 |
| Calmness | 2 | Heaven | 1 | Proudly happy | 1 |
| Exhilaration | | Relaxation | 1 | Excited | 1 |
| (relief) | 1 | Triumph | 1 | Good | 1 |
| Happy | 1 | "Oh!" | 1 | "Ah yes!" | 1 |
| Good | 1 | Tired but glad | 1 | | |
| Happy/good | 1 | | | | |

Table B—6

You have done some homework to your pleasure and satisfaction,
and as the teacher starts going through it you realize you are totally
wrong.

| Female | | | | Male | | | |
|---|---|---|---|---|---|---|---|
| Embarrassment | 5 | Shattered | 1 | "Shit!" | 3 | Broken | 1 |
| Shame | 3 | Degraded | 1 | Embarrassment | 2 | Stupid | 1 |
| Disappointment | 3 | Despondent | 1 | Shame | 2 | Humiliation | 1 |
| Frustration | 2 | Inevitability | 1 | Disappointment | 2 | Deflated | 1 |
| Annoyance | 2 | Unbelief | 1 | Disbelief | 1 | | |
| Depression | 2 | Sick | 1 | Guilty/disbelief | 1 | | |
| Stupid | 1 | Upset | 1 | Self-disgust | 1 | | |
| Pissed-off | 1 | Heart sinks | 1 | Sinking | | | |
| "I don't believe | | Shock | 1 | feeling | 1 | | |
| it" | 1 | Anger | 1 | "What?" | 1 | | |
| Annoyed | 1 | | | Secretive | 1 | | |

Table B–7

The teacher hands you a wooden block puzzle, the pieces of which you have to fit together, and says that you can take as long as you like over it.

| Female | | | | | Male | | | |
|---|---|---|---|---|---|---|---|---|
| Intrigued | 3 | Fun | 1 | | Boredom | 4 | "What's the | |
| Puzzled | 2 | "OK" | 1 | | Interest | 3 | point?" | 1 |
| Interested | 2 | Contentment | 1 | | Amazement | 2 | | |
| Confusion | 2 | Bewilderment | 1 | | Puzzled | 1 | | |
| Boredom | 2 | Amazement | 1 | | "Oh, no!" | 1 | | |
| Puzzled and | | "What in the | | | Resistance | 1 | | |
| interested | 1 | world?" | 1 | | Stunned | 1 | | |
| Anticipation | | Suspicious | 1 | | Relief | 1 | | |
| (pleasurable) | 1 | Frustration | 1 | | Irritation | 1 | | |
| Pleased | 1 | Anguish | 1 | | Suspicious | 1 | | |
| Excitement | 1 | "Do I have to?" | 1 | | "What"? | 1 | | |
| Delighted | 1 | Negative | 1 | | Insulted | 1 | | |

Table B–8

The teacher returns after a short while and says "Haven't you done it yet?"

| Female | | | | | Male | | | |
|---|---|---|---|---|---|---|---|---|
| Annoyance | 5 | "It's hard" | 1 | | Annoyance | 3 | "Yes" | 1 |
| Anger | 3 | Justified | 1 | | Hostility | 2 | Pushed | 1 |
| Ashamed | 2 | "All right" | 1 | | Confusion | 2 | Worried | 1 |
| Confusion | 2 | Injustice | 1 | | Anger | 1 | Faith | |
| Frustrated | 2 | Depressed | 1 | | "Get lost!" | 1 | shattered | 1 |
| Fury | 1 | Frightened | 1 | | "Leave me | | Relieved | 1 |
| Cross | 1 | Dejected | 1 | | alone" | 1 | Panic | 1 |
| Growly | 1 | Panic | 1 | | Found | | Nil | 1 |
| Puzzlement | 1 | Rising panic | 1 | | justification | 1 | | |
| Challenged | 1 | | | | Resentment | 1 | | |

Many speculations arise when we look at these results. Each provides an idea for further investigation. Let us leave this fascinating area with just a few questions:

1. Do men have significantly different responses from women? Do they respond more strongly to attacks and record anger rather than dismay?
2. What does "relief" mean? Is it an escape from a threat (an antigoal) or can it have positive meanings?
3. Is the word "elation" very specific, and does it merit particular investigation?
4. What are the specifics of situations that create despondency rather than panic? Are they equally undesirable but different in character?

# Bibliography

The work described in this book is largely my own. The theoretical background I have used is that of Richard Skemp. I have deliberately not read widely in the general field of psychology. My inquiries into specific references to help me with my investigation of panic, and to provide a taxonomy of emotion, have yielded little.

Ausubel, David P. 1978. *The Psychology of Meaningful Verbal Behaviour.* New York: Grune and Stratten.

Bion, Wilfred. 1961. *Experiences in Groups.* London: Tavisback Publications.

Brearley, Mike, and Dudley Donst. 1979. *Ashes Retained.* London: Hodder and Stoughton.

Buxton, Laurie. 1985. "Cognitive-Effective Interaction in the Learning of Maths." Doctoral thesis, University of Warwick,

———. 1984. *Mathematics for Everyone.* New York: Schocken Books.

Chomsky, Noam. 1965. *Aspects of a Theory of Syntax.* Cambridge: MIT Press.

Davitz, J. R. 1969. *The Language of Emotion.* New York: Academic Press.

Eagle, Ruth. 1978. "Self-appraisal in the Learning of Maths." Unpublished paper.

Koestler, Arthur. 1967. *The Ghost in the Machine.* London: Hutchinson.

Krutetskii, V. A. 1971. *The Psychology of Mathematical Ability in School Children.* Chicago: University of Chicago Press.

Magee, Brian. 1973. *Popper.* London: Fontana.

Paterson, T. T. 1966. *Management Theory.* London: Business Books.

Popper, Karl. 1973. "Indeterminism Is Not Enough." *Encounter* (April).

Russell, Bertrand. 1967. *The Autobiography of Bertrand Russell, Vol. 1 (1872–1914)*. London: George Allen and Unwin.

Shanker, S. G., ed. 1988. *Gödel's Theorem in Focus*. London: Croon Helm.

Skemp, Richard. 1979. *Intelligence, Learning, and Action*. New York: John Wiley.

———. 1976. "Relational and Instrumental Understanding." *Maths Teaching* (March).

———. 1971. *The Psychology of Learning Mathematics*. Harmondsworth: Penguin.

———. 1959. "Difficulties in Learning Maths by Children of Good Intelligence." Doctoral thesis, University of Manchester.

Tobias, Sheila. 1978. *Overcoming Math Anxiety*. New York: Norton.

Wilson, John. 1967. *An Introduction to Moral Education*. Harmondsworth: Penguin.

# Index

attitudes 174
71
70